The Poverty of Life-Affirming Work

The Poverty *of* Life-Affirming Work

Motherwork, Education, and Social Change

Mechthild U. Hart

HV
699
.H 345
2002
west

Contributions in Women's Studies, Number 194

GREENWOOD PRESS
Westport, Connecticut • London

Library of Congress Cataloging-in-Publication Data

Hart, Mechthild U. (Mechthild Ursula), 1948–
    The poverty of life-affirming work : motherwork, education, and social change /
Mechthild U. Hart.
        p.   cm.—(Contributions in women's studies, ISSN 0147–104X ; no. 194)
    Includes bibliographical references and index.
    ISBN 0–313–31776–3 (alk. paper)
    1. Poor women—United States—Social conditions.   2. Single mothers—United
States—Social conditions.   3. Welfare recipients—United States—Social conditions.   4.
Public welfare—Government policy—United States.   I. Title.   II. Series.
HV699.H345   2002
362.83′0973—dc21   2001045123

British Library Cataloguing in Publication Data is available.

Copyright © 2002 by Mechthild U. Hart

All rights reserved. No portion of this book may be
reproduced, by any process or technique, without the
express written consent of the publisher.

Library of Congress Catalog Card Number: 2001045123
ISBN: 0–313–31776–3
ISSN: 0147–104X

First published in 2002

Greenwood Press, 88 Post Road West, Westport, CT 06881
An imprint of Greenwood Publishing Group, Inc.
www.greenwood.com

Printed in the United States of America

The paper used in this book complies with the
Permanent Paper Standard issued by the National
Information Standards Organization (Z39.48–1984).

10 9 8 7 6 5 4 3 2 1

Copyright Acknowledgment

The author and publisher gratefully acknowledge permission to use the following:

Mechthild Hart, "The Experience of Living and Learning in Different Worlds," *Studies in Continuing Education*, 20/2 (1998), pp. 187–200. Permission granted by Taylor & Francis Ltd., 11
New Fetter Lane, London EC4P 4EE, England.

To Dante Hart, the messenger from a brighter future

Contents

Preface

In 1948, when I was born, Germany was still a heap of rubble. I slowly learned about the war as I was growing older. Although I saw ruins and houses damaged by bombshells from the window of the train my mother took us on every month to visit her mother in Nürnberg, it took many years to begin to understand what happened. I heard stories about how my grandmother sought shelter with her daughters when the bombs were falling; I heard my father exchange war stories with old cronies. But this was all part of growing up.

Only in high school did I begin to piece together the history of the war. It was a young German teacher who finally broke the taboo on even mentioning the concentration camp horrors. Our teacher gave us books to read on the medical experiments performed on Jews by German doctors, and we listened to Hitler's speeches. This started years of questioning my parents on their part in these horrors, years of struggling with the knowledge that my mother somehow did not know and that my father was a member of the Nazi party.

At the same time, both my parents, especially my father, instilled an unshakable faith in the importance of education in me. My mother's aspiration of becoming a pediatrician was dashed when her older sister took her out of school during the war and sent her to a farm where she had to learn housekeeping. My father's hopes to study literature were squelched because his family could not afford the cost of a university education.

In 1987 I moved to Chicago. Although I had heard and read about racism, mainly in connection with colonialism and imperialism, before moving to Chicago I had not had an opportunity to be confronted with its direct consequences. While I saw some of these consequences, I was engulfed by my professional work at a university, and I was also "shielded" from racism. As is typical for white people in the United States, at that time "race" had nothing to do with being white.

Through a variety of connections, the opportunity to work with a literacy group in one of Chicago's highly racialized public housing projects was offered to me. I attended weekly sessions of a woman's literacy group, carefully listening, observing, and offering assistance wherever I saw it was needed. Later I had many conversations with women taking care of children in another public housing complex. I have learned, and am still learning, about people's very own struggles and survival strategies in an environment that has become a kind of war zone.

I clearly had to learn what it means to see the "colossal unseen dimensions" of a system of white privilege (McIntosh 1995). Slowly but steadily I have been moving beyond simply knowing about and seeing signs of racism and of having the "other" world right in front of my doorsteps. I have been trying to meet this situation more head-on: looking at what the "whiteman" has done to all "non-white" people, but also at how I am myself implicated in this scheme—externally and internally. I can never lose sight of this fact, no matter where my work or life places me.

This is where the two major strands of my own personal, political, and intellectual history come together: My belief in the importance of social and political change is inseparable from my belief in the importance of seeking and speaking the truth. My mother's work anchors these beliefs in the necessity and importance of everyday living and care. Since my parents were very poor and every single penny had to be accounted for, my mother had to work extremely hard to get her family nourished and clothed. We had a big garden that was carefully cultivated to grow most of the food. We had no refrigerator, which also meant that my mother had to devote a lot of work to preserving food in different ways. Working meant growing fruits and vegetables, taking care of the garden (including weeding and fighting caterpillars or ground squirrels), harvesting, and preserving fruit and vegetables, grocery shopping every day for fresh dairy goods, cooking and baking in a way that made the most out of scarce resources, doing most of the laundry by hand, hanging the laundry up, repairing clothes, sewing almost all of the children's clothes and taking care of them so they could be passed on, feeding the bathroom oven once a week for making hot water, feeding the tiled oven in the living room for at least one warm room in the winter, and, of course, daily cleaning with equipment that required a lot of hard work.

But this was only part of the work. Somehow my mother had to do all this work and take care of her children who required more than food and clothes, but also a kind of care that cannot so easily be translated into a list of clearly identifiable, specific tasks. All the work she did, and all the tasks she had to perform on a daily or weekly basis blended into each other. They were a necessary and meaningful part of caring for the lives of her children and her husband.

When I listened to the stories of inner-city mothers, I heard stories about tremendous anxieties or fears about their children's well-being in the midst of poverty and destruction, but also stories of pride and joy, of laughter and play. And I could make connections with my mother's experiences and those of the women I met in Chicago's inner city. I was fully conscious, however, that there is a qualitative difference between living in poverty while at the same time being able to cultivate fruits and vegetables for daily needs on privately owned land, and living in poverty and owning next to nothing. Nevertheless, the intensity of caring for the well-being of children provided a connection to what I learned from my mother's work. It built a bridge of understanding between myself, a German-American middle-class academic, and African-American women depending on public aid, often without a high school diploma. I am used to being a cultural outsider, an "alien resident," and at least from that perspective I am an "outsider within" (Lorde 1984). I am also a German whose search for truth has guided me in learning about the complexity of Jewish history and tradition. This has helped me to learn not only about Jews, but also about non-Jews who have been "othered" by various dominant cultures. It has also helped me see where this othering process undermines or destroys the basic internal and external conditions for any kind of life-affirming work, and to see where parts of this work are still alive, although the workers, such as the "motherworkers," are struggling against overwhelming odds.

Acknowledgments

I have to thank many people who accompanied me during various stages of my writing journey. All of them helped me in numerous ways to push beyond but also acknowledge my limits, to bring the journey to a halt, and to enjoy the landscape that stretches out in front of me, begging for future visits.

Special thanks go to the friends and colleagues who took time and energy to critically read (and re-read) parts of my writing in various stages of development—although they may not recognize the way I took their comments to heart: Frida Furman, Ann Russo, Ann Stanford, Beth Kelly, and Corinne Benedetto made many critical suggestions and raised questions that kept me motivated to search for answers without being afraid of generating even more question during that search. Michelle VanNatta took it upon herself to go over the entire manuscript, and she gave me a wonderful combination of praise and detailed, specific criticism.

I also want to thank people whose interest in my work took the form of encouraging me to make it available to others by presenting it at conferences or by putting it in writing. Special thanks go to Angela Miles, Michael Newman, Michael Welton, Peter Willis, Jean-Paul Hauteceour, Budd Hall, Elana Michelson, Ron Cervero, Arthur Wilson, and Phyllis Cunningham. Phyllis has been the one whose comments sometimes threw me off balance, making me see some of my blind spots, propelling me into the pursuit of what for me were old, but had to become new themes in a new context and a new phase in history. After she reminded me that I did not sufficiently address race and ethnicity in my previous writings, she also pointed out that the issue of class is never absent in discussions of social inequality.

Phyllis Cunningham was one of many people who engaged in conversations with me, sometimes over vast geographical or cultural distances, sometimes close by. Their intellectual integrity and inquisitiveness, and their commitment to social justice kept me on my intellectual, emotional, and political toes. I was particularly influenced by Aimee Horton's untiring commitment to making this world more livable, Claudia von Werlhof 's uncompromising ways of confronting injustice in any form, or Deborah Holton's gracious ways of reminding me of my racial blinders or ignorances. They, like many others, inspired me to re-think some of my old ideas, and to see the world in a new light.

It is difficult to put into words the profound appreciation and gratitude I feel for Elio DeArrudah, Almetta Russell, Sue Sago, and Mica Godbold. Some of the most inspiring gifts I received during my journey was their relentless criticism of "our system," their wit, spirit, courage, and dedication to work with or care for others in order to stem the tide of social destruction all around them. Not only did they cause some badly needed jolting and shifting of my consciousness, but they also lived the promise of a better world in the midst of hardship and devastation.

My students, of course, need to be thanked for what they taught me about the possibilities, and limits, of my educational work. They sometimes threw some big questions my way, making me pause, think, and reflect on the social and individual sources of these questions, how I may have contributed to raising them, and how they could be addressed in our collective educational endeavor.

Many thanks go to my family abroad and here whose love and respect for my work nourished my soul and spirit. Special thanks go to my daughter Jenni Hart for modeling motherwork in an admirable way, allowing Dante to unfold in a loving and inspiring environment, and to Tama Weisman for being particularly supportive by never ceasing to encourage me while putting up with the toll writing a book takes on loved ones.

Finally, thanks also to the Dean of the School for New Learning, and to DePaul University for granting me two research leaves.

Introduction

Only when I sit in-between different chairs can I truly encounter the real problem. It gives the problem itself the opportunity to criss-cross me, which then gives me the opportunity to transform this event into a sometimes quite painful experience, and to develop this experience into communicable knowledge.

—Claudia von Werlhof, *Mutter-Los*

What my mother teaches me are the essential lessons of the quilt: that people and actions do move in multiple directions at once.

—Elsa Barkley Brown, *African-American Women's Quilting*

Throughout the chapters of this book, I let the many different facets and practical implications of motherwork unfold, especially when done under the harsh conditions of poverty and single motherhood. I show how society expects solo mothers in poverty to nurture their children without very little or no personal, social, or political support, and how developments in the world economy blend into the mix of economic deprivation and ideological vilification. It was one of my main goals in writing this book to allow the women who live under extremely harsh conditions speak about their own experiences. Since their voices are practically never heard outside of their own environment, I try to "become the conduit of those silenced" (Boris 1998, 30).[1] Moreover, their stories, and the strength and courage expressed in them, directly contradict the way they are misrepresented or defamed in the media, the only social public that makes information about their lives available to the general population. Instead, I dismantle the stereotypes surrounding Black[2] mothers on welfare in the way Duneier (1992) demolishes those of Black men who are seen as belonging only to two groups: the middle class or the underclass. Duneier tries to undermine the social, media-driven assumptions behind such a dichotomy, and to bring to light the respectability, civility, and wisdom of Black working-class men.[3]

Most of the women whose words are recorded here relied on public aid, and they were therefore members of the jobless poor (Wilson 1996). Although their poverty is generally not associated with the notion of class whose meanings in employed Black men's lives Duneier investigated, class is nevertheless interlaced with the experiences of all poor mothers, regardless of whether they are members of the working poor or the jobless poor, and regardless of their racial-ethnic background. The women's stories are therefore anchored in concrete, individual life circumstances, *and* they exemplify the lived experiences of complex, multilayered social and economic forces that shape autobiographical actualities.

The women's stories are stories about motherwork. They are stories about sustaining and affirming life in a social context that directly disaffirms life, both psychologically and physically/materially. Seen from a critical social-political perspective, motherwork can be placed under the larger, more encompassing rubric of "subsistence work," a category that summarizes all kinds of work whose main orientation is the sustenance of life rather than the extraction of profit from life. Subsistence work is rooted in the materiality, the physicality of life, of staying alive, or of simply surviving. This is true especially when surrounding economic and social conditions are not only not supportive but rather directly detrimental to keeping alive and cherishing the life-affirming orientation of subsistence- or motherwork.

In this book I trace the conflicting, contradictory, but also complementary experiences of poor mothers, and how these experiences get shaped or distorted by a social and political context that disregards or vilifies the life-affirming dimension of their work. I also trace the many different kinds of individual and social survival strategies, and how they rely or build on the survival of life-affirming cultural traditions—even where they appear in rudimentary or fragmented form. I address this situation from a variety of perspectives, and with different purposes in mind. These range from listening to these mothers' stories to examining the larger social and economic context that shapes their lives, and from describing their learning desires to discussing how their stories, their world, can become the focus of emotional, intellectual, and political learning experiences that take place in a quite different world.

Fostering or developing a subsistence orientation is impossible without tremendous learning processes, especially in a society, and a world, that thrives on the opposite. Depending on where one is placed in the social order of things, and how one lives and sees the world, these processes can be experienced or witnessed in an endless variety of ways. Based on my own experiences as an educator, I narrow the vast range of possibilities and focus on three different educational contexts: my work and observations in a literacy center, at the office of the public housing youth center, and at my own university. I look at various educational efforts that take up the struggle of learning or relearning a subsistence orientation from very different perspectives. These educational endeavors occur in quite different social or institutional contexts, and they cover a range of possibilities and challenges. They all demonstrate, however, that the learners (myself included) are working against severe emotional, intellectual, and structural (material) obstacles placed in their learning path.

Finally, I discuss how the experience and basic orientation of motherwork influences the political work of "mother-activists." The very meaning of political work here builds upon motherwork by implying a subsistence perspective or orientation. The driving force behind the construction of the entire book is my belief in the importance of such a subsistence perspective because it is oriented toward preserving life and surviving rather than toward mercilessly competing, warring, accumulating, and winning, and that such a perspective can be nourished or developed.

CHAPTER OUTLINE

Chapter 1 presents an outline of the conceptual and political framework that provides the theoretical underbelly of the book. I discuss why the term "motherwork" is more useful than "mothering." While motherwork holds on to the nurturing, life-affirming connotation of the term mothering, it also takes the latter out of the conceptual box of "nonwork" where the multitude of efforts and activities that comprise motherwork are usually kept under ideological and material/financial lock and key. By placing it under the analytical, social-economic rubric of "subsistence work," its economic underside becomes apparent, retroactively clarifying and giving meaning to the history of capitalist development. This history always relied on locally or regionally bound indigenous subsistence economies. Defining these economies as primitive or precapitalist—a view that is intimately linked to Western notions of progress and development—meant turning them into grounds for exploitation and eventual destruction. Subsistence laborers were therefore drawn into the orbit of capitalist class relations although the latter remained, and remain today, fully dependent on various kinds of subsistence labor. In the ongoing process of capitalist development, subsistence work has, however, lost a great deal of its original orientation toward cherishing life in all its richness and diversity. Instead, under conditions of social and economic deprivation, it has become mere "survival work."

In transnational capital's relentless search for cheap labor, economic growth has always been accompanied by a worldwide growth in poverty and misery. Not surprisingly, the slave and the housewife have provided ideal models for the cheapest, and therefore most profitable, kind of labor. Both work for free, and together they tell similar but also fundamentally different stories of the intersectionality of race, class, and sex. "Sexual economyths" (Beasley 1994), however, tell that part of the story that has to do with the fact that children come out of a woman's body, and that worldwide it is mostly women who take care of these children. I more firmly join the concepts of motherwork and subsistence work by examining the economic underpinnings of the process that de-economized motherwork—calling it at the most reproductive rather than productive—and turned the ability to bear children into an affliction that follows all women into the labor market. I analyze how mother/subsistence work weaves in and out of class relations, and instead of jettisoning class as the primary concept for looking at the social and economic implications of work, I examine how it interconnects with notions of private and public, market and nonmarket work, race and ethnicity, and, above all, with the physical, bodily dimension of life.

In chapter 2 mothers' voices tell stories of at times insurmountable personal and structural obstacles in the way of raising children, but also stories of moments of abundance, joy, and laughter. As Fine and Weis (1998) observed, poor urban mothers do "mother work" without a net, but "despite the financial stretch, the social difficulties, and the personal pain they experience, these women take great pride in their children and great pleasure in their moments with 'the kids'" (203). By placing the "joys of motherhood" into a larger social-economic framework, this side of motherwork illustrates how pain and effort are as much a part of any kind of work that is life-affirming as are joy and playfulness.

I focus on a concrete local area, and on political struggles that are by nature local or place-bound. This does not mean, however, that I lose sight of an understanding of the effects of global maneuvers or strategies on local living and working conditions. One of the most devastating effects of globalization is the growth of a new urban poverty (Wilson 1996). The internationalization and industrial restructuring of the U.S. economy are directly related to the recent growth of poverty in segregated neighborhoods in which the majority of adults are either unemployed or have dropped out of the labor force altogether (19). We have to add the sexist division of labor to the combined results of "racial segregation, class subordination, and social isolation" (xviii). It leaves mothers to fend for themselves and their children without any moral public support.

All African Americans who live in racially and economically segregated public housing areas on Chicago's West and South Side are struggling against tremendous odds. The work of raising children—a responsibility almost exclusively placed on women—faces many external and internal obstacles. Public housing areas in Chicago show how conditions necessary for raising children have been rapidly eroding. Destruction and destructiveness are all around, affecting every aspect of the conditions for motherwork. These are material and physical conditions, including poverty, abysmal public housing complexes with apartments badly in need of major repairs, public schools that have been the worst in the nation, no public spaces such as parks, and no affordable grocery store in walking distance. Psychological conditions are also deteriorating. Without any prospect for financial or emotional stability, people have lost a sense of future. And there is spiritual devastation. This ranges from a loss of community and, increasingly, a loss of connections to previous generations living in the

South, to loneliness, despondency, seeking refuge in alcohol or drugs, or collapsing into a state of passivity in front of the TV.

TV is most frequently the only contact with "society" or the "outside world." The inner city population, like anybody else in this society, is inundated with commercial images of a dreamworld where the social is defined by the ownership of shiny material goods that have turned into status symbols. The slogan "the more the better" determines success or failure. Its omnipresence proves that "the economy" has become entirely unlimited and that anything truly social has been destroyed. Where unemployment is high, where jobs are no longer available because they have moved "elsewhere," and where there are very few or no financial resources, dealing drugs has become the prime avenue for getting more material goods. The drug culture has become omnipresent, and with it violence, or the threat of violence, around and in one's own house.

In a context of poverty and isolation, surrounded by violence and utter public neglect, caring is of a troublesome, multi-layered nature. Social exploitation and self-oppression are highly intertwined, and caring is caught in a dense web of pain, fears, anguish, and concerns that are intimately connected with motherwork. Caring signifies an overwhelming emotional burden. Because it is at the core of motherwork, however, and because it involves a multitude of tasks, skills, abilities, and forms of knowledge, it also signifies an overwhelming amount of work and responsibility.

Women who live in these areas are doing an inordinate amount of survival work, especially around children. This does not get any public recognition, and often the women themselves do not acknowledge the incredible strength and courage they are mustering twenty-four hours a day while they talk about their tremendously complex and demanding tasks and responsibilities. These tasks require a vast array of skills, abilities, competencies, and knowledge, and they range from financially providing for, feeding and clothing the children to nurturing, teaching, and protecting them. Because they live in the shadow of a violent drug culture, the mothers constantly have to move in different directions all at once, have to see and know everything. The women also talk about the heavy personal price they must pay for never-ending care. There is little or no reprieve from its demands because there is little or no support, either from the fathers of their children or from society in general.

Chapter 3 examines larger social trends that are behind the current punitive measures against single mothers on welfare, women who are engaged in subsistence work with children—a very vulnerable population. In addition to not being paid for their work in the home, poor solo mothers "are forced either by law or by economic circumstances to choose wages over children" (Mink 1998a, 58). As expressed by the right-wing Heritage Foundation, mothers who are financially dependent on government assistance are stereotyped as uneducated, immoral, and destroying "family values" by bearing children outside of the patriarchal control of a husband. The Foundation therefore claims that "there is now a widespread understanding that . . . providing cash subsidies to never-married women who have children out of wedlock . . . destroys marriage and promotes illegitimacy. Unless Congress and the Administration make curing illegitimacy the central component of a strategy to reduce welfare dependence, [welfare] reform will fail" (Rector 1994, 27). While motherwork has never been in the forefront of public acknowledgment, the new welfare laws passed by Congress in August 1996 have officially turned being a mother into a form of moral deficiency. Consequently, welfare reform's primary agenda is to reform the "welfare mothers" themselves.[4]

Welfare mothers violate one of the primary social rules that govern motherwork: It needs to be done quietly and invisibly in the bosom of the private sphere, whose most worthy manifestation is still the heterosexual nuclear family. Once the work of raising children goes public and claims to be in need of public resources because private ones are not available, it incites tremendous political rage. It is the political public (aided by the social public of the mass media) that makes sure this work is taken out of the public realm by withdrawing any public support. As the new welfare laws and regulations show, this act is accomplished by forcing these mothers to find a job. Where the work of raising children has become superfluous within the logic of the capitalist economy, it is no longer "repressed" (Beasley 1994). Instead, it is put under the glaring searchlight of public scrutiny, vilified, and then dismissed. The main image of the welfare mother or welfare queen, that is, the young Black teenager who does not work but only breeds and takes from the government, is the most striking example of an intricate blend of class-bias, racism, and sexism. It turns welfare mothers into "scapegoat stick figures" for everything that is wrong with our economy (Childers 1997, 101).[5]

Moreover, the current emphasis on workfare rather than welfare is fueled by the realization that welfare recipients have placed themselves outside the economic exploitability network. Thus, woman's true calling is transformed into a character deficiency because that calling is no longer exploitable. Pulling poor mothers into the workforce makes this deficiency somewhat reformable. Otherwise, poor mothers need to be cut off the dole altogether, letting them fend for themselves and their children among the hungry and, most likely, the homeless.[6] The fact that these welfare children are not really needed as future wage laborers is one of the reasons there is no heated public debate about the anticipated increase in homelessness, hunger and despair once the new welfare laws have fully taken a hold. These children are part of a growing surplus population, and so are the mothers if they cannot be employed. This leaves unanswered the question whether mothers who are pushed to the margins can retain the subsistence orientation that is an integral part of their caring work and responsibilities.

From March 1994 to April 1995, I attended weekly meetings, called the Women Empowerment Hour, at a literacy center in one of Chicago's public housing complexes. Chapter 4 describes how my observations at the literacy center take up the theme of subsistence work, this time placed in a very specific learning situation. As a participant observer I record and interpret the concrete, deliberate learning desires and efforts by women this society has pushed to the very margin. I locate the particular situation of the women in a larger social and political context and ask how this context influences how and what they learn. The main question underlying this chapter is how the many dimensions of motherwork—physical, psychological, social, emotional, intellectual, or spiritual—appear in different fragments in the actual learning process.

Although the work of raising children, or motherwork, was never an explicit topic—children, taking care of them, protecting them, and relying on the assistance of other mothers (often the children's grandmother)—were constant themes similar to the ones that appeared in the narratives of the mothers I interviewed.

These themes moved between two extremes. Most of the time discussions addressed various aspects of never-ending care, of having sole responsibility for caring, and of the children's ongoing demand for love, protection, and attentiveness. The other extreme was the neglect or abuse of children due to the mother's despondency. While this theme was mostly mentioned in reference to women who were not participating in the literacy group, sometimes it was also raised by participants who were trying to escape their own drug or alcohol addiction, or whose children had been abused (or, in one case, killed) by former boyfriends.

These mothers denounced in the most glaring way the social destruction of the outer and inner survival base of motherwork. They were also in the best position to indicate where struggle, resistance, and change on many levels are needed and are of primary importance. As it became clear to me, the women had overwhelming responsibilities for themselves, their children, and people around them, and they were clearly in need of mutual support, affirmation, and help. But all these could only be given by nurturing a sense of power in themselves— a sense of power that was needed to swim upstream, to be a source of strength for their children.

This was the main purpose of the Women Empowerment Hour. It placed the gaining of this kind of "literacy" at the center of the participants' efforts, a literacy that is "hidden" according to official definitions which do not include vital abilities, forms of knowledge, and skills related to motherwork (Hautecoeur 1990). The women employed a learning method that combined the telling of personal stories and anecdotes with attempts to gain a reflective distance. This sometimes happened when stories were shared and when commonalties were discovered or emphasized, and sometimes when visitors came to talk about a recurring problem in more general terms. Often the ability to be self-critical, to acknowledge one's own responsibility in perpetuating pain was also called for. This could only happen after trust was built, and it relied on consistent support. Narrating one's personal stories and gaining some reflective distance by developing a larger perspective was a slow, painful process that sometimes meant taking a few steps forward, sometimes also a few steps backward.

Chapter 5 offers a glimpse of what guides my educational work: to acknowledge and to develop in all participants in a learning situation a holistic, practical approach to life, and to see and appreciate the many facets of sustaining life or staying alive. Gaining a life-affirming perspective is a process that often involves personal, social, and cultural transformations, an unlearning of ways of thinking that are heavily influenced, if not shaped, by patriarchal bottomline thinking and a discernment of other possibilities.

Since the production and acquisition of knowledge, skills, and competencies is a primary challenge for educators, I also look closely at the way Western masculinist epistemologies reign supreme in the semipublic realm of higher education, turning subsistence work, and subsistence knowing into counter-concepts, into "categories of challenge" (Shiva 1989). I examine how I use, or could use, these categories of challenge in my own educational work, and how this attempt shapes corresponding teaching/learning processes.

I therefore look at my role and identity as an educator. I confront the questions raised by the fact that a woman such as myself, whose race and class background makes her at least a partial member of the dominant group, visits places where people experience the racist and class-biased repercussions of such a membership. Since interconnectedness and interdependence are core dimensions of a subsistence orientation, I try to come to grips with the implications of these social divisions and how they enter each educational situation in full force. I describe how such an orientation has to acknowledge and denounce relations of power and corresponding forms of oppression and exploitation. Such an orientation also has to cherish, and at times transcend, differences of experience, language, meaning, ways of knowing—all of which are anchored in one's cultural heritage. Educational work is very personal, but it also has strong cultural and political dimensions. All educational situations therefore involve learning processes related to acknowledging and denouncing, cherishing and transcending difference. In this chapter I analyze aspects of those processes by translating them into concrete pedagogical challenges.

In my educational work I try to create, or move about, in an environment similar to the structure Brown (1989) sets up in her African-American history course, a structure that resembles those of a "polyrhythmic, 'nonsymmetrical,' nonlinear" African-American quilt, where "individual and community are not competing entities" (926). While she selects the class readings and controls the time schedule for discussing the assigned readings, the overall structure of the class set-up gives authority to the students themselves. It guides them to assist and evaluate each other in the learning process, and to discover that "it takes a variety of skills, resources, and emphases" to collectively reach the goal of accomplishing their learning task (928). Just like strips of fabric can be sewn together into the dynamic whole of a quilt, in the course of a class, the many different bits and pieces of knowledge and experience can therefore lead to a fuller, more complete knowledge of oneself and the world. It is knowledge that emanates from the process of subsistence knowing, a way of knowing that is anchored in life-affirming work and a life-affirming orientation toward oneself, others, and the world around us.

In chapter 6 I more fully return to the notion and experience of motherwork. Motherwork is by nature political as it is inserted in a nexus of social and economic power relations. While mothers can, for instance, translate their concern for their children's future into active membership in a race-hate or right-wing organization (Blee 1997; Koonz 1997), they can also translate it into an organized social protest against some of the practical ramifications of a racist, economically exploitative society. In other words, mothers can make a leap from caring for the well-being of their own children to those of others, and of their community and society in general, by understanding and fighting against social or economic power structures.

Regardless of culturally different notions and experiences of mothering, and regardless of the specifics of the particular power nexus that shapes its practices, as a form of life-affirming subsistence work all motherwork contains within it the spark of radical change (Jetter, Orleck, and Taylor 1997). Placing the well-being of a future generation above anything else, that is, above making profit, is a truly radical challenge. As one of the women engaged in protests against toxic waste dumps in her working-class neighborhood said, "It appalled me that money could be more important than the health of my children" (quoted in Krauss 1998, 137). Thus, to be primarily concerned about the sustenance of life is part and parcel of a subsistence perspective that underlies mother-activists' struggles for social change.

Community is a recurrent theme in the different reports of the struggles of community othermothers, (Collins 1990, 1993, 1994; James 1993), activist mothers (Naples 1992, 1998a, 1998b), or mother-activists (Jetter, Orleck, and Taylor 1997). In the second chapter of this book, I report on how the women I interviewed voice their anguish about the loss of community and how their own efforts nevertheless still echo the important African-American tradition of community othermothers, in however beleaguered form. In the final chapter I bring together the many different reports written by feminist activist-researchers on actions and struggles that directly continue this tradition, or that illustrate different variations of the theme of activist mothering. The interconnection and interdependence of people's lives, whether they are young or old, is another important dimension of a subsistence orientation, one the term "community" tries to capture.

The political dimension of community motherwork is rooted in the life-affirming work surrounding the well-being of children. The community can therefore be seen as an environment where women are trying to sustain a homeplace by promoting community viability. This intermingling of the personal and political creates new spaces between private and public life, spaces that "cannot be read according to traditional separations" (Melchiori 1996, 18). How caring work crosses various boundaries is another recurring theme. It moves in-between the public and the private sphere, and in-between paid and unpaid work, whether it is done within the realm of one's own family, someone else's—as in the case of paid domestic work—or as part of an effort to improve social institutions within a particular community. Although the blurring of any distinction between paid and unpaid work is part of the very nature of caring work, it is also an outcome of the super-exploitation of both kinds of caring work, within the context of our economic system.

One of the primary insignia of such devaluation is the fact that community othermothers, just like mothers, "labor in obscurity," (James 1993, 48), that is, in the shadow of invisibility. Their political work therefore remains invisible as well. Just as the work of raising children is not considered real work—as illustrated by the term "working mother"—the work of mother-activists is likewise not considered real political work. It is ignored, either by official politicians or by male, formal leaders of political organizations where women did, or do, most of the daily grassroots work. Barnett (1995), for instance, who analyzed Black women's collective organizations, writes that poor and working-class women belong to a category that "is too often incorrectly assumed to be apolitical and thus inconsequential to social movement mobilization, maintenance, and success" (201). Cruikshank (1995) makes a similar point. She describes how during the War on Poverty a great variety of people, such as single mothers, alcoholics, Blacks, the unemployed, and many others was placed into the uniform category of "the poor," or "The Other America," as Michael Harrington termed them in his best-selling book (1963). The poor are represented as apathetic and politically inactive (Cruikshank, 37).

Women's engagement in many different kinds of political protests has been well documented.[7] However, looking at the political struggles of poor mothers in particular provides "an important corrective to the rhetoric of politicians and the cardboard characterizations of writers and scholars who see poor women as a distinct and alien species, somehow not quite as human as the rest of us" (Orleck 1997b, 89). The most important, most challenging, and most radical aspect of this corrective is the fact that

First and foremost, women have participated as leaders and as participants in organized struggles to attack problems that directly threaten their *economic survival* and that of their families and children. Most often, cross-nationally, they have been involved at the local and community levels around daily issues such as obtaining food, welfare, jobs, housing, and other needs—taking part in food riots, welfare protests, labor struggles, tenants rights, and similar collective actions. (West and Blumberg 1990a, 13)

These kinds of struggles are the focus of this chapter. They are the daily survival struggles that have no name, as they do not fit the language of "normalized workers" or "normalized mothers" (Polakow 1993), that is, the class-biased, racist, and sexist stigmatization of abnormal mothers and nonworkers who allegedly victimize the system. This final chapter looks at collective forms of organizing and protesting against the often life-threatening material and structural implications of an unjust, exploitative nexus of political, social, and economic power relations. I examine how these practices and struggles contain the potential for envisioning a way of life that places the affirmation of life at the center of its soul.

MOVING IN DIFFERENT DIRECTIONS

Although the chapters in this book are thematically connected, they are also rather discrete, separate entities. This certainly poses some challenges to the readers of this book. I hope that it also provides some benefits. While individual chapters can be read without necessarily following a particular order, the reader is also asked to keep track of how I make connections among the chapters and to make her or his own connections by placing them into a larger, unifying context.[8]

"This reminds me of quilting," said a friend to whom I was trying to describe the process of putting this book together. I have always admired the art of quilting. Most of all I admire the women who could produce a colorful and complex piece of art by spending many nights carefully stitching together patches taken from pieces of fabric, making the quilt the combined result of long hours of physical, spiritual, and creative work. As Aptheker (1989) wrote, "In this way women gave meaning to their daily lives, the cumulative effects of their quilts finally transforming the ragged and the mundane into discernible patterns, beautiful, sturdy, enduring" (68).

My book clearly doesn't have the fanciful, artistic design and flavor of an African-American quilt, where women create "the impression of several patterns moving in different directions or multiple rhythms within the context of a controlled design" (Brown 1989, 923). I am not part of the culture that developed a "polyrhythmic, 'nonsymmetrical,' nonlinear structure" of seeing and thinking about the world which is expressed in such artistic creations (926). Instead, I was brought up in a culture whose linear notion of the world is behind the "rigid, uniform, repetitive, and predictable" designs of European-American quilts (924). However, the process of my work has been similar to the one described by a South African woman in terms of putting down ideas for her quilt: "I write my thoughts down on little scraps of paper . . . a quilt is like a book of many stories done up together, and many people can read it all at the same time" (quoted in Lorde 1988, 102). I have questioned the Western view of the world for some time, especially in terms of its epistemological ramifications. By putting the pieces of this book together, I have learned to "pivot the center," that is, to center my work and teaching in the lives of "nonwhite, non-middle-class, non-Western persons" (Brown 1989, 921)—although I am not one of them.

Quilting represents the knowledge and experience of a process Elsa Barkley Brown learned from her mother: People and actions do move in multiple directions at once. My intellectual and my emotional work also constantly and simultaneously push and pull me in several different directions. Underneath this constant movement flows, however, the strong and steady undercurrent of an ethical–spiritual and political belief. It is the belief that such simultaneous movement into many different directions offers positive possibilities for seeing, understanding, and recreating a world whose patchwork shows the fundamental interdependence of people and their movements.

Such a belief places rather tremendous intellectual, emotional, and political challenges in front of me. First of all, from an academic perspective, simultaneously moving into different directions means crossing disciplinary boundaries, thus occupying a "'space' between the disciplines" (Pryse 1998, 4). In her analysis of the interdisciplinary and cross-cultural nature of women's studies, Pryse offers a detailed critique of how the disciplines represent "an administration of knowledge in which control over academic boundaries contributed to weakening concepts of interconnectedness and interdependence between or across those borders" (5). Instead of romanticizing such interconnectedness and interdependence we can construct a *critical interdisciplinarity* that borrows and applies knowledge and insights from a standpoint and that is nourished by a commitment to "seeing the relation between dominant activities and beliefs and those that arise on the 'outside'" (Harding 1991, 131–32). Thus, critical interdisciplinarity crosses borders "among vectors of oppression" (Pryse, 12). Within the order, or rather disorder, of our world, this implies cultural border-crossing as well as "cross-cultural epistemological coalition(s)" (10).

Cultural border-crossing and cross-cultural epistemological coalitions require the ability to improvise, to experiment—but not in the traditional scientific sense—and to take personal and professional risks. Without such an open-ended willingness to listen, to know, and to experience rage when systemic injustices and abominations are confronted and without joy in understanding the different ways of seeing and experiencing the world, border-crossings are meaningless forms of tourism. Or, to put it more bluntly, they can easily become acts of intellectual colonialism.

By moving between cultures and countries, by leaving my white, middle-class academic world and visiting the Black, impoverished world of Chicago's inner-city ghettos, I have also learned to wonder and to admire. My desire to learn has been nourished by my political commitment to understand and respect lives that have been separated from my own, and to understand how this separation is embedded in a larger system that extracts profit from rather than nourishes life. The motivation to visit and learn from fairly unknown worlds does therefore not arise from the voyeuristic inclinations of a tourist. Rather, it is nourished by a deeply held belief in the vitality of ways of living and working that cherish life in its many different forms instead of living off its substance, and in the process destroying it.

I have also learned to recognize my ignorance and to acknowledge how my own cultural, racial, and class background limits the possibilities of surpassing such ignorance. Visiting the mothers living in Chicago's public housing has taught me to see that my skin and class privilege is a form of deficiency because it is part of my ignorance concerning vital experiences of people who live there. I can only partly improve this ignorance by recognizing the many concrete obstacles in the way of my own true learning about the situation, background, or histories of the people living in public housing, and by overcoming some of these obstacles. Many of them will remain intact.

METHODOLOGY

The six chapters of this book are the result of different methodological ventures. Chapters 2, 4, and 5 are ethnographic in nature, combining field work (onsite interviews, participant observations) with theoretical analyses. These chapters examine concrete manifestations of "situated knowledges" (Haraway 1988, 1991). These are "marked knowledges," not only of the people whose lives and stories I studied, but also of my own. They are marked by our specific location in the power matrix of this society, and they represent local knowledge claims that are made by women living under concrete, specific circumstances. Chapters 1, 3 and 6 represent the more conventional academic–theoretical approach of investigating and discussing the larger social, economic, and political context of the individual experiences and stories presented in the other three chapters. When doing the direct ethnographic research, I was, of course, also working within a certain theoretical–analytical paradigm regarding various forms of injustice and exploitation, a paradigm that certainly guided the selection of recorded conversations and the translation of women's stories, our interactions, and written material into coherent texts. In many ways I tried to follow Dorothy Smith's description of a feminist method. This method goes beyond "interviewing practices and our research relationships to explore methods of thinking that will organize our inquiry and write our sociological texts so as to preserve the presence of actual subjects while exploring and explicating the relations in which our everyday worlds are embedded" (1987, 111).

A feminist researcher who claims to be an ally of people whose lives she studies and who live in worlds pushed to the very margins by the dominant groups of which she herself is a member finds herself moving through methodological, ethical, and political thickets. I cannot ignore, and certainly not undo, the power hierarchies our different worlds represent. This poses questions concerning testimony and advocacy, questions about who can speak for whom, especially when issues of power and the politics of knowledge construction are at the center of attention (Alcoff 1991). In her discussion of ethical dilemmas in feminist research, Kirsch (1999) puts it quite bluntly:

We need to recognize that we may not be able to avoid speaking for others, that we are always implicated in the social and cultural hierarchies we study and seek to transform. As scholars, we cannot escape a position of power or the potential for misappropriating the voices and experiences of others. . . . We also need to recognize that inequities—differences of power, knowledge, education, and resources—continue to shape our relations with others, no matter how emancipatory our goals are as scholars and teachers. (85)

To the extent to which this is possible, self-reflexivity has to be continuously practiced in order to alleviate the impact of these differences, since "autobiographical, reflective statements . . . do not change the power dynamics between researchers and participants, between interviewers and interviewees" (83). This does not mean, however, that reflective accounts are unimportant. While they do not erase power differences, they nevertheless can unmask them. Moreover, "they remind readers that scholars are always products of their culture and history, that observations are always limited and partial, that interpretations are complex and contradictory, and that all accounts of research are open to revision and reinterpretation" (82).

I agree with DeVault (1999), who writes that fieldwork is usually "all about text" and that "we produce, interpret, and present data only through our writing" (220). Obviously, I contribute to these publicly circulated documents by giving "physical existence" to stories told to me by the women I interviewed. I thereby construct what Borland (1991) describes as a "second-level narrative based upon, but at the same time reshaping, the first" (63). In a way, I translate spoken words into their written rendition. As Phillips writes, a "conversational account involves translation in a number of senses" (1996, 23). Since she observed and interviewed women in Ecuador but wrote in English, Phillips was engaged in the most direct, immediate act of translation. She also reports, however, that translating involved "transforming oral conversation into text: I have turned women's spoken words into sentences, inserting commas, paragraphs, and exclamation marks in places where the women themselves of course do not specify." In other words, she turned the women's words into "flat text" (23). Similarly, I myself used standard English spelling when editing the interview transcripts, especially since I have no training or experience in transcribing an English that is in a number of ways different from what I learned as my official second language. At the same time, I also look at this process as a way of building a bridge over the divide that separates the spoken word from its written rendition.

Regardless of my belief in the importance of an egalitarian, reciprocal relationship between the researcher and the people who are the subject of her research, I nevertheless have ultimate control over the research process. I keep drawing on "text-based sociological and other institutionally related discourses" (Naples 1996, 91), and I undoubtedly reshape the women's own narratives in accordance with my political and ethical reasoning and beliefs. Although similar to Naples, I broaden my understanding of these discourses by carefully examining the stories and observations recorded in my field-notes, I nevertheless claim "interpretative authority" over the material I gathered.

In addition, presenting material also means taking into account the audiences I have in mind when producing the text. In that way audiences "bring themselves to the product" (Hertz 1997, xiii), giving me the ultimate control over reshaping or rewriting the research product, thus making it even more my own (see also Ribbens 1989). As Stacey puts it with respect to ethnographic research in general, "With very rare exceptions it is the researcher who narrates, who 'authors' the ethnography. In the last instance, an ethnography is a written document structured primarily by a researcher's purposes, offering a researcher's interpretations, registered in a researcher's voice" (1991, 114). Not only will the "informants" therefore not benefit directly from the research, they also have no or very little control over its content (Cotterill 1992, 605). This is clearly the case with the women I interviewed or observed, and it opened a Pandora's box of questions and difficulties.

For instance, I have to ask myself what influences or guides my interpretation and what are the bases of my "interpretive authority" (DeVault). I also have to examine how my control over the results of my research affect my relationship to the women I observed or interviewed. By striving for an egalitarian, reciprocal relationship with my informants, it remains a research relationship and therefore contains elements of power and control. Research is a privileged activity, and I can simply walk away with the words of the people I interviewed, transposing them into an interview transcript. Gorelick (1991), however, points to one of the potentially quite useful dimensions of the difficulty of interpreting and representing people who are differently located in the nexus of power relations. She states that the researcher can use her analytical tools by placing individually experienced instances of oppression into a larger framework, thereby contributing to a kind of understanding of general social power structures that can be useful for all participants in ethnographic research. Enslin (1994) makes a similar point. She considers writing about women a powerful weapon although it contains feminism "safely within academic institutions and texts rather than connecting it with women's struggles in the streets, farms, factories, forests, kitchens, bedrooms, hospitals, and prisons around the world" (559). Nevertheless, this writing is powerful because it "has the potential for challenging hegemonic assumptions about human histories and futures" (559). By having written this book I hope to contribute to this kind of knowledge. Nevertheless, I will always be haunted by the question Patai (1991) asked herself when interviewing poor women living in slums in Brazil: "Does 'contributing to knowledge' justify the utilization of another person for one's own (academic, feminist) purposes?" (143).

Let me translate these theoretical–methodological difficulties and challenges into a description of the two ethnographic approaches I employed. They are different mainly with respect to the position of the "authorial I" (Kirsch, 78).

Conversation-Based Research

From March 1994 to April 1995 I attended weekly sessions of a women's literacy group in the ABLA Homes, a public housing development on Chicago's Near West Side.[9] Some women came only once in a while to the literacy sessions, some came fairly regularly. I had ongoing contact with about fifteen women. After my visits at the literacy center ended, from September 1995 until

April 1997, I had conversations with ten women who at the time lived or worked in one of several public housing developments: the ABLA Homes, the Henry Horner Homes (on the West Side, but to the north of the City of Chicago's downtown business section), or the Altgeld Gardens (on the Far Southeast Side). I had the special help of Jenna, who drew on her extensive network of friends in order to find women who were willing to be interviewed. Jenna was careful pointing out to the women that they had to see some benefit in talking to someone from the outside about what it means to be responsible for children when living under rather harsh conditions. The women ranged in age from their late teens to their mid or late fifties. Some of them depended on public aid, some worked at minimally paid jobs, one woman was a full-time city employee. All of them were biological mothers or grandmothers. Methodologically speaking, these women were not a sample. They were telling stories connected to my interest in seeing the world from their perspective and in examining how these stories expressed their own unique participation in general social structures.

I conducted what has been called "conversation-based research" by engaging in mutual or "interactive interviews" (Stern 1998, 108). During these kinds of interviews the participants are making sense together. The researcher employs a "bottom-up methodology." Stern describes this process as being "grounded in the perspective of those carrying the burden of the struggle" (108). It does not, however, reduce the researcher to a disembodied, unemotional, or, in the positivist sense, "objective" controller of the interview process. However, while I continually invited the women to ask me any questions about my own life circumstances, and while I frequently participated in a conversational back and forth by sharing ideas or experiences, most of the talking was done by the women themselves. [10]

Their willingness to talk to me was complemented by my wish to learn from them. In order to truly learn about and appreciate the knowledge that was embedded in the everyday and everynight worlds of the women who were telling their stories, I had to practice what Alarcón describes as the ability to "learn to become unobtrusive, unimportant, patient to the point of tears, while at the same time open to learning any possible lessons" (1990, 362). Only then can something like "empathetic cooperation" take place, an ethical and spiritual stance that should not be mistaken for a "sympathy that maintains the arrogance of 'I'" (Sylvester 1995, 957).

My listening also had the strong ethical dimension of caring for the people who spoke and for what they were speaking about. As Naples points out, "the 'ethic of caring' forms one strategy to break down power differentials and experiential differences between the researcher and the researched" (1996, 101). At the same time, what are the grounds for such an ethic? What is empathy, and what kind of listening is involved in this strategy to break down power differentials?

It is a kind of listening that is not a form of silent passivity. Rather, it is what Schweickart calls an intense "interpretative agency" (1996, 319). However, listening, just as gaining a voice or giving voice to, has become a rather contestable issue in various analyses of the value and ethic of anthropological and ethnographic research. DeVault, for instance, devotes a separate section to the theme of voice and silence in ethnographic research where speaking and listening or being silent weaves in and out of quite different research practices and texts (1999, 59–83). Likewise, Phillips asks feminist anthropologists who question Western notions of development to "explore and make explicit their *theory of listening*" as it addresses the "epistemological question of how we know women's voices" (1996, 21, 18; emphasis in the original). It will help the researchers to become clear about their assumptions that underlie their methodology. Consequently,

Listening should not be taken for granted as a nonjudgmental process . . . ; it is, like any social activity, a process steeped in ideologies that need to be explicitly examined if we are to avoid the old development traps. A theory of listening would tell us what researchers think is important, why they might think so, and how they have played a role in ensuring that the reader will agree with them when they make women's voices central to their projects. (21)

My own acts of listening demanded that I critically scrutinize the material with which I wove my interpretations. I learned that whatever I heard or saw was first filtered through the mesh of preconceived notions and interpretations I had to acknowledge, keep at bay, or dismantle. In other words, I had to probe more deeply into the way my heart and intellect selected, ordered, filtered, or dismissed the stories I heard and the knowledge they contain. At the same time, conversation-based research is a "jointly constructed verbal encounter" (DeVault 1999, 100). The women I had conversations with were in control over the kind of relationship they were willing to engage in with an outside researcher, and also over which stories to tell. Susan Tucker, who recorded the memories of Black domestics and their white employers in the South, states quite succinctly what this situation entails: "I was very aware, throughout the interviewing and editing, that, above all, the stories told were ones that these women were willing to share. They were stories selectively remembered, selectively repeated, and selectively recorded" (1988, 4).

Whether at the literacy center or in the office of the Youth Center (where I conducted the interviews), I always met the women in their own environment where they were surrounded by women they knew well. Before conducting the interviews my experiences at the literacy center had helped me to tackle a rather tremendous challenge: to become excruciatingly aware of my visible membership in the white middle class. At the literacy center, however, I was much more a silent visitor who could be ignored, or whose offer to assist women in their efforts to gain literacy skills could simply be taken up. The fact that the literacy coordinator had invited me to fully participate in the weekly sessions, that the women had formed their own group, and that guest speakers, that is, other outsiders, quite frequently came to the weekly sessions must have lessened some of the misgivings the women certainly had about my presence. Whether working with individual women on improving their literacy skills or conducting a reading and writing class, I was a quiet participant observer who neither taped the sessions nor took notes during the special weekly session I attended.

When visiting the women I interviewed I clearly was first of all quite visibly white, I had the more personal attribute of having a foreign accent, and I was a middle-class college professor. The fact that I am a lesbian came up during a conversation that took place not long after I started the interview process. The occasion arose because one of the women made a rather homophobic remark about gay men, and I briefly responded. A few months after this rather brief verbal exchange, two of the women (Jenna and Rose) and I engaged in a lively debate about the differences between racism and homophobia. We managed to mutually enlighten each other by telling stories from our lived experience of these different kinds of stigmatization and discrimination. Our quite frank discussion was, however, made possible because we had already established a certain measure of trust based on our shared concern for the well-being of the children, a trust that was heavily weighted by my being a mother as well as a grandmother. While being a white middle-class outsider was always greeted with silence, my being a mother, that is, "normal" in that respect, seemed to open most conversational spaces. This could push some of the rather pronounced differences between us to the very background of attention. My desire to listen to stories that the outside world is totally disinterested in except when they are presented as mangled, stereotypical media images, must have contributed to the women's openness toward other fundamental differences between our worlds. So must have our shared passionate concern for the well-being of children.

While I was clearly an outsider, I was not necessarily fixed to one extreme of the insider/outsider duality. My being a mother who wanted to hear how the women managed to live with children in a kind of war zone[11] and who openly admired them for the tremendous strength and courage they had to muster made me less of an outsider. At the same time, as a foreigner with an accent, I was also a "friendly stranger." As Cotterill reports from her own experience, the friendly stranger is someone who exercises less social control over the respondents. The relationship "exists for the purpose of the research and is terminated when the interviews are complete. Indeed, respondents may feel more comfortable talking to a 'friendly stranger' because it allows them to exercise some control over the relationship" (1992, 596). In other words, one's outsiderness or insiderness is not a fixed, immovable status where individuals or groups are placed on different sides of a fence, but a position that can shift or be negotiated around different points of connection or strangeness (see also Naples 1999).

Although the women seemed to be fairly comfortable telling me stories that contained a tremendous amount of pain, fear, and sorrow, that comfort did not lessen my ethical responsibility to try to perceive myself through the eyes of the women I interviewed. In order to address and experience some of the entrenched social power dynamics, I had to learn to look at myself as the "other" I clearly represented in the context of Chicago's public housing projects. I engaged in a difficult, sometimes successful, sometimes unsuccessful process of locating the center of my perception outside of myself. Mies describes this learning process in the following way: "The outside . . . is not, however, some imaginary reality, but rather the real, living woman who is looking at me, trying to understand me, posing unusual questions" (1991, 79). In other words, by trying to see myself through the eyes of the women I had conversations with, I became more conscious of my own otherness and therefore also more vigilant about not simply appropriating the women's stories from that very place of otherness. By honoring the trust and voices of the women, I hope my ethnographic inquiry contributes to learning about and from each other, and to cross-cultural understanding and communication.

Practice-Based Inquiry

Where I study my own experiences and practices as a teacher–learner, I move out of the shadows of the role of the observer who is documenting her observations in copious field notes, or of the role of the interviewer whose tape recorder captures people's words. Instead, I more fully engage in practice-based inquiry by focusing on my identity as an educator and what it means to be a teacher, a teacher–learner, or simply a learner. In particular, I examine my tasks and responsibilities and the kind of pedagogical challenges I face when trying to work within the parameters of "subsistence knowing," one of the categories of challenge emanating from subsistence work. Chapter 5, where I record the results of this kind of ethnographic study, is therefore what has been called an "author-saturated" text (Kirsch 1999). This represents methodological as well as ethical challenges.

One of the dangers of engaging in autobiographical accounts is to "become shallow and perfunctory," the other to become "self-indulgent and narcissistic" (Kirsch 1999, 77; see also DeVault 1997, 225; Hertz 1997, xvi). How do I therefore justify my use of the "authorial I" without falling into either one of these traps? To paraphrase Kirsch, how can I distinguish between personal factors that affect my work in terms of enabling me to see certain perspectives or blinding me to others (1999, 80)?

Instead of simply locating myself on the power map of individual and collective identities, I start with the recognition that educational endeavors are always personal, and that the participants' multiple or multi-faceted identities become an integral part of each educational situation. Being an active participant—as a student or as a teacher—in an educational setting therefore requires one to grapple with these identities and to recognize how some students or teachers are confronted with the difficult task of managing several stigmatized identities (Hurtado 1996, 375). Multiple identities always contain those that are socially devalued and lodged in corresponding experiences, and they are therefore not just bits and pieces of a thrown-together heap. Instead, they relate to each other in very specific, hierarchically organized ways. Whereas thinking and reading about these difficulties prepared me for an analysis of their reality in my own educational work, it did not take away the necessity of engaging in practice-based, contextualized inquiry. What inspired me to embark upon an analysis of my educational work was reading what others had to say about the challenges and possibilities of such an inquiry in Mayberry's anthology *Teaching What You're Not* (1996). Translating the various writers' insights into an examination of my own educational practice also asked me to draw deeper connections between my personal experience and the larger political-ethical agenda that motivates this practice. In turn, I had to translate the theoretical categories of challenge that emanate from a subsistence perspective into concrete practical endeavors that move everyone—myself included—in the direction of such a perspective, and of corresponding ways of seeing, knowing, and acting in the world.

I therefore place all three educational contexts—the literacy center, the office of the youth center, my own university—at the center of scrutinizing my own educational work around ways of knowing, forms of knowledge, skills, and competencies that are attached to experiences of creating and nourishing life, or the conditions of life. These contexts can be put on a continuum that shows their geographical and social connectedness as well as separation. My awareness of this interconnectedness of different worlds is the impetus behind my work, behind my venturing out of the relative safety and professional respectability of my college environment. I know that I cannot fully understand the university world (and what it represents in society in general) without understanding the world that is quite removed from it, and why there is such a distance between these worlds. Clearly, the knowledge I bring to these worlds, the knowledge I gain from working in them mutually enhance each other and contribute to my understanding not only of these worlds, and what it means to live in them, but also how it shapes my professional identity and my political commitment as an educator.

My ethical and epistemological coalition-building is rooted in my concern for preserving life-affirming ways of living and working. This concern glues together the different pieces of this book. Going back to the quilt metaphor, it is the thread with which I stitched the patches together into a complex, colorful pattern. Some of the patches are more sturdy, others more fragile, some have bright, some have subdued colors, but all of them are supported by a strong, resilient piece of fabric, one I started weaving together many years ago. In theoretical terms it is the notion and reality of subsistence and motherwork, and of a corresponding life-affirming orientation. Subsistence work therefore provides the background weave of my book, and throughout the book I unfold layers of its meaning in close conjunction with motherwork performed under very difficult circumstances, and with mother-activists or community othermothers who sustain and practice subsistence/motherwork.

NOTES

1. While I address this issue more fully in the methodology section, here I want to simply state that my "giving voice" to the women does not mean I ignore the uneven power relationship between myself, the middle-class white researcher, and the women who are located on the very margins of society. I also do not claim to "empower" the women, as is often pronounced by feminist researchers who do fieldwork (see Wolf 1996, 25–26).

2. I capitalize "Black" but not "white" because it signals more than skin color (with all its associated normative assumptions). In the United States "Black" rather than "black" speaks more clearly of a specific cultural identity while "white" refers to all that is differently located in the racialized power nexus of U.S. society. It can imply diverse cultural identities, such as Irish or Austrian.

3. Frida Furman pointed out these similarities to me, as she herself had been involved in an ethnographic study of older Jewish women who regularly attend a beauty salon, thus describing the complexities of the lives and experiences of a population that is socially devalued and kept in the shadows of invisibility. See her *Facing the Mirror* (1997).

4. Albelda and Folbre 1996; Sidel 1996; Abramovitz 1996.

5. The portrayal of welfare mothers as typically Black automatically associates race with the nonworking poor, or the underclass. It thereby underwrites the social dismissal of the existence of the Black working class. See Williams 1995; and Duneier 1992.

6. DeParle, for instance, reports in the *New York Times* that many homeless shelters have seen a sharp rise in single women who had to leave their children with relatives (21 February 1999, A24).

7. See, for instance, Cohen, Jones, and Tronto 1997a; Ferree and Martin 1995; Kaplan 1997; West and Blumberg 1990b.

8. I owe this observation to Narayan 1997, xii.

9. "ABLA" stands for the names of a cluster of four public housing projects: Grace Abbott Homes, which are an extension of the Jane Addams and Robert Brooks projects, and the Loomis Courts, adjacent to the Brooks Homes. As Bowly wrote in 1978 with respect to the Abbott Homes, and as I myself experienced when visiting that area, "More than any project built in Chicago to that date [early 60s], the overall feeling is forbidding, and the human scale is completely lost" (91). In 1992, before HUD (U.S. Department of Housing and Urban Development) and the CHA (Chicago Housing Authority) engaged in various redevelopment efforts, more than 2,700 families lived in 3,600 apartments (McRoberts, 1998b).

10. Patai writes about the eager willingness of Brazilian slum-dwellers to be interviewed by her. She observes that she "became convinced that not enough people are listening, and that the opportunity to talk about one's life, to reflect on its shapes and patterns, to make sense of it to oneself and to another human being, was an intrinsically valuable experience" (1991, 142). I think she articulates an important aspect of the public housing residents' willingness to talk to me.

11. The term war zone has become rather common in descriptions of inner city conditions (see, for instance, Garbarino, Kostelney, and Dubrow 1991; Jones, Newman, and Isay 1997; Popkin et al. 2000).

― *Chapter 1* ―

The War Against Subsistence

While motherwork and all it entails have never been acknowledged as vitally important work, the recent political move of "ending welfare as we know it" has twisted this work into a sign of moral failing. This historical move feeds on Western ideas about rights and laws which declare "nature" and "the feminine"—and everything or everybody associated with it—as Other, as being outside the norm of culture and civilization:

Women, nature and "the feminine" do exist, but get produced *and* abolished, are feared *and* denied, used *and* silenced. . . . The feminine "others" therefore appear as a vague and unspeakable "threat to civilization," as the potentially external *and* internal danger of being godless, fatherless, immoral, possibly independent from any social order but feeding off a terrible chaos without rules, obedience, or "humanity." (von Werlhof 1996, 35)

Von Werlhof's words are quite alarming because they fully summarize the political and media-driven view of welfare mothers in the United States. What is it these mothers are doing wrong? They are poor and they raise children. Poverty has traditionally been associated with some kind of "otherness"—such as being nonwhite, undeveloped, female, or somehow belonging to the realm of the "feminine" by being a nonwhite man—and with personal failure. It is precisely these categories that have been associated with cheap labor, a direct bonus for corporate profits. Most poverty in the United States is the result of jobs paying wages below the official poverty line (Abramovitz 1996; Sidel 1996; DiFazio 1998). Not surprisingly, poverty can be good for business, and although former President Clinton abolished "welfare as we know it," he certainly did not put an end to "poverty as we know it."

But why do poor single mothers get a lot of public attention while the working poor do not? Poverty itself is therefore not the main reason for stigmatizing welfare mothers. Can they be wrong because they have children, although this is still considered a woman's true calling? Yes, because they are having babies without the financial resources needed to do this unpaid work as inconspicuously as possible in the shadows of the private nuclear family. When mother-work relies on the bad dependency—on the state—instead of on the good dependency—on an income-earning husband or boyfriend—this work becomes highly visible.

Clearly, good mothers do their work in private, without pay. They don't bother their employers or the government by asking for special support, and their husbands or boyfriends may not be very willing to give that support either because, after all, raising children is still considered a woman's job. They are also good mothers if they adjust children to the parameters of the system by instilling in them the ability to look at their life in terms of economic calculation, or bottom-line thinking, as the primary, most important principle guiding their thoughts, feelings, and actions. Motherwork can therefore contribute to "domesticating, educating, and normalizing" children by socializing them into "proper producers and consumers of commodities" (von Werlhof 1996, 165, 169).

This tangled knot of ideological and material-structural norms and conditions includes all poor mothers, regardless of whether they are members of the working or the jobless poor. Their economic deprivation can therefore only partly be captured by the notion of socioeconomic class, the category usually employed in an analysis of economic welfare. Regardless of numerous variations in terms of who has access to what kind of work at what kind of pay, class represents a universal, across-the-board association with paid work or wage labor. Mothering, or motherwork, on the other hand, generally falls under the umbrella term of "nonwork," a categorization that is mirrored by its generally unpaid status. It is not considered real work in the official, normative sense of the word whose meaning is inseparable from a market perspective. It is, however, precisely this market-driven view that connects poverty and class, or socioeconomic status, notions that most directly refer to economic welfare. Since the majority of the poor are, however, women and children, how then does mothering relate to economic welfare, and thus to class?

This question underlies one of my reasons for using the term "motherwork" rather than "mothering." First of all, motherwork captures "a certain element of present social reality. . . that women mostly raise children" (Peters 1985, 16). In addition, not only does the raising of children comprise a tremendous amount of work, as unpaid (or minimally paid) work it also has direct economic implications. In DeVault's words the concept of work "does for mothers' activities what it had earlier done in research on housework—calls attention to the time and effort involved in mothering, and its social and economic significance" (1999, 80).[1] Motherwork is therefore not only a form of life-affirming work, it also provides an invisible basis for waged work. "Subsistence work" is the term that has been used by a number of feminist theorists, a term that summarizes the dual nature of this kind of work, that is, work that is both unrecognized (and unpaid) as well as life-sustaining.

THE DUAL NATURE OF SUBSISTENCE WORK

Subsistence work is a rather awkward term, "not easy and smooth. It demands explanation." (Bennholdt-Thomsen and Mies 1999, 19). However, while "life-affirming work" does capture the spiritual core of subsistence work, the latter is a more precise analytical, social-economic concept. As such a concept it names its underlying major orientation toward life, that is, survival or "subsistence" rather than profit. By being an integral part of critical economic analyses it also points to the economic imperatives that shape its dual nature.

Subsistence work is a concept, however, that has been used to summarize many different forms of unwaged or unremunerated labor, and it has been the focus of many debates.[2] In all cases the terms subsistence work, subsistence production, or subsistence economies are an integral part of discussions of the development of capitalism. By deriving their meaning from the history of industrialization (including its "post-" phase), these terms therefore signify a historical and geographical-political continuity. More precisely, subsistence work is a category that signifies the very "basis of capital accumulation and industrial commodity production, a basis which is constantly made subordinate and invisible" (von Werlhof 1991, 169). Although Marxist and mainstream economists alike have "repressed" (Beasley 1994) this relation of dependence, the history of colonialism and imperialism (and neocolonialism) shows that capitalist development has always depended on, and eventually destroyed, "precapitalist," "undeveloped," or indigenous subsistence economies.

Historically, indigenous economies were always locally or regionally specific. As place-bound economies their main orientation was to produce for their community's livelihood. Although goods were exchanged on the market, this exchange was also guided by a desire to trade locally produced goods for those that were offered on the market, and that were needed by the community. In *The Subsistence Perspective* (1999) Bennholdt-Thomsen and Mies discuss the many different exchange relationships that existed (and to some extent still exist) outside but also within market economies.[3] They also write about how work whose main motif was not the maximization of profit became "de-economized" under the auspices of a capitalist market perspective and was no longer considered part of the economy. In the case of European women who were members of the bourgeoisie, their work was attributed to love and affection in the private sphere. In the case of peasants, their work was considered irrelevant as long as it did not contribute to surplus value but was "only" part of the reproduction of the farm itself (115). As the two authors discuss, "There have never been societies without exchange relations; what there have been are exchange relations that

follow a different morality from the one dominant in the maximisation society"
(112). Planning economic exchange for the purpose of reaping and maximizing
profit or accumulating capital[4] was therefore entirely alien to these subsistence
producers. Instead, the well-being of the "whole house" (Brunner 1968), that is,
of all who lived in their community was dependent on everyone's work, not on
monetary income and external markets (Mies 1997, 14). In other words, everyone was guaranteed a "subsistence security." As Mies writes:

To guarantee this subsistence security on a given plot of land and within a given village
community in a given region, with a given geography and climate it was necessary to
maintain certain norms and institutions, in short a subsistence ethics . . . This subsistence
ethics was based on mutual help, village reciprocity, generosity (even sometimes forced
generosity), patron-client relations and, above all on the village commons, on which the
poor had a claim and a right. (15)

While Mies here refers to the European Middle Ages, manifestations of a
subsistence ethics, and therefore of a "moral economy," are still alive today, in
different parts of the world. They range from establishing community gardens
on recovered land following factory closings in Detroit (Dalla Costa 1997) to
the respectful and careful relationship to the land developed by women forest-
agriculturalists in India (Shiva 1989; Mies 1997).

Critics of a reductionist, free-market understanding of capitalism took issue
with the fact that subsistence economies were labeled "precapitalist," or "not-
yet-developed" as they engaged in production relations that moved entirely
within the scheme of money-commodity-money. Such hierarchical ordering
included the fantasy or illusion that subsistence economies had no market relations, or, if these relations were at all recognized, that they were obsolete remnants of preindustrial exchange relations. Since all this fit the Western notion of
progress and development it gave the green light to destroying subsistence
economies. This destruction was considered a necessary part of the bloody but
inevitable beginning of the history of capitalism, the time period associated with
the original, "primitive" accumulation of capital. As capitalism expanded its
influence, so the story goes, precapitalist societies became developed, and violent conquests were therefore no longer necessary. A direct quote from Marx's
Capital may most directly give a sense of this view:

The discovery of gold and silver in America, the extirpation, enslavement and entomb-
ment in mines of the aboriginal population, the beginning of the conquest and looting of
the East Indies, the turning of Africa into a warren for the commercial hunting of black-
skins, signalised the rosy dawn of the era of capitalist production. These idyllic proceed-
ings are the chief momenta of primitive accumulation. On their heads treads the commercial war of the European nations, with the globe for a theatre. (taken from Tucker 1978,
435–36)

War against subsistence means war against century-old knowledges and abilities of preserving seeds and growing food in harmony with the specifics of regional or local ecological conditions. In the process of development, of cultivating the various monocultures of export-oriented cash crops, of becoming dependent on chemical fertilizers and pesticides, and of monopolizing and controlling the production and use of seeds (which now extends to genetically modified seeds), these knowledges have become useless. Moreover, they contradict and undermine mass production for a global market (Bennholdt-Thomsen and Mies, 1999; Shiva 2000).

The anti-life dimension of the Western view of progress and economic development has left its mark on the remnants of subsistence work itself. As von Werlhof describes in *Mutter-Los* (1996), today subsistence work has a two-fold character. On the one hand it is a remnant of an older orientation that cherished and affirmed the richness, diversity, and multiplicity of life. On the other hand subsistence work has become part of, and thereby contributes to, the local and global context of exploitation. Thus, subsistence production, and a corresponding perspective, have either been directly destroyed in countries and regions that were "developed" by the colonial and neocolonial world capitalist system, or have been undermined and made to crumble.[5]

Seen from a global but also from a local perspective, in the majority of cases the conditions of subsistence work have been damaged or destroyed to an extent that the term itself is more accurately replaced by the term survival work—doing everything just to barely stay alive (Mies and Shiva 1993). Thus, subsistence work has been robbed of its spiritual, emotional, or cultural foundations. It appears as a burden, an unwelcome chore to be "contracted out" to those seen fit for this kind of work—to women, racially or ethnically marginalized people, and immigrants. It appears as the isolated work of mothers at home, often without sufficient material and social support, the work of nannies, the work of cleaning ladies, the work of domestics, the back-breaking work of farm workers. The only connection to subsistence work is the subsistence level of its wages. Or, subsistence work is performed as survival work, as the work of surviving under extreme conditions of poverty, scavenging for food among garbage, collecting scraps of material for constructing shelters, or growing food on parcels of land, a land unforgivingly barren.

Modernization and development have created poverty in the modern, entirely material sense of the word (Bennholdt-Thomsen and Mies 1999; Harcourt 1994). It is a form of poverty marked by endless toil and drudgery, the only survival strategies. This is one of the reasons that the term subsistence has primarily negative connotations. As Dalla Costa so vividly describes throughout her essay on "Development and Reproduction," "*from the human viewpoint, capitalist development has always been unsustainable* since it has assumed from the start, and continues to assume, extermination and hunger for an increasingly large part of humanity" (1995, 15; emphasis in the original). And as the example of Chicago's inner city illustrates, "even in the 'core countries' development today means scarcity, insecurity, violence and chaotic living conditions for more and more people" (von Werlhof 1996, 179). If any effort of staying alive moves within into the orbit of despondency and violence, the hope-inspiring, life-affirming essence of subsistence labor vanishes.

According to theorists who continued the Marxian analysis, this is all part of the ongoing and unstoppable social-economic development. Consequently, with the development and thus disappearance of self-sufficient subsistence econo-mies and, correspondingly, subsistence workers, the working class became the primary focus of critiques of capitalist exploitation. Marxian analyses have therefore moved exclusively within the orbit of a conceptual framework that centered on a bipolar class structure: the relationship of the working class to the ruling class, the owners of "the means of production."

Feminist sociologists who see the connection between the international and sexist division of labor[6] are the staunchest critics of this view. Their analyses pivot around the core observation that subsistence labor, in whatever form, re-mains the perennial basis of capital accumulation. Consequently, by moving out of the conceptual constricts of a the bipolar class structure, social relations are entirely retheorized, thus contradicting both Marxist and mainstream, neoliberal economic theories.

As Bennholdt-Thomsen and Mies (1999) discuss, a multitude of apparently heterogeneous production relations makes them unfit for the umbrella term wage labor that floats in and out of discussions of bipolar class relations. Housework in the industrialized countries, subsistence work of women in the Himalayas, or the work of small peasants in Mexico all signify variations of subsistence production relations. At the same time there are commonalties among geographically and culturally quite differently situated populations. As subsistence producers they are primarily, above all, concerned with creating and sustaining the means for living and staying alive rather than with finding a job that would give them the money to buy these means and *then* live. In other words, their subsistence work lies outside the imperatives of wage labor. Sec-ond, although they are primarily engaged in subsistence work, they do not live in a pre- or noncapitalist world. By being fully integrated in a world-capitalist system, their work is being exploited in several ways. For instance, its contribu-tion to people's chances for survival are calculated into providing the lowest pay possible, that is, a nonlivable wage, for market-work they may otherwise be engaged in. In other words, the wage does not cover people's subsistence. Or the products of their labor are simply taken away from them, or are minimally paid, and they appear as luxury items in the supermarkets of the First World (Bennholdt-Thomsen and Mies, 11). In reference to Mies's writings, Ebert (1996) summarizes the key aspects of this critical approach:

Building on the broad concept of productive labor in Marx as the transformation of natu-ral matter and his theory of primitive accumulation, Mies understands the production of surplus value and the accumulation of wealth as based, in part, on the appropriation and exploitation (the *superexploitation*) of subsistence labor. In doing so, she . . . provides an important means of theorizing the oppression of women, people of color, workers, and the colonized across various modes of production and historical social formations, but especially in global, imperialist capitalism. (80)

As this quote indicates, any discussion of subsistence labor and production does not involve a dismissal of the notion of class, or a class analysis. Quite the contrary is true. Although the meanings of class shift or become more fluid, especially when paid labor is examined in close relation to a number of other categories such as race–ethnicity, nationality, or sexual difference, an understanding of other forms of work—and motherwork is one of them—cannot bypass an understanding of class. Before making more direct connections between subsistence work and motherwork, the focus of this book, an overview of the various interpretations of class, how they relate to the sexual division of labor, and thus to the social devaluation of motherwork is appropriate.

THE INTRACTABILITY OF CLASS

What is class? When the focus is on its economic dimension, class can be seen primarily in terms of material interests that have two dimensions. As described by Wright (1997), one is *economic welfare*, or the total package of toil-leisure-income available to a person. Wright here agrees with all other, often quite diverse class analyses that range from Marxist to structural-functionalist or mainstream versions of formal social theory. In all cases class is associated with material interests and with the ability or power to pursue those interests (Hall 1997). Thus, despite an abundance of different definitions and analyses, class is always linked to a certain position in the economic structure and therefore to financial assets. As Folbre (1994) writes, "Assets are clearly important to class, whether described in terms of initial inheritance (as in 'the propertied classes'), current economic position (as in 'the top 1 per cent of all income recipients'), or control of particularly crucial assets (as in 'ownership of the means of production')" (57). While class implies a certain position in the economic structure, "class is also associated with a certain political position or ability to influence certain political outcomes" (57). Class therefore signifies "an interplay of economic interests with markets, economic organizations, political power, and cultural distinctions" (Hall, 31).

The other dimension of class Wright discusses is *economic power*, or the control over the "surplus product," and corresponding control relations. The surplus product, a core concept in Marxist analyses of the class structure, is "that part of the total social product that is left over after all of the inputs into production (both labor power and physical capital) have been reproduced" (46). Managers, for instance, occupy a capitalist location within control relations by dominating workers, but they also inhabit a working-class location within ownership relations by selling their labor power to capitalists (52). In other words,

they do not control the surplus product. Professional credential holders provide
another version of this indeterminacy of class location. They do sell their labor
power, but they are "privileged" by virtue of being less exploited than other
employees.

Hall describes how *economic class* becomes *social class* in relation to "social constructions of identity, class-as-status group cultures, processes of inclu-
sion and exclusion, in relation to group boundaries, and cross-cutting versus
aligned solidarities in relation to ethnic, racial, gender, and other social institutions" (31). Folbre makes a similar point with respect to race:

Most individuals feel a certain solidarity with others of a similar racial background, and
there are many historical examples of race-based strategies of collective action that have
effectively reinforced the importance of racial identity. Racial inequality cannot simply
be attributed to social norms or individual preferences for "racism," because it has economic and political dimensions. Many political rules, including restrictions on rights to
vote or own property, have been race-specific and, partly as a result, assets such as
wealth and educational attainments vary systematically by race. (1994, 57)

Thus, while "inequalities in the class structure distinguish social functions and
individual power," these distinctions "carry over to race and gender categories"
(Mantsios 1996, 102). Both gender and class can therefore be racialized in "societies where racial demarcation is endemic to their socio-cultural fabric and
heritage—to their laws and economy, to their institutionalized structures and
discourses, and to their epistemologies and every custom—gender identity is
inextricably linked to and even determined by racial identity" (Higginbotham
1992, 254). At the same time divisions of waged labor are not only based on
racialized norms and values, but also on material arrangements that are "embedded in a gendered divison of labor" (Brewer 1993, 19). Brewer illustrates this by
examining how regional as well as international economic changes since the
1980s have affected Black women's labor and all women's relation to work.
Despite a partial collapsing of race/gender divisions in the creation of the new
service working-class, a disproportionate number of Black women are employed
in the service sector that is known for its low wages, a financial disadvantage
that is exacerbated by the high unemployment rate of Black men (24). Brewer
summarizes the complex interplay of class, race, and sex in the following way:
"The working poor as a significant segment of the working class must be understood in a gendered context. Black male joblessness alone does not account for
the tremendous disadvantage of the Black poor. Race/gender segmentation and
low wages as reflected in the positioning of African-American women are con-
ceptually central to African-American class inequality today" (24).

Racial formation theory uses the term "racialization" for summarizing "the
processes by which racial meanings are attributed, and racial identities assigned"
(Winant 1994, 23; see also Omi and Winant 1986). Despite the many different
forms and intensities of these processes, and regardless of the terrain on which
personal, cultural, or social experiences or actions take place, all social-

institutional arrangements and practices are marked by processes of racialization. As a term that summarizes the multitude of corresponding processes, racialization can therefore provide a powerful "analytic tool that allows us to map the changing and contested negotiation of different racial-ethnic groups and subgroups as they insert themselves and are inserted into new social, political and economic environments" (Naples 1996, 95).[7] Not only are forms of racial or sexual oppression historically and geographically changing or shifting, they also cut across class lines, *and* "class oppression permeates other spheres of power and oppression, so that the oppression experienced by women and minorities is also differentiated along class lines" (Mantsios 1996, 102). Consequently, while class is an analytically distinct category, it is so interwoven with other categorical distinctions that it becomes almost intractable. Where it is explicitly expressed in feminist studies of economics, labor, and class, these studies are "almost entirely confined along disciplinary lines," and they are relegated to the terrain of specialist knowledges and excluded from an integrated transdisciplinary inquiry into gender and sexuality, thus marginalizing these issues in feminist theory itself" (Ebert 1996, 23).[8]

Where the intersectionality of class with sex, race, ethnicity, or nationality is more explicitly addressed, class is mostly mentioned with respect to social inequality, low wages, or poverty, but not necessarily specifically defined or analyzed.[9] More, or most, of the analytical weight is therefore placed on an examination of the workings of racism and sexism behind various forms of financial and cultural disempowerment. Patricia Hill Collins's analysis of the race-class intersectionality is an exception. She expands the concept of intersectionality developed by Crenshaw (1997), who primarily explores the intersection of gender and race, although she emphasizes that the concept can be expanded to factor in other issues such as class, sexual orientation, age, and color (551). Collins draws on a variety of social and economic theories and teases out specific features of economic class analysis that are "germane to conceptualizing how race-class intersectionality in the United States constitutes a particular type of group formation" (1998, 212). Collins marks four specific features. First, the dual meaning of class derives from its location in economic analyses *and* from the way "social groupings are actually organized within historically specific capitalist political economies," that is, by actual lived Black experience of complex economic conditions shaped, among other things, by institutionalized racism (213, 214); second, race, like ethnicity or nationality, has always been part of processes of exclusion and separation that visibly marked economic inequalities among groups; third, class is not an entity or "thing unto itself, because such a class could not exist without other economic classes to which it is linked in relationships of, at best, mutuality and, at worst, exploitation" (215–16); fourth, group culture and consciousness are a central component in approaching class as a dimension of group formation (216).

While Collins places her discussion of Black women's unique relationship to the intersection of race and class at the center of her book, Amott and Matthaei

(1996) provide an example of analyzing capitalist development in the United States with respect to "women's works" in general. The plural indicates the complex and multileveled intersection of class with racial-ethnic and gender formations, sex/race-typing of jobs in the formal and informal (including underground) labor market:

> The operation of gender, class, and racial-ethnic power in the labor market has had two main consequences. First, disempowered groups have been concentrated in jobs with lower pay, less job security, and more difficult and dangerous working conditions. Second, workplaces have been places of extreme segregation, in which workers have worked in jobs only with members of their same racial-ethnic, gender, and class group, even though the particular racial–ethnic group and gender assigned to a job may have varied across firms and regions. (318)

Mohanty widens the circle of analysis by illuminating "the minute and global processes of capitalist recolonization of women workers" (1997, 27): "Third-World women workers (defined in this context as both women from the geographical Third World and immigrant and indigenous women of color in the U.S. and Western Europe) occupy a specific social location in the international division of labor which *illuminates* and *explains* crucial features of the capitalist process of exploitation and domination" (7; emphasis in the original).

Although Mohanty focuses on women workers in various parts of the world and on how class intersects with race-ethnicity and culture, her notion of class is firmly tied to paid work. In that respect she does not part company with other radical, especially Marxist, writers. Likewise, Wright, who revises and expands the typical, Marxian bipolar class structure, nevertheless continues the Marxist notion of productive work as being equivalent to waged labor, and discusses the multiple, mediated, or temporary class locations a person may occupy within this structure in terms of paid work.

Other theorists such as Wallerstein (1979) have examined the multiplicity of both unwaged and waged labor, especially as they are tied to various international divisions of labor, and therefore to the capitalist world economy. The world-wide web of capitalism unifies the diversity of multiple forms of waged and unwaged labor, such as factory work, tenant farming, share cropping, or self-employment. Instead of generalizing waged labor, and thus corresponding forms of labor control, Wallerstein's theory includes more directly coercive forms such as slavery or peonage. However, the overall economic purpose of maximizing and expropriating surplus value is the broader, unifying context that makes the multitude of forms of labor highly interdependent.

This adds another dimension to the issue of class. Seen from the perspective of profit maximization, wage labor is expensive, and other forms of labor may therefore be much cheaper and thus much more profitable. The slave has always been a model for the ideal wage laborer (von Werlhof 1993a, 1023). Bales's *Disposable People* (1999), for instance, gives a detailed account of different kinds of a new slavery that is part of the global economy, and he describes how slaves are cheaper than the most ill-paid workers in the Third World: "In our global economy one of the standard explanations that multinational corporations give for closing factories in the 'first world' and open them in the 'third world' is the lower labor cost. Slavery can constitute a significant part of these savings. No paid workers, no matter how efficient, can compete economically with unpaid workers—slaves" (9–10). The history of capitalism with the global economy, that is, the new phase of capital accumulation and the free unencumbered flow of capital where trade rather than production signal its latest, most "advanced" version, is not only a history of economic development. It is also a history of genocide, slavery, and often deadly working conditions. Indentured servitude in the sweatshops of the late twentieth-century garment industry in the United States and new forms of slavery are a logical implication of unfettered bottom-line thinking.[10] The fact that "we" in the industrialized countries can jog in our expensive Nike shoes adds another dimension to the ideal worker. These commodities have been assembled in militaristically organized, extremely unhealthy production sites, or sweatshops, that is, the "Niketowns" of Southeast Asian or Latin American factories where workers are paid below the abysmally small minimum wage (Moberg 1999; se also Louie 2001).

The latest version of this trend is continued in the welfare states of the late twentieth century. In his discussion of the transformation of welfare to workfare states Peck (2001) points out that the tremendous variety of national, regional, or local policy shifts and ensuing welfare practices are embedded in a broader, international trend. A number of different national welfare systems that previously regulated various aspects of needs-based entitlements to welfare benefits transformed these systems into various forms of labor regulations. As a "new regime of labor" (171) that takes its cues from the labor market, workfarism contributes to the profitability of low-paid, highly unstable, that is, "flexible" jobs.

In the United States the "economic logic of welfare" (351) became quite apparent in August 1996 when Congress passed the new welfare regulations that created a virtually indentured labor force of welfare recipients. Significantly, Aid to Families with Dependent Children (AFDC) whose very name faintly echoed the ethics of subsistence security was replaced by Temporary Assistance to Needy Families (TANF). Consequently, "the seduction of cheap or '*free*' labor, combined with the requirement that states enroll increasing numbers of welfare recipients in work, has produced gross exploitation and immiserated low-wage workers who have lost their jobs." (Mink 1998b, 111; see also Peck 2001). Welfare mothers are therefore flooding the job market, and as "additional jobseekers" they "intensify competition for low-wage jobs and increase unemployment, making it easier for employers to keep wages down and harder for unions to negotiate contracts" (Abramovitz 1997, 17).

In many ways, what rules transnational capitalist maneuvers to make profits at the lowest cost possible—where "cost" is defined in entirely financial rather than social terms—has seeped in and gotten a hold of large numbers of people.

Their working and living conditions are themselves inseparable from the process of creating profit margins (Luttwak 1999). If people cannot be exploited because they are not part of the new slavery and do not come close to the possibility of a paid job, they become members of the "superfluous overpopulation" (von Werlhof 1994a, 169), somehow surviving on their own. This is true on a national as well as international level, especially with regards to "the genetic manipulation of food and the industrial and commercial policies that sustain that manipulation, [making] food increasingly inaccessible to the vast majority of humanity" (Dalla Costa 1997, 28; see also Shiva 2000). Dalla Costa points out that this leads "not only to a progressive destruction of nature's reproductive capacity, but also to the progressive annihilation—through wars, repression, epidemics, and hunger—of populations rendered superfluous by the expropriation and poisoning of land due to the use of pesticides and landmines" (28).

"SEXUAL ECONOMYTHS"

The search for cheap labor is a crucial aspect of the sexual politics of global capitalism. By drawing on ideologies of race, class, and nationality, the sexual politics of the global market tie in with cheap labor's versatility and flexibility. Mohanty (1997) therefore places the following question at the beginning of her analysis of common interests and a common context for struggles of women workers: "How does global capitalism, in search of ever-increasing profits, utilize gender and racialized ideologies in crafting forms of women's work?" (5). She delineates "the intersections between gender, race, and ethnicity, and the ideologies of work which locate women in particular exploitative contexts" by studying workers in the electronics industry in the Silicon Valley, and homeworkers in Narsapur, India (11). By drawing on a study by Mies (1982), she shows how the Indian lacemakers are "located as *housewives* and their work as *leisure time activity* in a very complex international market," and how "Third-World women in the electronics industry in the Silicon Valley are located as *mothers, wives*, and *supplementary* workers" (14–15; emphasis in the original). Mohanty thereby exposes "a domesticated definition of Third World women's work to be in actuality a strategy of global capitalist recolonization" (28).

By investigating the intersection of gender and work Mohanty points to the possibility of making "cross-cultural comparison and analysis which is grounded in the concrete realities of women's lives" (8). Moreover, domesticated definitions of women's labor structure the entire matrix of normative assumptions about real or "productive" work and provide fodder for corresponding ideological justifications of various forms of discrimination and exploitation. Clearly, as Mohanty writes, "part of what needs to change within racialized capitalist patriarchies is the very concept of work/labor, as well as the naturalization of heterosexual masculinity in the definition of 'the worker'" (11).

Motherwork is almost exclusively associated with women of all races or nationalities. This has a cost-saving underside: In order to be most profitable, that is, most exploitable, all workers have to be born and raised free of charge to the corporate world. Ironically, the white middle-class trope of the "housewife" has become the prototype for truly cheap labor and therefore an affliction that follows all women into the marketplace, irrespective of their racial-ethnic identity. The free market economy has always been extremely dependent on the low cost of women workers.[11]

As Mies (1986) points out, Marx's analysis of the value of labor power is based on the idea that "the worker has a 'non-working' housewife. . . . After this all female work is devalued, whether it is wage-work or housework" (110). In terms of feeding the profit motif the housewife, similar to the slave, constitutes one of the least expensive forms of labor. Corporations that travel around the globe in order to find a labor force as cheap as possible have therefore set in motion a trend that has been termed the "housewifization of labor." As Mies writes, "housewifization means the externalization, or ex-territorialization of costs which otherwise would have to be covered by the capitalists." While this means that "women's labour is considered a natural resource, freely available like air and water" (110), it provides a useful model for any labor that can be paid as little as possible.[12]

To consider women's work a natural resource is an integral aspect of the Marxist critique of capitalism. Folbre (1993) therefore correctly points out that "childbearing and childrearing were considered not only unproductive of surplus value but also irrelevant to its realization. Domestic tasks were never described as aspects of a creative labor process; they were relegated to the noneconomic world of nature and instinct, analogous to a spider weaving a web or a bee building a honeycomb" (103). Consequently, where the wage is seen as the only connection to the appropriation of surplus value and to exploitation, "women may be said to be even more exploited than paid workers since their labor is appropriated without a wage" (Glazer 1984, 65).

In *Sexual Economyths* Beasley (1994) discusses how mainstream or Marxist/Neo-Marxist economists alike equate the economy with the class system (68), thereby exacerbating the social disregard of work typically performed by women within the household:

Western women's domestic labour, and versions of this that penetrate the public sphere without payment, are extinguished (rendered invisible) because they are 'naturalised' as non-work and therefore not capable of social appropriation . . . Domestic labour is naturalised in the sense Marx outlines, yet it is also made to seem fixed or inevitable as a consequence of a literal linkage with nature/the body and of an association by extension with the 'biological' bases of personality, family, emotional life and sexual identity. (25)

Beasley developed the notion of an "emotional economy," thereby challenging "economic assumptions that exclude/marginalize women's experiences" (107). The emotional economy is instead "founded in the specificity of women's labour and the household economy, in their difference from market labour and the market economy." To assume the perspective of an emotional economy allows one to look at the "complex interweaving of the creation of services/goods with the experience of love/affection/care" (13), and to place "power relations between the sexes at centre stage."

SUBSISTENCE/MOTHERWORK

Although Beasley focuses on the work (white) women perform within the heterosexual nuclear family, her notion of an emotional economy comes fairly close to a description of core dimensions of subsistence labor. She writes that the economy cannot simply be equated with the class system, but that the household economy may also be viewed "as a repressed dimension underlying the market economy and integral to its existence" (115).

It is important to see motherwork, like any other kind of subsistence work, in relation to commodity or market-work. These different kinds of paid and unpaid work fall into a host of quite different categories and realities, and they relate to each other in equally numerous variations (see Hart 1992). In terms of motherwork there is, for instance, the typically unpaid, private work of maintaining a household and raising children. Where this work enters the private market in more direct ways, it takes on the form of the low-paid, "hidden occupation" of paid domestic work characterized by "non-specialized, diffuse menial tasks" (Hondagneu-Sotelo 1998, 202). This work is part of the informal sector comprised of jobs that are largely unregularized, unprotected, and precarious, and that take place in the shadow of a privatized environment. Such work is invisible, devalued, as well as super-exploited, especially when it is performed by undocumented workers (Hondagneu-Sotelo 1994, 1998). In the United States the history of African-American women workers speaks volumes about their concentration in private domestic service and agricultural work after the abolition of slavery, since they were barred from most other jobs. After the great migration to northern cities in the 1920s, African-American women continued their tradition of (minimally) paid work, one of the reasons being the low wages Black men were paid, wages too low to support a wife staying at home (Amott and Matthaei 1996, 165; see also Glenn 1997).

Whether subsistence work is unpaid or minimally paid, it refers to all kinds of work whose main orientation and primary and immediate purpose is to create or sustain the daily conditions of life. It maintains, cultivates, cleans up, mends, repairs, nurtures, comforts, heals for the sake of maintaining, mending, and sustaining life itself—above anything else. Where its main orientation is to affirm and sustain rather than profit from the conditions of life, this work also implies an intricate blending of the economic and social-cultural aspects of work and production.

Because subsistence work is interlaced with every aspect of daily and nightly life, it goes against the grain of what is generally referred to as "the economy," that is, a central but separate social structure. Moreover, by being involved in the daily care of our bodily existence, it violates the guiding principles of the

Western political-philosophical framework. Subsistence work is work that is associated with the old horror of "processes of growth and decay through which nature forever invades the human artifice, threatening the durability of the world and its fitness for human uses" (Arendt 1958, 100). This horror lives on in the current glorification of computer-mediated work—work that has been robbed of its sensuous dimensions and is most removed from the living, organic, or material conditions of economic production that always takes place "somewhere else." Likewise, the horror of being dependent on a woman's body for one's existence translates into the hope of assuming a god-like position by cloning a new human being in the lab. This may very well be "the final chapter in the long history of fantasy of self-generation by and for the men themselves—men of science, but men of the male kind, . . . and fascinated by their power" (Braidotti 1994, 88).

No matter how much scientists can control the making of human beings, however, we cannot ignore the fact that we are dependent on this "other," nonscientific, nontechnological work, the "bad" kind of work that administers to the body and its needs, a body that gets born and dies and that gets us in touch with the earth and its materials, with dirt, blood, and excrement, that is, with life in the primary, "primitive" sense of the word. The cultural denial of our dependence on this work translates into its disregard or neglect, and the exploitation of those whose work is most directly oriented toward life, toward the creation and sustenance of life.

NOTES

1. DeVault (1999) addresses "the vexing problem of labeling the unpaid work of raising children" (80) and stresses the use of different labels that capture different parts of reality: housework, family work, caring, the work of coordination, and interpersonal work (81). My construction and use of the term motherwork includes all of these parts of reality.

2. See, for instance, Bennholdt-Thomsen and Mies 1999; Hart 1992; Mies 1986; Mies and Shiva 1993; see also von Werlhof 1993a, 1993b, 1994a, 1994b, 1996.

3. Bennholdt-Thomsen gives a unique example of a female-dominated trade in the town of Juchitán, Mexico (the region of Oaxaca). As she writes,

Juchitán has a subsistence economy and remains this way insofar as the items and goals of the transactions serve to provide for the daily needs of the inhabitants. Trade in this rural town is considered nothing less than an art, a natural gift most women are born with. The specifics of trade nevertheless have to be learned, and the senior market women are proud and more than willing to pass on their special knowledge. This perception prevents the skill of trade from becoming the duty of dependent employees, thus preventing this economy from transforming into a capitalist business enterprise" (1996, 167).

4. Capital accumulation refers to the process where money begets money (goods) or commodities are produced and traded on the local or global market in order to reap profits. Once these profits are accumulated, they are used to expand the production and dis-

tribution of commodities. The Marxist term "primitive accumulation" refers to the genesis of the industrial capitalist where European merchants looted the colonies by appropriating material as well as aboriginal labor in forms that not only were coercive and violent but often also included genocide.

5. See, for instance, Braidotti et al. 1994.

6. I discussed how this connection is made by several feminist sociologists in *Working and Educating for Life* (1992).

7. See Brodkin 1998 for a detailed analysis of why race and ethnicity "almost define class" (23).

8. Bettie (2000) makes a related point with respect to the failure of feminist theory to transform class analysis and to conceptualize women as class subjects (3).

9. See, for instance, Chow, Wilkinson and Zinn 1996; Jameson and Armitage 1997; and Young and Dickerson 1994.

10. See, for instance, Anderson, Cavanagh, and Lee 1999; Figueroa 1999; and Moberg 1999. See also various contributions to *Women Transforming Politics* (Cohen, Jones, and Tronto, 1997a), particularly the essays by Jones and Jones, and Kwong. There are a number of organizations or coalitions of unions, student groups, or community organizations that fight against sweatshop conditions both here in the United States and abroad, such as the Campaign for Labor Rights, the National Labor Committee, or Sweatshop Watch. In 1998 Justice, Labor, and State departments created the National Labor Exploitation Taskforce in response to the rising numbers of immigrants and U.S. citizens being forced into servitude.

11. If we look at just a tiny slice of some of the basic capitalist-patriarchal mechanisms at work in the United States, and particularly in Chicago, women are making less for the same kind of work (and with the same level of education) than men (*Two Sides of the Coin* 1994). In other words, they are afflicted by the housewife syndrome.

12. See Hart 1992 for a detailed discussion of this point.

━ *Chapter 2* ━

"I Ache when I Think of My Children": Raising Children in Chicago's Public Housing

Chicago is fraught with a history of racial segregation. Today, its Black inner-city population lives surrounded by poverty and violence. Living in this environment also means being confronted with highly sensationalized media images of a generally deficient or deviant ghetto population where welfare mothers keep having babies society doesn't want. Motherwork is therefore confronted with numerous, and at times insurmountable, external and internal obstacles.

Listening to women who are part of this population, and reading about racism, poverty, and welfare made me realize that the women who are doing the inordinate amount of survival work, especially around children, do not get any public acknowledgment. Although the life-affirming substance of motherwork is still alive in their stories, these stories are utterly invisible to the public— defined as what gets attention in the public media, and what gets written about, documented, and reported by members of various institutions. Not surprisingly, the women I listened to themselves hardly every acknowledged the incredible strength and courage they were mustering twenty-four hours a day. This chapter documents their strength, courage, and creativity, and how their resistance to the devastation wrought upon an inner-city population builds on traditions that are still alive in however beleaguered form.

The women welcomed me with an amazing abundance of stories, perspectives, and analyses, something I can hardly do any justice to by presenting only small portions of their stories. As described in the Introduction, the selection and presentation of parts of their stories is clearly the product of a reflective and interpretive process that combines years of fieldwork and theoretical work. However, it is also the product of suggestions and ideas that came from the mothers themselves. When a colleague of mine mentioned a conference that was held in praise of Paolo Freire's work, I asked Rose and Jenna, two of the women I had regular contact with, to come with me and talk about the work they were doing with the children at the Henry Horner Homes, one of Chicago's public housing complexes. I asked these two women in particular because their emotional and spiritual responses to motherwork illustrate opposite ends of the entire spectrum of demands and expectations placed on women. Rose lives and breathes caring for children, and Jenna therefore rightfully calls her a "saint." Rose epitomizes the African-American tradition of putting children at the center of one's being. It is her core value, the core of her sense of self. Jenna, on the other hand, looks with some disdain at the infinite expectations placed on mothers, asking them to take care of everybody else's needs first, their own last, if at all. Jenna is a fighter who has developed a number of different ways to resist and undo the core traits of feminine training. In many ways she is on a war path—without, however, in any way shunning any of her more immediate or direct motherly or grandmotherly responsibilities.

Rose and Jenna organized their presentation around several themes that summarize the major characteristics of motherwork under extremely difficult circumstances. This not only sensitized me to a number of issues I was only vaguely aware of, but it also helped me structure this chapter. They stressed the fact that mothers had to juggle the many different roles of providing, nurturing, teaching, and protecting children, and they talked about the multitude of tasks, responsibilities, and skills mothers had to have or develop in order to be able to meet the omnipresent, all-encompassing challenges of their work. A second strand of their stories therefore dealt with the heavy demands these challenges place on individual women. Such demands range from never-ending care, where no space or time is left for the mother herself, to the draining worries and fears about the dangers surrounding the children twenty-four hours a day. They also spoke of the overwhelming intellectual and emotional demands placed on them because they have to see and know everything, have to be able to give attention to many different things at the same time. Finally, they accused society as a whole for providing little or no support for the work of mothering children, and they chided individual men for sharing the underlying belief that taking care of children is a woman's job rather than "real work," or that it is work of little or no value. Jenna's and Rose's presentation encapsulated the endless array of contradictions many Black mothers, especially mothers living in public housing, continuously have to wrestle with.

What follows is a brief history of the environment public housing creates for its residents and a discussion of how violence due to drug trafficking has permeated all living conditions. I then describe various dimensions of motherwork and how it is embedded in the matrix of a general social devaluation that feeds on a sexist division of labor. An indication of the many forms of knowledge, skills, tasks, and responsibilities mothers have to develop or shoulder under these extremely difficult and complex conditions is also given. I show how the women experience a loss of community and how it affects their motherwork. Despite many expressions of hopelessness and despair, stories of learning and unlearning convey a sense of agency and inspire hope for change.

PUBLIC HOUSING

"I'm Living in an Outhouse Now"

When I moved here in 1975 the people could sleep outside on the benches. Wouldn't nobody mess with them. People would leave their dogs out, wouldn't nobody mess with them. And that went on for a while and this year you could tell the changes. . . . And then it got to the point where there was always something happening. Then eventually drugs moved in and the gangs moved in. And then the people started moving out because CHA wasn't hearing anything and making it better for the people. Then we got down to where it was only three people on the eleventh floor. Me, Rose, and her sister Regina. And the building was real empty. People had moved out like crazy. The building was in the place where they were saying it was condemned. And we started marching, going to meetings, knocking on doors, passing out flyers. And then, eventually, I say like the end of eighty-nine, people started listening to what we was complaining about. They sent the fire people in here, saying that the place was a hazard to our health. That we was living in danger. And we didn't want to move. So we marched and we protested. And then they eventually sent someone in. That's when they did the first rehab.

They came in and did the building and put in security. Then after a while they changed them and put in the bad security and it's been going on ever since . . . that was in the nineties, that was like ninety-one or two. That is when they did the first rehab. Then after that they put in the security, then after that they put in the contract security. You know, hired from a private security company. Then after that they went from one security to another. Then there was just nothing.

When Cora told me this story, she was still living at the Henry Horner Homes, but she was hoping to move into one of the new townhouses the city was building across the street from the Homes. We were talking in the office of the Youth Center. "Office" here refers to an empty apartment on the ground floor of one of the dilapidated high-rises still standing, with very little so-called office equipment. There was a desk with a phone, a table, some chairs, and a refrigerator. The people meeting in this place tried to keep it tidy, which was particularly difficult with a muddy playground right in front of the building and with everything roach-infested. There were iron bars in front of the windows, with some of them boarded up. The first time I visited the Homes I went to the building but could not see the hand-written sign "Youth Center" behind the bars, and after wandering around for a while, two police officers tried to find it as well. When they finally found it, it was locked and nobody was there. They strongly advised me to drive away if I wanted to stay out of danger.[1]

Teresa, a woman who was living at the ABLA Homes said "I am living in an outhouse now." Khia, a woman who was living at the Altgeld Gardens, one of the earlier public housing settlements on the Far Southeast Side, complained about the often sickening smell people living there had to endure in the summer because "all this [the Altgeld Gardens] is built on a swamp. Waste and all that garbage and stuff, that's what this is built on top of. They had to evacuate everybody from Altgeld years ago, it was smelling so bad." Living on a waste dump was exacerbated by some of the actions of people who live there and by the city's lack of basic services. Khia's friend Darlene, for instance, complained about garbage being thrown on her back porch, and that everything was roach-infested. CHA maintenance people left calls for basic repairs mostly unanswered: "My tub has been stopped up for three whole weeks. So I been calling up there, and calling up there." Khia responded to Darlene's complaint by saying that "you got to go up there and just smack them. They just did this sink and I had a work order for this for two years."

Calls for repairs weren't the only calls left unanswered. So were calls for police. As Jenna said, "Police don't come when you call, firemen *may* come." This was a story repeated by several other women living in different projects. People are often scared of the CHA police.[2] Not only do they not come when called, but "a lot of policemen are in on it too, 'cause they're getting a cut of something." Khia's words indicate some of the possible drug-related reasons behind the CHA police's reluctance to respond to calls. As described by Rose in a story called "The Table Was Turned,"[3] when the CHA came to their building as part of a drug raid they kicked in doors, tore up property and simply left it up to the janitor to clean up. Moreover, police officers' behavior was seen as particularly scary for children, especially boys. As Regina said:

Sometimes you are a little scared to let your kids go out and play because they never can decide when they're going to shoot. You think about that a lot, and sometimes you think about how the CHA police come around and how they do people. I guess they use their badge as an excuse for how they do it. And ain't nobody going to say nothing. Sometimes you worry about whether they're going to shoot the kids by pulling out their gun. Going after one of them boys, they might shoot the kids that's playing.

Regina's concerns were affirmed by Ruth, who was living in a different project. She was constantly worried about her sixteen-year-old son because the dangers of living in a gang-controlled war zone are exacerbated by the behavior of the police. Ruth told of how one time the CHA police mistook her son for someone they were looking for. She said they threw him in a garbage can, knocked some of his teeth out, and almost killed him. Other women told of similar incidents.

These stories offer a glimpse of the reality these women face. There is a history behind Chicago's public housing developments, a history of blatant as well as insidious structural racism that is only dimly captured by the term segregation. As Wilson (1996) writes, "The segregated ghetto is the product of systematic racial practices such as restrictive covenants, redlining by banks and insurance companies, zoning, panic peddling by real estate agents, and the creation of massive public housing projects in low-income areas" (23). Through these and other measures, the federal government contributed to the early decay of inner-city neighborhoods and to the growth of jobless ghettos.

Several of the women I had spoken with talked about the rather pleasant living conditions—at least compared to the current ones—which were still in place when they first moved into public housing in the early seventies, and how the most dramatic changes started happening in the eighties. Rose, for instance, told me that she never had a problem with letting her children play outside when she first moved into the Horner Homes. Ruth and Marge also said that times weren't as hard as they were now, and that when they first moved into these Homes they were "nice and clean." Marge said, "I was proud of coming to the Henry Horner Homes, I thought I was doing something big . . . and I had good heat, a long bed to sleep in." There were also walking security guards, and "you couldn't spit on the floor. If you did, you were gonna pay a fine." Marge also said that she would "take her kids and a blanket, let them sit in the grass," while Ruth reported that "you could leave your doors open all night," to which Marge responded by saying that "I wouldn't take my cat out there now, or my dog."

Cora told me that in the seventies most people she knew had jobs, especially in the steel industry. She also mentioned that "a lot of people still have jobs today, but these are many different little jobs. They may not be long-term." Seen from that angle, the inner-city adult population does not substantially differ from the current trend of many workers holding more than one job, and this during a time when overtime is at a record high (Wilson 1996, 26). Rose also observed that the many little jobs held by public housing residents pay minimum wage, but "how can you live on a minimum wage job?"

History and Politics of Chicago's Public Housing

The history of Chicago's public housing and of the Chicago Housing Authority (CHA) is a history of Chicago politics. The CHA was formed in 1937 as part of the United States Housing Act, which transferred responsibility for constructing public housing from the federal government to local officials. Although the CHA was not an agency of Chicago but a nonprofit municipal corporation, its commissioners were appointed by the mayor. Decisions related to public housing, such as selection of sites, were therefore an integral part of Chicago's political machine. When the mayor fired the liberal, social-change oriented executive secretary of the CHA in 1954, public housing was no longer viewed as a vehicle for social change, as it had until then. No matter how unrealistic corresponding expectations for fundamental social change might have been, the shift in control from liberal to conservative politicians opened the doors very wide for the CHA to head for a virtually all-Black family occupancy: All locations for new projects were selected by the CHA and by the political leadership of Chicago, and these selections were aimed at constraining, segregating, and isolating the poor Black population, creating a "second ghetto" (Hirsch 1998). In chronological terms this meant that the rowhouses that comprised 90 percent of public housing construction between 1941 and 1946 were almost completely replaced by the CHA's eleven high-rises constructed between 1950 and 1969 (Bowly 1978; Popkin et al. 2000; Venkatesh 2000).

Originally, the CHA's dual purpose was to provide affordable housing and to remove slums and other blighted areas. Since racial segregation was federal policy when the CHA was formed, the prewar public housing projects were rented exclusively to white tenants, with the exception of the Ida B.Wells Homes which in 1941 finally opened exclusively for Black tenants. When temporary housing was built for war-industry workers, and later for World War II veterans, a small number of Black families were let in, especially since the housing shortage was particularly severe for the Black population (Bowly 1978).

Aside from earmarking a small number of two-room apartments for elderly couples, the CHA accepted only "complete families" with children. In order to minimize the occurrence of incidents of racial violence where whites sometimes fire-bombed the home of a Black family who had moved into their neighborhood, the housing authority even arranged for Black families to move in during the day when the white men would be at work (Lemann 1991, 71). Many of these families, Black or white, did not stay very long in the projects because public housing was seen as the first step on the road toward a family's economic recovery.

In 1949, when the CHA received funds for 80,000 new public housing units, and after lengthy arguments concerning whether the new projects were to be built on unused land in white neighborhoods or inside the overcrowded Black belt, the City Council approved a plan to build the units on land that would be made available by tearing down existing poor Black neighborhoods, that is, engaging in widespread slum clearance. As reported in the *Chicago Tribune*, "brute local power begot the physical isolation of Chicago's worst public housing projects when the City Council in the 1950s and 1960s located nearly all of them in areas that remain overwhelmingly poor and black" (Kamin 1995b, 9).

Building high-rises was the logical answer to the city's decision not to build projects in the vacant areas of white neighborhoods but rather confine them to already crowded Black neighborhoods. By 1957 the first Henry Horner Homes were built, and by 1962 the Stateway Gardens, Cabrini-Green, and the Robert Taylor Homes. The Taylor Homes—a South Side development with twenty-eight identical sixteen-story buildings—are the largest public housing complex in the world, fittingly called public housing's "crowning achievement" (Lemann 1991, 91–92).[4] Crowning achievements such as these meant that "the new high-rise concrete towers heaped poor people upon poor people, boxing communities inside their walls" (O'Neill 1997c, 1). Along with reinforcing racial segregation by building a major expressway one block west of a strip of public housing high-rises came overcrowded Black public schools. White schools in adjacent areas were half-empty.

By the mid-1960s the developments began to show signs of decline. Mayor Daley's push for the projects to be built and filled up as quickly as possible certainly contributed to the deterioration of the quality of life in public housing. Originally, the screening of applicants included an interview by a social worker, a verification of one's employment, a check of one's police record, and a home visit by an investigator (Bowly 1978, 32). The tenant screening process had become too cumbersome to keep up with the pace at which public housing units were being filled. By the time the last three Taylor Homes were finished, the tenants were barely screened at all. Because of the lack of screening, many projects soon became crime-ridden. In the late fifties and early sixties, gangs had a visible presence in the projects.

In the summer of 1966, the CHA was sued by a group of civil rights lawyers representing several tenants and applicants for public housing for violating the Civil Rights Act and the Fourteenth Amendment by building segregated housing projects. The case was named after its leading plaintiff, Dorothy Gautreaux, a public housing tenant and civil rights activist. Both, the CHA and the U.S. Department of Housing and Urban Development (HUD), were charged with racial discrimination. While the HUD case was held in abeyance the CHA case proceeded. In 1969, a federal court ruling stopped the construction of large-scale public housing developments in Black areas and ordered the CHA to engage in a "mobility" or integration effort by developing a scattered site program.[5] The HUD case was finally settled by the federal Supreme Court in 1976, ordering relief through Section 8 certificates as a means to help people move out of public housing areas.[6]

By the mid-1970s, the unemployment rate was up to 50 percent in many buildings. There are a number of social, political, and economic reasons behind this shift from "institutional to jobless ghettos" (Wilson 1996, 46). As crime in public housing got worse, working families steadily moved out. They were replaced by single mothers on public aid because an amendment to a housing bill had set public housing rent at a fourth of each tenant's income. The amendment meant to help the poorest residents, such as families relying on welfare, by making their rent cheaper, but it caused the rent to become too expensive for the working families who were not on public aid. Many of them left. The original mix of families dependent on public aid and the working poor that had provided some stability disappeared.

However, the high rate of unemployment has not only been fed by government policies but by macroeconomic trends as well, especially those related to industrial restructuring. As reported by Wilson,

Fifty-seven percent of Chicago's employed inner-city black fathers . . . who were born between 1950 and 1955 worked in manufacturing and construction industries in 1974. By 1987, industrial employment in this group had fallen to 31 percent. Of those born between 1956 and 1960, 52 percent worked in these industries as late as 1978. But again, by 1987 industrial employment in this group fell to 28 percent. No other male ethnic group in the inner city experienced such an overall precipitous drop in manufacturing employment. (30)

It is therefore the combination of joblessness, declining wages, and a rapid de-
pletion of employment opportunities that have contributed to the recent growth
in ghetto poverty, and to the economic and social dislocation that has affected
Chicago's inner city. One of the results of this process has been a steady decline
in population density, which severely impacts the overall social organization
and sense of community in a ghetto neighborhood.

By the early 1980s as many as half of the units in projects were vacant, due
to the unlivable conditions brought on by massive maintenance neglect. These
apartments became centers of gang activity, prostitution, weapons storage, and
drug dealing. Because of easy access to drugs, and because of the desperate
conditions in the projects, many of the residents were becoming drug addicts.
Crack cocaine was first introduced to Chicago projects in the late 1980s. This
highly addictive and easy-to-make drug has been the center of many residents'
life ever since.[7]

Angered by mounting evidence of mismanagement and CHA's overall failure, HUD took over public housing management in May 1995.[8] Its stated purpose was to "reverse decades of decline, rehabilitate the dilapidated housing
stock with limited funding, reform the management structure." Because "the
depths of the problem were staggering," HUD promised to address the problem
of "miles of poorly maintained high-rises filled with very poor people, plagued
by crime and bureaucratic resistance to change" (Chicago Housing Authority
1997). Consequently, since 1996 six of Chicago's public housing developments
have been drawn into a scheme that is alternatively called "redevelopment,"
"renewal," or "revitalization," depending on the specifics of planned or ongoing
changes.

The ABLA Homes and the Henry Horner Homes are two of the six developments that became prime candidates for redevelopment efforts. Their geographical location is seen as "a real estate agent's dream" (Simpson 1996, 8).
They are close to Chicago's downtown business district, public transportation,
major expressways, and a large medical complex. Redevelopment therefore
translates into "commercial gentrification," where the public housing problem is
being 'solved' by evicting many tenants and importing a better class of people"
(Venkatesh 1997, 38, 34). As pointed out by the leader of a local fair-housing
group, "there is a lot of focus on the land-rich areas like Cabrini and Horner and
some discussion about Taylor, but I think there has to be a comprehensive plan
that includes the Altgeld Gardens, which is sitting on a waste dump" (quoted in
Gordon and Ylisela 1998, 17). From a developer's point of view, the Altgeld
Garden's Far Southeast Side location provides absolutely no corporate and municipal impetus for redeveloping or revitalizing its abysmal conditions. Moreover, as EPA reports show, several kinds of carcinogenic toxins can be found at
dangerously high levels in the soil on which Altgeld was built. Residents therefore report a high incidence of cancer, asthma, and liver and kidney disease.
Karl Grossman (1993) attributes this attitude to environmental racism whereby
areas get dumped on because they are largely inhabited by African Americans

or Latinos. Hazel Johnson, a resident of the Altgeld Gardens and the head of People for Community Recovery said that "they figure that we're not going to come out and protest and disagree" (Grossman 1993, 326; see also Lyderson 1998).[9]

Public housing residents get caught in various redevelopment snags. For some of them the rehab of low-rise units produced some benefits, others keep living among broken steam pipes and flooded basements. In January 1999, for instance, the dysfunctional heating system at the Taylor Homes caused an infant to freeze to death. Pipes burst throughout the development and 800 families were relocated in the emergency. Some residents may be on the Section 8 waiting list, whereas others may have been able to utilize their Section 8 voucher to find an affordable apartment. Until recently, however, five out of ten residents had to bring their vouchers back because they could not find a place to live. Since Section 8 is far from being a guaranteed replacement program, there is a long waiting list of families hoping for vouchers. With market rates on the rise in the city, landlords may choose not to renew a lease after a year, and a family may have to find a new apartment every year.[10] In addition, in 1995 almost two thirds of poor renters in the Chicago area paid more than 50 percent of their income for housing (Fischer 1999, 8). Every low-cost unit is faced with more than two low-income renter households and almost 20 percent of low-income families are doubling up or living in overcrowded conditions (9). This makes Section 8 practically the only housing alternative for people vacating developments.

Space does not allow me to go into the tremendous bureaucratic complexity of current redevelopment schemes,[11] but I want to address two major points. First, regardless of the terminology being used or the plan being pursued, whether it is redevelopment, revitalization, or renewal, the fundamental issue of poverty is never addressed by reporters or city officials discussing aspects of these plans. If it is mentioned at all, it is presented as part of the public housing population's personal failure—and this regardless of the fact that the CHA's territory covers nine of the ten poorest areas in the United States (McRoberts and Wilson 1998, 1). As Wardell Yogathan, the cofounder of the Coalition to Protect Public Housing, stated, "If there's a tremendous economic problem in public housing, they're going to be the same disadvantaged people wherever they go" (O'Neill 1997b, 6). The poor who are blighting sections of the urban landscape do not, of course, fit into the real estate agent's dream about the good, profitable location of these sections. Jennie Dunn, vice president of an ABLA tenants organization, therefore rightfully said: "I don't call that renewal. I call that removal" (6). As stated by a Chicago housing attorney who is suing the CHA for violating tenants' rights, eviction can be used as a "replacement tool" (O'Neill 1997a, 1). CHA's *Plan for Transformation* will make it easier for CHA to evict families (Garza and McRoberts, 1999, 10). Not surprisingly, the eviction rates are highest in four developments slated for revitalization: Addams-Brooks-Loomis-Abbott, on the Near West Side; Cabrini Green, on the Near

North Side; Henry Horner Homes, on the West Side; and the Robert Taylor
Homes, on the South Side (Rogal 1998, 1).

As critics of redevelopments point out, the demolished high-rises will "resur-
face as sprawling low-rise ghettos" (O'Neill 1997a, 9). The Woods Fund of
Chicago reports that in 1998 80 percent of relocated families were living in 90
percent African American census tracts, and the other 20 percent where the
population is at least 50 percent Black (Fischer 1999, 7). Not only has the supply of affordable housing for the poorest generally declined, with a particularly
tight market outside traditional Black areas, but families are also confronted
with the legacy of a dual housing market that still governs perceptions of where
Black and poor people can and cannot live (15).[12] Race is still the main divider
where white people can move anywhere where they can afford a home, but
Black people are funneled toward their own.

Not surprisingly, white and Latino residents are resisting the attempts of
having scattered site public housing developed in their neighborhoods, or of
having Black families move in (Fischer 1999, 3; McRoberts 1998b,1; Rubinowitz and Rosenbaum 2000).[13] In addition, developers, city officials and yup-
pies are gentrifying inner-city areas at a rather rapid pace, and corporations are
increasingly industrializing the suburbs. Thus, by pushing poor people to the
suburbs Chicago may start to resemble European cities where impoverished
suburbs surround wealthy inner cities. Section 8 housing is typically found in
areas farther from the city center than public housing, that is, farther from jobs,
schools, hospitals, churches, and social services. This is also the area where the
absence of a level playing field with respect to Section 8 hits hardest—by making it possible that a family may have to move every year. By pushing the poorest people to the suburbs, communities are transformed into desperate pockets
of nomads who are forced to abandon their only resources: personal relationships and community institutions. In the words of Deborah Young, vice president of the Robert Taylor Local Advisory Council, "It's like we've become the
new Indians of the Street Corridor, so let's find a new reservation to put us on"
(Hanney 1999, 3).

Thousands of people are still living in the old reservations, however, that are
marked by poverty and social isolation. One of Rose's comments was particularly insightful regarding the interplay of general economic deprivation and personal responses to it, an interplay that, in turn, creates its own economic dynamics:

The economy is so bad, you got people here who would love to hold down a job. A lot of
the men here, they want to work. There's no place for them to work, they can't find jobs.
So the next best thing is to get high. When you get high, you have no responsibilities,
you have nobody you have to care for except getting high. You're addicted to getting
drugs now. You don't think about you got a baby that needs feeding. A child needs shoes
on. Somebody that needs a coat or whatever the case may be, food on the table. You
don't think about that. And there is no place for these men to work and call themselves
men. There are minimum wage jobs out there. But how can you work a minimum wage

job, pay to get to these jobs and then come home? You don't have enough in your pocket to give.

Rose's words indicate the rather complex relationship between economic deprivation, men's loss of a stable sense of self tied to the role of economic provider, drug addiction (and drug dealing), and neglect of family responsibilities. At the same time, she—like all the other women—is also suffering from a constant fear of the dangers posed by gang activity.

DRUGS AND VIOLENCE

"You're Addicted to Getting Drugs Now"

Every Friday they gather around in their circle, and they was Vice Lords. So I thought they was all together. Then I went back upstairs to check on my daughter Kionna . . . And then as I was going to come back downstairs to finish washing, you know, to look at the washing machine, there go three shots. And the second shot . . . that sounded like that was the window. And then I heard another one, and that's when we all got down on the floor. I was telling them you all get back. And then I was going downstairs to open my door, and the screen glass was all in the door. So I called the CHA police out here, they did not come.

In Darlene's words, "I don't let my son go to school out here. Because it's just entirely too bad. Because I remember that day, my little nephew, he was going over here to this school and they was just shooting and shooting. Bullets just flying all over. My little nephew had to jump into that dirty dumpster, and he is just in fifth grade."

Other women also had many stories about their constant fears that their children could be in the wrong place at the wrong time. However, their own lives were not excluded from these worries. Some of the women at the ABLA Homes literacy center, for instance, on occasion mentioned rather sarcastically that they never knew whether they would be able to come to the next literacy meeting because they couldn't be sure they would still be alive.

During the mid-sixties, gangs were becoming large criminal organizations, gaining control over all high-rise housing projects. This was the beginning of a trend that eventually changed projects such as the Robert Taylor Homes "from the oasis of decent housing for the black poor they were meant to be, into a hellhole whose residents were terrorized by constant violence" (Lemann 1991, 227; see also Popkin et al. 2000). Managers of projects often had to get to know gang leaders and negotiate with them in order to maintain order.

Where drug trafficking has become the main means of employment for tenants, it becomes nearly impossible for young people not to be lured into joining gangs.[14] The absence of jobs (especially jobs that would pay a livable wage) is no excuse for the violence rampant in the public housing war zones. Nevertheless, it seems to be the major reason for gang activity having developed a more economic focus, a focus that coincides with the appearance of cocaine on the underground market. One could therefore argue that the institutionalization of unemployment provides good economic opportunities for the corporate "super-gang" to be the main employer who engages in underground mercantilism, observes monthly drug-sale quota, and requires street taxation (Venkatesh 2000). The underground entrepreneurs of an entrenched drug market work within the confines of a rigid organizational hierarchy where leaders act as middle managers (168–69). In other words, the outlaw capitalist who makes money dealing drugs is not fundamentally different from "the yuppie who manages an investment portfolio" (Marsh 1997, 20). Or, as Luttwak (1999) poignantly observed, "Those who entered the drug trade were making a rational choice based on correct information, and could not have been otherwise directed by any competent management consultant. They were certainly better off than their equals who preferred the alternatives of unemployment or causal labor at the minimum wage" (100). The machinations of the street gang are therefore not entirely different from the machinations of corporate America as issues of control, mergers, subcontracting of work, submitting to formal wage structures, and protection are all part of the drug business. These corporate practices often include apparently random kinds of violence. They are random only for the innocent bystanders, but carefully planned and executed by the actors engaged in a gang war.

Media portrayals of the entire public housing population have almost exclusively focused on gang violence. During the past decade such portrayals of life in the projects have been complemented by the stigmatization of mothers relying on public aid as character-deficient (see the next chapter). Jenna captured this continuation of "othering" inner city Blacks well:

See, you're keeping the liars pumped up and the people that are regular, ordinary people are just trying to survive. They are grouped with the negative part. You never hear about women like Khia and Darlene. You hear about the woman that's out there trying to bribe the police, and not taking her son 'cause he's stuffing drugs on him. And those are the people you hear about. And those are what people think when they think of projects, 'cause that is all that lives here.

However, the permanent fears for one's own and one's children's lives take a devastating toll on the work of mothering. Although the mothers interviewed here had a good understanding of the larger issues that were feeding despair, greed, and violence, their fears and the tremendous demands being placed on the women responsible for the well-being of children always took center stage in our conversations. They underlined one of the observations made by Puntenney (1997) who points out that an extraordinary amount of time is consumed by caregiving responsibilities when surrounded by the permanent threat of gang violence, and that the constant fear for children's safety places a toll on mothers' labor force participation (146).

The current legal requirement for mothers on welfare to find employment certainly adds another thick layer of difficulty, in many cases making it next to impossible to take care of children while participating in a required work program. As Roberts (1999) describes, in some states this opens wide the door to terminating benefits if the woman fails to report to work, or this may also trigger a home visit by a welfare caseworker who may notify child protective services (163). Not only are the new welfare regulations certainly contributing to the "neglect" of children, many of the entry-level jobs have work schedules that include nights, weekends, or rotating shifts.[15] As reported by Carol, a woman with a job, this makes the children "latchkey kids, and they don't even know about family. So when gangs approach them, well, 'Somebody loves me'" (quoted in Puntenney, 158).

CHILDREN AND GANGS

"They Call Them Family, So They Can Have Somebody to Turn to"

The women who came to the interviews made it clear that they were used to constant shooting. For some of them the never-ending violence moved them very close to being convinced that "this is the end of the world." Horror at witnessing a girl shot in front of their eyes was accompanied by outrage because little kids have to constantly duck on their way to school. As Andrea exclaimed: "These are little kids, they are really innocent!" Fear and anger were inextricably mixed in accounts of the constant fear to which the children themselves are exposed. Ruth gave a vivid example. With a mix of anger, sadness, and resignation in her voice, she talked about a "remarkable little girl" she knows, a girl who "cares for her siblings, and is making A's and B's in school. But there is nothing for her when she grows up, and she is shivering all the time out of fear. Fear is there all the time. Living in constant fear."

In a little book called *My Neighborhood: The Words and Pictures of Inner-City Children*—a book excruciatingly painful to read—children's essays, poems, and drawings tell about the terror and pain in their lives. As described by the editor (Waldman 1993), violence "is an ever present reality that lies in wait each time a door is opened. It hangs in the dark corners of the hallways, hovers over the playgrounds, and strikes out from the windows of passing cars. It violates the innocence of childhood" (iv). Bakari, an eight-year-old child, writes: "Some days I'm scared to even walk to school by myself thinking that I'm gonna get killed, kidnapped, or just plain kicked around by some older guys who wanna have a little fun before school. Then there's even more fear when walking home because face it I live a block away from school but in this world we'll live in today that's a long walk home anything could happen" (3).

Puntenney, who interviewed mothers living in a West Side public housing project, summarizes the effects constant and unpredictable shoot-outs have on the residents, especially the children. She writes that "the effects of this kind of disruption in daily life include unrelenting fear and nervous tension, the scrapes and bruises that result from a fall to the ground, the need to focus large amounts

of energy on awareness and avoidance, and the extraordinary expenditure of
time invested in negotiating existence under these conditions" (154). As reported by Popkin and Olson (1995, 74), "even preschool children in some developments learn to hit the ground at the sound of gunfire and to avoid open
areas where shootings are common. Those who are physically injured by violence in public housing often receive media attention, but all children who live
in high-crime developments are at risk for the psychological trauma and intellectual deficits that result from chronic fear of victimization." Garbarino, Kos-
telny, and Dubrow included a chapter on the Robert Taylor Homes in their book
called *No Place to Be a Child: Growing Up in a War Zone* (1991), where they
describe children's many troublesome reactions to their constant fear, and to
having witnessed people being killed in front of their eyes, killings that sometimes included children's own mothers (see also Popkin et al. 2000).

Fear about children's safety is also inseparable from the fear about boys
joining gangs. "Joining gangs" covers a whole range of issues. Children live in
their own world and may see the world around them without capturing all the
serious implications of the existence of gangs in their lives. For instance, making easy money makes kids "think they are having a good time" because they
"don't know anything else." Rose's words barely touch upon the complex, multifaceted interplay of children's ways of experiencing the world and the omnipresent power dynamics behind official gang membership. Forming friendships
with other children is inseparable from the significance attached to who is talking to whom, associating with whom, or walking about in whose turf. Children
have to learn quickly, and they need the support of adults who know the inner
workings of territorial wars. Cora's words describe the complicated dynamics
children are drawn into when associating with others or distancing themselves
from them: "If they [her boys] walk in or out of a building and they don't speak
to them or they don't say anything to them then they get an attitude. And then,
if they talk to them and if something happens then they say, well, you be with
him, you socialize with him, then you are part of them too. So it is a no-win
situation."

Children do not only have to learn the territorial implications of associating
with others, they also have to become aware of how their established friendships
may take on new, dangerous meanings. Cora described the anguish of little children who "didn't want to stop speaking to them [other children] because they
are gang-related," especially friends who "stay about, stay out at their house, . . .
eat at their table, . . . spend the night at their house. . . . Little kids don't see that
if you're a friend of a friend, then I am not your friend."

While Jenna stressed the fact that gangs are not recruiting boys, and that
some gang members walk the kids to the bus or send them off to school,[16] boys
who are "gang-related" in various ways may not be so restrictive in approaching
other boys. Again, boys learn from adult male models that the ability of exerting power over others is a prime insignia of male authority. For older boys picking on younger ones is an easy way of exerting power over others. As Cora ob-

served, "A lot of times you could sit up and look and you see little boys, nine and ten years old, you see the older boys giving them ideas." Cora was especially worried about her son who did not want to join a gang other boys were trying to "coax him to join." Because of his refusal they saw him as someone who "thinks he's more than anybody" and therefore decided to "pick on him."

Cora made another important observation. When she talked about the older boys giving ideas to the younger ones, she was talking about boys "that want to hang out, and the parents do not want to give them no curfew." It is, of course, difficult to enforce a curfew on older children, but there is another important dimension behind children or young people joining gangs, especially those who either do not even have a brittle shield of protection, or who are simply neglected by their parents. At the literacy center some of the women, especially Tammy, talked about kids needing a sense of belonging and love, which many of them don't get at home—and the gangs give it to them. In a similar manner Regina summarized the tangle of emotional needs and demands mothers as well as children experience: "Kids. You do get scared about a lot of things, and you start to wonder if your child is going down the wrong path. And then you do try to pull them back to the right. Like a lot of them at school: They get scared 'cause the gangs at school threaten to jump them and stuff. And lots of them are joining gangs. They call them family, so they can have somebody to turn to. But I wish they didn't have to feel that way."

Jenna, who works at the Youth Center with children who were rejected by any other formal after-school program due to their behavioral problems, said that most of the children were "just neglected. . . . Few children—where I work at—are physically abused. But parents ignore them." There are a variety of reasons behind such neglect. Jenna makes a clear connection between neglect and the fact that "people just get beat down." These words were echoed by Marge, who saw a link between people simply being weak and the fact that "most people are now on drugs, running the wrong household, and they forget they got a family. But they don't mean to. That's their weakness, they forget they got a family."

The weakness that Marge talked about, or the sense of being beaten down, of having no hope for a better future, must be seen within the context of extraordinary amounts of strength needed by people who have to work within the tiny range of possibilities left to maintain their own dignity and sense of self, and to nurture their children in a way that at least prevents them from being subjected to the most visible damage. An acknowledgment of the need for superhuman strength does not, of course, deny the fact that there were many examples of bad mothering in the women's neighborhood. The women I had conversations with gave me several examples of bad mothering and how they tried to undo some of the resulting damage done to the children. Their observations, however, and their criticism as well as understanding of larger problems that clearly transcend individual weaknesses and failures, came out of a profound understanding of the work of mothering—in general, but especially within a context of extreme hard-ship.

WOMEN'S WORK/MOTHERWORK

"Cooking, Cleaning, Nurturing, Loving, Keeping Them Straight"

I am on public aid now, trying to work towards becoming independent. I used to work downtown, but I always worked all my life. This job I lost a couple of years ago. Then I went back to school and was unable to find employment out there. So I started working with children all the time, I mean it's better than sitting around and doing nothing. So I spend all of my time at the school or down here. I was tutoring the kids, 'cause you know we don't have a lot of kids down here that read well. And once during the summer, I have bake sales. I sell food, rent buses, and take the kids skating, take them to amuse-ment parks, museums, stuff like that.

Society don't see us as that [working mothers]. My time never ends 'cause I have neighbors knocking on the door: "The baby's running a fever, the baby cut the finger, the baby bumped the head." So it's like I am a built-in nurse, a doctor nurse. Then I am a nanny, 'cause I baby-sit a lot so their parents can go and do things they need to do for themselves. Like going to the doctor, take care of some business, go get groceries. Yeah, I do everything, I am an all-around-jack-of-all-trades-handyperson.

I'm on welfare. I don't abuse the system. To me they say I'm not working every day. I get up every morning, I go to Dett School, I be there at eight o'clock, I leave at two thirty. I'm tutoring, . . . I'm xeroxing, I'm cutting out letters, I'm watching classrooms while they're doing staffing for kids who have learning disabilities. (Rose)

If I could start all over thirty years ago, I still would have liked to be a student, taken some kind of course. Try to battle my life and not be on public aid. I've always been working. I got real bad asthma too, and I have always worked. Then I got to where I couldn't work no more. If I could turn it around, I would have worked on that. (Regina)

Rose's and Regina's words illustrate the tangled knot of issues associated with the work mostly performed by women. It is work that is generally invisible to the outside world, and whose invisibility takes on a perniciously punitive di-mension when it is performed under conditions of poverty and dependence on public aid. Whereas the following chapter discusses the class-biased and racist implications of the American welfare system and how that system feeds on and perpetuates a sexist division of labor, here I want to describe how this general social devaluation of work women do is experienced by the women themselves, how they see it, analyze it, and approach it.

"In Some Families Men Don't Do Anything"

The difference between raising boys and girls certainly feeds into the sexual division of work and into the hierarchy of values associated with this division.

So do different expectations parents and peers place on them, and the lessons they learn from observing the women and men around them. High rates of male unemployment and the vitality of women's ongoing work of "cooking, cleaning, nurturing, loving, keeping them straight" seem to reinforce rather then blur or even crumble that division. As one of the women said, unemployed fathers could help, but "they still don't do nothing. They just don't want to do nothing." Jenna observed a link between the phenomenon that "in some people's families men don't do anything" with the fact that "they aren't required to do anything."

This comment contains, of course, a hornet's nest of problems. Not only does the traditional sexual division of labor reverberate in Jenna's comment, but "traditional" is here combined with rather extreme life circumstances. This places a heavy demand on women, especially on mothers of boys. While "men aren't required to do anything . . . we tend to hold on to those boys too, 'cause we don't want them hurt. . . . Black men have always been the target for people to hurt, and do everything with. These women [are] holding these little boys, but they're grown when they get out in the street." Jenna finished her comments by stating that "we cannot save kids from everything." While that may sound like a matter-of-fact observation, it contains a tremendous amount of fears, conflicts, and contradictions. Some of them may have to do with the fact that mothers have only limited influence on their children's behavior, but there are a host of other, more structural causes for this mix of fear, caring and hopelessness. Above all, the boys have hardly anything to look forward to. Regina, for instance, wished that there were "a lot of jobs around here. Maybe some of the boys would have jobs instead of selling drugs." Because decent-paying jobs are not available, especially not to young Black inner-city men, women are being drawn into the caring demands of protecting their sons and of trying to counteract the onslaught of social stigmatization or downright dismissal of these boys and young men.

The women I talked to were aware of the injustice behind various manifestations of the sexual division of labor, of how they participated in or reinforced this division, and also how they engaged in a daily struggle of resisting or counteracting it. When asked whether it would make a difference if boys and girls were raised more equally, in the sense of making both of them feel equally responsible for their share of work in a family, Jenna gave the following response: "I think it would—if they would see, if they had been in a family structure that would get everybody an equal chance, even if they came home and they saw their father sitting down, not doing anything while their mother was running around." Jenna then gave an example of her refusal to participate in this kind of set-up:

[My husband] told me the other day, I'm hungry, what's for dinner. And he had just walked in the door! Are you on drugs? Or you better get some, you got to be crazy! I work too, but my work, since it isn't physical work, since I'm not out there cutting my fingers and pushing stuff through a machine, my work isn't anything. Because his work is harder, therefore it's more valuable. But when it is time to pay the bills, my money spends like his money. So I don't cook and do a bunch of things.

The participants of the literacy group also saw a close connection between the sexual division of labor and the fact that boys and girls are brought up differently. The quote that initiated the discussion was the following: "Who's raising black men in this country? Black women. So if black men are not being very conscious of black women, then it is our fault. I think that black women tend to love our sons and raise our daughters. We tend to not give men responsibility, not hold them accountable the way we hold our daughters" (quoted in Summers 1989). There were several stories told about how girls are taught that they won't be able to keep a man if they don't learn how to cook and bake for him. There was also a lot of laughter when the women recommended sometimes quite funny ways of taking revenge—such as putting laxatives into the food—on what was perceived as a form of exploitation. The women who engaged in this humorous conversation were very clear about the importance of this rather hard aspect of motherwork, and how adult male behavior the boys were exposed to made it even more arduous. It was also the women's sense of humor that seemed to give them the strength they needed practically all the time in order to be "friend, disciplinarian, mother" (Rose) to their children. This threesome of roles easily unfolds into the endless list of skills, knowledges, competencies, efforts, and responsibilities all motherwork entails. As Ruth simply stated, "It's so hard. I don't care what you got in these times and who you hear, even if you got a lot of money and you don't live in a poor neighborhood, it's hard, period."

"I Think Even in Our Sleep We Are Thinking about What We Are Going to Do for Them Kids"

If they need me I'll be there for them. If they're sick, can't nothing keep me away but death. If they're in trouble, can't nothing keep me away but death. And you know, even in death you still can have that bond, 'cause it is a certain time that you will still feel that love that you had, that you gave them when they were alive. Can't nobody take that away. (Ruth)

Never-ending care is a story that should be familiar to anyone who has the main responsibility for the well-being of a child. Rose's and Ruth's words, however, also tell the story of how the dangers around them push mothers toward caring far beyond so-called normal boundaries. To raise a Black child in a white supremacist society gives caring complex, often contradictory, dimensions. African-American women have written about the tremendous demands on mothers to prepare the children for the many different small and large dangers lying in wait in a racist society, without running the risk of curtailing or damaging the development of their children's strong sense of self.[17]

The women whose words are recorded in this book expressed similar concerns. They talked about the fact that the world outside is cruel and makes you want to be strong and help your children to grow up strong by staying away from it. During a conference workshop Jenna talked about telling her son that everything was fine until she realized that she didn't tell him the truth, and that she had to correct her mistake. One of the women in the audience responded by saying that "you have to tell your children exactly what is going on out there, about racism. You need to arm them, otherwise they are disarmed." As Rose said during one of the interviews, "You have to get out there and show them what the world is like, prepare them for certain things that they can avoid," otherwise "it's like taking a kid that has been sheltered in the mountains and throwing them into the big inner city. He's not gonna be ready for nothing if he hasn't been prepared." Rose's image of the mountain captures a mother's overwhelming need for sheltering her child.

Protection is a vital element of care (see Ruddick 1989, Bowden 1997), but in the inner city's war zone, it becomes an overwhelming and often impossible task. The women I talked to kept emphasizing that they never let their children out of sight, or at least made sure that someone watched all the time. Regardless of this constant oversight, a child might still be shot. After talking for a while about her life at the Henry Horner Homes, Cora told me the story of her son's death. It was particularly painful to hear her talk about the last few minutes she saw her son well and alive. Shortly after he left the house and celebrated a friend's birthday at a nearby McDonald's, he was killed by a man who wanted to steal his car.

What does caring mean in an environment where one's work and effort could be undone in a second? What if the caring person is just an ordinary human being rather than one endowed with superhuman strength? There seems to be very little or no space for simply being such an ordinary mother who should have some leeway for making mistakes and correcting them, or learning from them. Listening to the women at the literacy center or at the other public housing environments led me to believe that there are only three different ways of responding to the need for never-ending care for children who have very little or nothing to look forward to: (1) The mothers give up, get involved in drugs or alcohol, and neglect their children; (2) they care not only for their own children but also become "othermothers" (Collins 1990) for all the children around them; or (3) they decide to put a stop to what had become even grown children's expectations for never-ending care by engaging in acts of refusal.

As regards acts of refusal or downright rebellion, Jenna was the most deliberate and the most outspoken. I want to point out, however, that the meanings of refusal, or rebellion, have to be seen within the context of demands for care and protection that go far beyond the ordinary pull towards self-sacrifice contained in official social norms regarding good mothering. While these norms are clearly in action in the lives of all people responsible for raising children, in the case of public housing residents, they are also woven into the realities of rather extraordinary living conditions, and they comprise a tangle of social and individual expectations, demands, or d/evaluations.

From "I have given all I can give," "My life was my children's life," and "You will lose your mind. You're in the house and nothing in the house belongs to you" to "Listen, it's my time, everybody go, get away" (Jenna), these observations can be seen as setting limits to self-sacrifice, as working against the onslaught of social expectations on women to be the caretakers of everyone:

With my kids . . . I was their homemaker. I was sewing, cleaning, cooking. I was having a good time until I said what the hell happened to me. I didn't come into a marriage, I was Jenna. When you get married or you're with somebody else you never notice that the man is still himself but you're turning into somebody else. He was husband, a father, and Jerry. And supposedly I was Jenna and mother and this and that. But then I started being everybody. But he was going to work and coming back home with a life. My life was my children's life. So I said: What happened to my life? I came into this marriage with a life, I didn't find it anymore. All I was doing was being a wife and mother. Jenna didn't have a chance. I used to say, I'm going out, and oh, I'm having so much fun. But I wasn't. I was doing a lot of other things other people wanted to do then. So I said, forget it. I'm through with this bullshit. Jenna got to live again. I got to find her. And she don't live in my house. She lives out there chatting with people, shopping, going to museums, going to libraries. Every time I go to the library I get about eight books. Then I drag the books in. That's who I looked to be. I don't like to come in and feed a meal 'cause somebody is hungry. They're big enough now, if they're hungry they're hungry 'cause they don't want to cook. I guess they'll just eat each other.

In an essay called "Who Is Me?" Cora makes a similar point. She writes about having a full-time job, taking care of her four children, cooking and cleaning, and at the age of forty-one she has to admit that "I still don't know who me is. I would like to take the time to find her and talk to her and get to know her. So far, I haven't found her. I hope before I leave this earth I find her."

Jenna's refusal to give in to what are women's well-trained responses to people's needs extends into her nonfamily work as well. She told me how she simply left a CAP (Chicago Area Project) meeting she had at the office because the men immediately sat down and expected her to serve lunch. Her fury seethed in her when she asked: "Why do women come into a room and try to find out what needs to be done while men simply sit down?"

Not surprisingly, taking care of oneself was a recurrent theme, and it appeared in many different variations. Connotations of this theme reverberated in the women's regrets about the times in their life when they did not take care of themselves because they let their youthful ignorance take over, interrupted their education, and had babies. While none of the women I spoke with ever regretted having children, some of them stated very clearly that now, in retrospect, they realized that they should at least have finished their high school degree. Some of the women were trying to get this degree by taking GED (General Education Development) classes. For others the need to have space and time to themselves was paramount, and almost impossible to find or defend. When asked whether she had any time for herself, Rose said "when they go to sleep": "When they go to sleep I read, I meditate, I cry. Boy, do I cry. I think about old times, new times, the future. Now, since they have gotten older, on weekends they like to go to my brother's house. When they leave Friday evenings I lock the door, I won't do anything. I don't even eat. I just be so happy to be just by myself."

Books are as important for Rose as they are for Jenna. Rose said that "the only thing I would really want to do is travel, but I can't afford to do that. So how I travel is read. I go anywhere I want to go, any place I want to go to. Any time of day I read."

"We Are All Grandmother-Mothers, Because Even Though They Are Grandkids They Are Like Kids because We Have to Keep Them All the Time"

Most of the women were grandmothers who were fully involved in the care-taking of their grandchildren. As Ruth said, "O.K., we're all doing the grand-motherly thing." While the support of kin, extended families, and othermother-ing are integral components of the African-American communal tradition, under the devastating conditions of deteriorating external and internal resources, grandmotherly responsibilities can easily become an unwelcome additional bur-den the women are nevertheless taking on, out of necessity. Some of the women gave me quite different reasons for the fact that they became involuntary grandmothers, some of which I could only surmise. Hearing that a grandmother had sole custody of her grandchild allowed me only to guess the reasons why her daughter had lost custody to begin with. Another woman had to take care of "two grandkids, for the time being." The children were nine and ten years old. Cora who had a job at the school also talked about the importance of being able to rely on the children's grandmothers. She emphasized the impossibility of finding a good baby-sitter, "especially one you can trust." Her daughter "was trying to get a job to work at night. That way when I get home in the evening I could watch the baby at night." Her rather ironic statement that "the grand-mother never gets tired taking care of kids, *so they say*" clearly indicated that she had more than her share of motherly burdens to carry. In an essay called "My Life as a Grandmom," she writes: "My life as a grandmom is a very hard life because when you become a mother all over again your child don't know how to take care of a baby right. You have to stop and think about all the things you did with your children when they were born." After giving a detailed de-scription of the endless demands placed on her, she says, "You love them, but you get tired and want some peace of mind. But things don't work like that."

Rose emphasized the reality of double or triple burdens for the grandmothers by talking about a woman who became an involuntary grandmother. Not only was her daughter only fifteen when she became pregnant, "but she still has chil-dren herself. I guess that's more of a burden to her. Being a young mom, she has got a daughter with a baby, then she has children of her own, and she got to cook and clean."[18]

As indicated by Rose's words, the grandmothers are not only burdened with the extra responsibility of taking care of their grandchildren, but they also have to work with their young daughters to teach them how to take care of a child. This became very clear when one of the teenage mothers said, "To tell you the truth, I really don't know [what it means to be a mother] 'cause I don't have him [her son] all the time." This double responsibility of a grand/mother who has to teach a very young person how to take care of her child while she is taking care of that child herself becomes even heavier when the grand/mother must watch a young daughter curtailing her chances of moving away from dependency on public aid or on low-skilled, low-wage jobs by focusing on her education. In their responses to their daughters' problems the women sometimes worked through their own history of having and loving children when they were very young, and of being engulfed by social and individual expectations of never-ending care—expectations coming from the children and the men in their lives. Marge and Rose were very outspoken about feeling outraged when they learned about their daughters' pregnancies. Marge reported that "when she got pregnant, I said oh my God, make this the first one and the last one." Rose, who would pull her daughter's hair during the nine months of her pregnancy, felt that all her efforts to "model her into a daughter I wanted her to be" had failed, "and for her to mess up, it hurt me. It hurt me. Because I didn't want her to go through these things."

"Momma, Everybody Wishes That You Were Their Mother"

An exclusive focus on the burdensome aspects of grand/motherhood neglects to take into account the African-American communal tradition of extended family ties, multigenerational families, and othermothers.[19] Not only did this tradition echo in many of these women's stories, but it also manifested itself in the strength of individual mothers to take on the care of other, neglectful mothers' children.

At the literacy center women sometimes expressed gratitude for other women, including mothers who were living close by and who were helping to take care of the children when they had to leave. The importance of grandmothers or other kin in helping with the work of raising children was quite apparent. Darlene, a very young woman, captures the importance of extended family support in the most vivid ways:

I really don't have too much problems. Because their father do help me, so my son's father is sending my son to Catholic school. His grandma on his daddy's side, she helps me out a real lot. Now, like during the summer times I would just have to buy my daughter Kionna clothes. His grandmother buys Mumu clothes. So if I did not have her, then I would be in a jam. Then my other daughter, now she don't hardly ever be at my house. And my auntie buys all of her clothes. I don't even remember the last time I bought something for Trina. You know, I have help. If it wasn't for them I don't know what I would do.

Terms such as "activist mothering" (Naples) or "community othermothers" (Collins) capture the broad and complex cultural (and political) meaning of mothering in the African-American tradition (see chapter 6). Ivy gave an example of othermothering by describing a kind of groupwatch over children, or—in Jenna's words—a form of "community raising." Luceta emphasized that this "makes it better for the kids 'cause they think somebody's always watching them."

The women Sparks (1998) had conversations with confirm this tendency. However, she also reports that the overall picture of kinship networks, and the help they provide, is far from uniform and should therefore not be romanticized. First of all, help may not always be readily available, or particularly stressful life circumstances may leave women on welfare "with very little to give (either emotionally or materially) to others in their extended families. And when resources in kinship networks are similarly depleted, available supports are meager and insufficient to meet mothers' needs" (233). The overwhelming presence of poverty and the dangers associated with living in a war zone have a tendency to eat into kinship networks so "that sometimes in the face of economic cutbacks and emotional crisis [people] must however reluctantly 'let go' of family members who cannot pull their weight" (Stack and Burton 1994, 41). Most women spoke about the importance of having help from sisters, mothers, or aunts in terms of watching the children, paying some bills, or simply giving them a break from their motherwork responsibilities. However, observing their state of exhaustion and noticing a sense of hopelessness that continually crept into our conversations made it clear that they were not receiving sufficient help from anybody, at least not on an ongoing basis. Their relatives could not automatically be relied upon, especially when they were themselves entangled in extremely stressful life circumstances. The women in this study were clearly the primary and often the only caregivers. They were also quite aware of what it meant to place more responsibilities onto their relatives' shoulders, and they tried to avoid this situation as much as possible. As Cora said, "My mother would help, or my sister. I didn't want to give my mother the responsibility of watching my kids. So [they took care of them] when I went some place that I had to go and couldn't take a child with me. But most of the time I took them with me wherever I worked."

Against a backdrop of social negligence or stigmatization—aggravated by the conditions of the inner-city war zone—being an othermother requires extraordinary strength that must be anchored in an ethic of care, or a "whole philosophy" (Rose). As Rose remarked, if the mother is not engaged in an ethic of care, if she is "not doing it, somebody should be doing it, so you have to do it." Rose has clearly been nourished by and carries along the tradition of othermothering. She told about how her "parents were everybody's grandmother and grandfather, or everybody's momma and dad," and that they "fed everybody in the neighborhood." She also made it clear that this tradition of "being surrogate moms and fathers" is particularly needed when many mothers neglect their own children:

Living here I found out there was a lot of children who didn't have a mommy like me. So I started taking time up with their children in this building and the ones in 3410. And giving them of myself, it was sort of like an extended family. A whole bunch of kids. I had boys on a daily basis, I would have a house full of kids. And I try to come back and instill in them the same values my parents instilled in me, that I was trying to give my children, so they will be able to pass it on to their children. And then I wanted to help these kids out so that somewhere along the line we can stop the cycle of this violence that's going on out here. If all of us stop running away from things and start facing them, then we could make a difference. We may not see it right then and there, but eventually everybody would start taking up time with these kids. And playing the role of the mother or the father that these kids are not getting at home. Then it'll change.

Rose goes on to describe in detail the many dimensions this work entails, from trying to get to know the children to setting firm ground rules, especially concerning the use of gang sign language or talk about gangs, "unless we're talking against gang violence":

I just set down rules. And I believe that kids want boundaries, they want guidelines, so they kept coming back. And they would bring others with them and they would already have given them the rules, before they get there. And I would say you got to learn what goes on in here, they say I already know, they told me. I know I can't do this and I know I can't do that. So I think that's the reason why they kept coming back was I was what they wanted.

Rose also reported that she talked to parents or mothers who were on drugs, that their children were coming to her, and how hard it was "to work with people like that" because drugs "make the mind warped," and "tempers high." During an earlier conversation Marge and Ruth had talked at great length about various experiences and encounters they had with children who were not getting the love they needed at home because their parents were on drugs and were "running the wrong household." Marge kept coming back to the story of a little girl who had come to see her because she had found an eviction notice under the door of her mother's apartment, and the steps Marge took to make the mother get her life back together again, at least enough in order to be available for her nine-year-old daughter. While Marge gave the mother some ideas about how to postpone the eviction, her drug addiction kept the little girl coming to Marge for comfort or for having her clothes washed.

During one of the discussions at the literacy center, other women, especially Tammy and Andrea, also chided mothers for letting children come to school in filthy clothes, with their hair all matted, and not having been fed. Tammy had brought a newspaper story that reported the killing of a two-year-old boy by his severely drugged-up stepmother. The ensuing discussion showed that neglect or abuse of children was a common phenomenon in the women's experiences.

Ruth and Marge, the oldest women present, could not grasp the cruelty, and I could see their pain in simply acknowledging or witnessing such cruelty. As Marge said: "A baby is just a precious thing." One of the women could barely talk because she was crying, telling the group that her two grandchildren were in foster care. The women did not ask her why. I had the impression that this was a quite familiar story.

The discussion also illustrated how everyone was wrapped up in personal and social or institutional conflicts or contradictions. Andrea talked about how one of her children was bruised by simply falling down, but that teachers immediately suspected abuse. The doctor whom she visited to immunize her two children kept asking about the bruise on the child's forehead. That doctor also did not believe that the pockmarks on the child's feet came from the chickenpox the child had recovered from only ten days earlier. This story gave an example of how the women themselves could not escape their entanglement in contradictory expectations. They strongly criticized the Department of Child and Family Services (DCFS) for placing children in foster homes that were not carefully checked so anyone could pretend to be an adequate foster parent, and there was quite a bit of contempt, hatred, and resentment expressed against an incompetent child welfare agency.[20] This resentment, however, was also fueled by the idea that the agency *could* take care of all the problems or horrors if adequately staffed, and if it had the right attitude. Anger and resentment were, however, often replaced by a general sense of hopelessness, especially when conversations turned to questions concerning possibilities for improving life circumstances.

"Even Though We Live in the Projects, if People Get Together and Stand behind One Another, and Get Closer, We Could Make Things Better. But a Lot of Them Will Not Do It"

Regina's words articulate a wish heard many times, although it was usually expressed with a sense of resignation, hopelessness, or even despair. While there are still remnants of a previous sense of community, accompanied by the ability to rely on mutual support, the words describing a severe loss of such a community were quite strong.

Social organization has rapidly deteriorated in public housing developments, fed by a rise in joblessness and a decreasing population density resulting in abandoned buildings and vacant apartments—providing havens for drug trafficking (Wilson 1996, Popkin et al. 2000).[21] The external structures that provide the very foundation of a sense of community, that is, a feeling of safety, have therefore been destroyed by the constant fear of violence, and by the abysmal physical conditions of the buildings and apartments themselves, conditions that include "darkened hallways, abandoned apartments, graffiti, trash, and street prostitution" (Popkin and Olson 1993, 74). At the same time, as Venkatesh (1997) observed during a period of four years during which he spent as much time as possible at the Robert Taylor Homes, there is nevertheless an invisible community as well where tenants "continue to rely on important social supports that are located in the community. Peer and kin networks provide invaluable child-care assistance, temporary shelter, and friendship. Moreover, myriad social control mechanisms, such as tenant patrols and floor watches, provide a relative measure of safety and enforcement, not to mention available lobbyists for more effective policing" (37).[22] This is one of the reasons residents often protest enforced relocation. As Deborah Young, the president of the Local Advisory Council of the Robert Taylor Homes said, "This is our community. We know who's above us, who's below us and, who's around us. . . . When we go beyond that invisible wall, we don't know nobody, we barely get a 'hello' when we say 'good morning.' We get the snob treatment" (Hanney 1999, 3).

As previously mentioned, under current public housing conditions, the meaning of community othermothers has a layer of desperation. Taking on the anguish, the emotional, and, at times, physical survival issues of children who do not get the steady, reliable love, care, and attention from their own mothers (or fathers), these othermothers are trying to stem the tide of destruction that has washed over their neighbors, or other members of their racial and economic community. The destructiveness of a system that relies on a multitude of social divisions and hierarchies in order to feed the economic bottomline has clearly seeped into the interior of many people living in public housing. At the same time, public housing residents belong to a population that has been encased in a host of racist assumptions and corresponding social and political institutional structures. The experience of social and economic marginalization has also, however, always been the major impetus for maintaining and creating communal countercultures (see chapter 6). Yet mutual support, an integral part of any sense of community, barely exists anymore:

Everyone needs to support and be there. It would be better . . . if every neighbor who is somebody had proof that they would get together and support each other—when they really had a problem, a special problem—that they could get together instead of fighting and killing each other. See, it ain't too many people you can go to now. Because you know what, it's just messed up. . . . Yes, we do have each other. But see, it ain't too many of us. We're supposed to stick together. (Ruth)

Any observation that things could be better if people would stick together was always accompanied by the statement that people wouldn't or couldn't do it. A variety of explanations covering a range of issues was offered. A few times a woman would move onto the macrolevel of analysis by talking about the different ways this society has wronged Black people, and how the men in power set things up in a way that makes people kill each other—the most effective way of getting rid of an unwanted population. As Ruth said, "This is what I meant when I say society. And they're bringing it [drugs] in here. And it's somebody in power. This is their secret. This is the way that will kill them all out." Viewing the influx of drugs as a weapon of genocide was shared by women on the

utmost margins of society whose life histories Pettiway documented in *Workin'
It* (1997): "That's a nice way to get rid of us, 'cause it is doing that. I mean they
think that the next war gonna be with guns and stuff. It might not be 'cause the
drugs is about the best killer I've seen. And it's definitely doing that in one form
or another" (xvii).

The women made connections to larger, systemic problems that, in effect,
divided them from other social groups. They also, however, talked about the
wrongdoings committed by the Black inner-city population itself, weakening a
sense of racial solidarity and community. During conversations that mainly focused on children, one of the most frequently mentioned internal divisions piv-
oted around good and bad mothers. Oppressive and therefore divisive relationships between women and men were also addressed, mainly in terms of absent
or neglectful fathers. Ruth, for instance, was not the only one who passed a
harsh judgment on the men who do not take care of the children they had "fathered," but she—like the other women—was also very conscious of the fact
that Black men, especially young Black men, are up against an onslaught of
negative associations and labels.

Pitts (1999), who discusses the link between obsolete fathers and the social
and economic marginalization (or criminalization), of Black men does not,
however, spare them from severe criticism. As he points out, while there is "no
shortage of reasons" for Black men's marginalization, these reasons can easily
be used by the men for self-excuse or self-delusion in terms of shunning their
fatherly responsibilities (71). The women who came to the interviews concurred
with Pitts's admonitions, but this concurrence was mostly expressed in the form
of a steady undercurrent of anger. This anger was directed against the men who
were the biological fathers of some of the women's children but who never
really fathered them. Only occasionally did the anger flare up, and stories about
the way a father manipulated, cheated, or simply neglected his child were
shared. Most of the time the women were silent about the men in their lives, or
they emphasized that they did not want to have relationships with men. Abusive
boyfriends came up a few times as well. In one case the mother had to take in
her daughter and grandchildren because they were escaping an abusive boyfriend. In another case a woman and her child had moved away from a battering
boyfriend and sought refuge in the Henry Horner Homes. It was clear that my
contact with the women I interviewed was too short-lived to allow for building
sufficient trust between us in order to address an issue that carries a particularly
heavy burden of social and historical implications. Only once did three women
engage in rather hard-hitting man-bashing banter while my presence was fully
ignored. This was similar to what sometimes happened at the literacy center
where I was mostly a quiet, unobtrusive observer while the literacy coordinator
was leading the group and assisting the women in engaging in collective story-
telling. The women were not concerned about whether or not an outsider understood them, and they felt free to openly talk about sensitive issues. During my
eighteen months at the center, I therefore heard many more stories about male

violence against women, some of them rather gruesome, dealing with rape or physical mutilation (see chapter 4).

Aside from the rather complex and multilayered division between the sexes that undermined a strong internal sense of community, another theme that was frequently mentioned and that spoke of a loss of community was isolation and not being able to make friends because people would turn against each other or were mean to each other. As Khia said, "You can't trust them." When asked to describe what it means to raise children in the Altgeld Gardens, she pointed out that while it is not easy, "It's all right as long as you keep to yourself and don't get friendly with everybody." While she elaborated on this experience to some extent, she kept coming back to the story of her daughter going outside and getting "jumped on," and that she could not talk to the parents of the children who jumped on her daughter because they wanted to fight and "act ignorant." Not only did distrust permeate all relationships in the Altgeld neighborhood, but the need to protect children from other children, and from their parents and other adults in general, pushed that distrust up to a level where it destroyed the very foundation of community-building.

When Khia said that "it feels like an island around here," however, she was referring to both her own personally experienced as well as social-structural isolation. The Altgeld Gardens are similar to the Taylor Homes, which have been described as "the site of a massive camp for America's internal refugees, the families who are displaced from 'regular' communities in the city" (Garbarino, Kostelney, and Dubrow 1991, 131). The Altgeld Gardens were, however, from the start extremely isolated by being "built on the edge of the city, far from any residential areas, and without mass transit except for limited bus service," mainly in response to the needs of war-worker housing for Black workers in the Far South Side–Lake Calumet area (Bowly 1978, 45). In addition, as previously mentioned, not only does the city not provide money for basic repairs, it also does not provide any means to alleviate the problem of carcinogenic toxins contained in the soil upon which the Altgeld Gardens are built. It would therefore be entirely unrealistic to ask for provisions to set up public places such as parks or community centers. As recently as September 1997, the city also stopped the bus service to the Altgeld Gardens, making Altgeld even more isolated (Frago 1997). Since most people living at Altgeld are dependent on public transportation, it became next to impossible for single mothers to take trips with their children to a different environment.

A feeling of entrapment due to the violence around them was therefore exacerbated by the absence of public transportation. These issues were not, however, the only culprit for making people feel isolated and distrustful of the world beyond their own public housing environment. The coordinator of the ABLA Homes literacy center talked about the women's distrust and fear of the outside world in general, and she used the example of her suggestion to walk downtown. The women insisted on taking a street that led through their own Black neighborhood rather than through a neighborhood consisting of stores, restaurants, and the various facilities of a public university. While the university can pride itself for having a good racial-ethnic and cultural mix of students, and while the downtown area has a high percentage of African-American employees, the most visible difference is clearly related to the markings of middle or lower class. The need to be around people with whom they share the experience of economic marginalization is one of the many contradictions people living in public housing environments have to wrestle with. And because their neighborhood is a place of much pain and suffering, the ability to move away, to move into the other world, becomes a sign of hope and success. Their neighborhood is, however, also the source of their "spatial identity" (Gregory 1998), the place where people know each other and the material and psychological conditions of their lives.

The women's fear of leaving their own treacherous environment can be seen as a rational psychological response to their systemic marginalization. There are other, larger social divisions and hierarchical fragmentations that have also settled into people's interiors. According to Jenna, many Black people do not want to hear the truth about "important things," or that things are not okay, despite knowing deep down in their hearts that things were indeed not okay. And there is the whole barrage of meanings associated with internalized racism. This could take on the form of being accused of "stand-offishness" because one's skin color is light; being seen as "too black" because one wants to talk about racism; thinking that "the white way is still the right way," especially when "white" means "all the things white people have."

Jenna's comments are, of course, interlaced with anger and resentment. They also chide the general, highly entrenched materialistic vision of the good life represented by all the good things white people have. Such a vision speaks of the larger spiritual void that accompanies this way of seeing and relating to one's internal and external world, and that finds its most direct expression in the programmatic junk food of American television. As Jenna pointed out, "When you get sad plus you're depressed, plus you can't get your hands on things, and you're looking at TV, it's all about money, it's all about sex, it's all about drugs." Drug dealing and the selling of sex are therefore rather rational responses to making good money in an economic ghetto, especially since they are the only avenues for any kind of lucrative business deals. For people who are not the main actors in these underground corporate transactions, getting high on drugs, numbing one's mind and soul by drinking or endlessly watching TV can therefore also be seen as rather "normal" responses to a hopeless situation. As Darlene said, nobody cares, and "you just have a vicious circle of apathy. . . . It's a shame, when you get them [the neighbors] here, we're talking, and they break down and start crying. You can't hardly sit here and think of anything positive to say. I can't see it getting any better."

The church has played one of the most important roles in African-American history and tradition. While this history and its current implications are too vast and too complex to address here, I can at least report that religion and "faith in the Lord" were common themes. For some of the women, this faith and church attendance were one of the few ways of keeping a sense of hope and dignity, of feeling less alone. Ruth and Tammy, for instance, emphasized on many occasions that without the Lord they could not go on. Not being able to go on without believing in the Lord has a ring of hopelessness as well as hope. Jenna expressed this mix of despair and hope by saying that "You got to come out of this, even if it is doing little things."

HOPE FOR CHANGE

"People Have to Change. We Will Have to Change. We Have to Want to Do Things for Ourselves"

Although hopelessness and despair were intimate companions of many of the women's stories, hope would sometimes glow, like embers under a big pile of ashes. While the fire of hope seemed to be dying, sometimes tiny sparks also rekindled it. From what I could see, those sparks had many different sources: some external, such as hope for a changing economy and for fundamental public housing improvements (which during the interviews were still in an early planning stage); some internal, such as strength drawn from religious or spiritual beliefs, or from believing in the importance of internal changes, including unlearning old patterns of behavior and learning new ways of being in the world.

All of the women who could at least envision changes would draw on the importance of "needing to get together and getting organized." They were drawing on their own tradition of collective struggle, especially in the form of woman-centered action concerning immediate living conditions. Cora told me how in the late eighties she and some women friends "started marching, going to meetings, knocking on doors and passing out flyers" as part of their effort to get the CHA to do something about the worsening living conditions at the Henry Horner Homes. She also told me that as a result the CHA did the first rehab, but that since then gangs and drugs have taken over, so "people started moving out, then people started destroying everything that was around here." Thus, when they were engaged in direct political action things had just begun changing for the worse and there was therefore still room for freely going door to door at apartments without fear of trespassing into dangerous territory. Nevertheless, Cora and Rose were members of the Henry Horner Homes Resident Committee, which is directly involved in the current revitalization process. They therefore attend numerous meetings. As Rose wrote in an essay, these are "meetings to select a contractor to build housing, another to select a private management firm, and others to assess the needs of the residents. This process of change is tedious and long, but I am very honored to be part of this tremendous challenge."[23]

Hope and hopelessness were inextricably intertwined in talks about social change. Just like the mothers who want to make their children flourish in the midst of destruction have to be endowed with superhuman strength, so do people who are committed to staying where they live but want to create more livable conditions. However, this strength is not simply the inner, spiritual kind required to stem the tide of despair. It is the strength derived from a vast amount of outer resources community activists would have to call upon in order to get at least some fragments of the system working in their favor. That the system is fully working against them was expressed by Regina. She was angry at and worried about "these boys around here" who are not going to school and are selling drugs. As she said, "I wish time would bring a better change because we do need jobs and I wish it was a lot of jobs here. Maybe some of the boys would have jobs instead of selling drugs."

Regina clearly expressed the need for fundamental economic changes, and these would call for vast and intense social–political struggles for community-based economic development. The women I had conversations with were not involved in any of these efforts, but their concerns pointed to some essential groundwork needed to bring about economic change. As discussed in the final chapter, those working for larger changes are in need of an already existing fabric of social support. There were some relationships of mutual support among the women interviewed, and the importance of getting together and working together as a group was mentioned several times, sometimes expressed as a wish that lacked the strength of conviction, sometimes expressed in the form of a plan. In either case, getting together was seen above all as a means to stem the tide of destruction, to make the neighborhood safer. As Ruth said, "It [the violence] can be stopped."

A small but important first step in trying to stick together to end the violence would be to get away from a sense of isolation, a sense of having the whole world against you. Jenna talked about trying to get a group of women together who would just talk and listen to each other:

If you start a core group, there are more people like you out here, you just don't know them. And they don't have anywhere to go where they feel like they got to tell what they got to tell and get it done. So, you get overwhelmed. The Housing Authority is against you, the police is against you, all the negative forces are working against you. Sometimes you're like a slave, you got to come out of this, even if it is doing little things. These people are even on my block, where your mother lives at, where my mother lives at— they need to get together and get organized.

Jenna has a radical political history herself, and her comments show that she is trying to revive a tradition of getting together, getting organized, and struggling for social and political changes. She was quick to take on a fighting pose while Rose's vision of getting together was most intimately connected to other-mothering, to a communal care for children. As she said, "If all of us stop running away from things and start facing them, then we could make a difference.

We may not see it right then and there, but eventually everybody would start taking up time with these kids."

Learning and unlearning were some of the recurrent themes during discussions of possible or necessary changes. These themes were embedded in a multitude of emotions and tasks, depending on where learning had occurred or where people hoped it would occur. Learning was tied to the teaching of children, to what the women had to learn about mothering, about themselves and the world they were living in, or what they expected other people to learn. The latter aspect was expressed in the most strikingly skeptical if not resigned way when the issue of men learning to be nurturing instead of simply being biological fathers came up. Cora, for instance, said that it "would be a good change" if "men play mother for a while, and you let me play father for a while. But men ain't going to take that responsibility. Everything is going to fall on you." Aside from the anger some of the women expressed when talking about the sexist division of labor, there was also pain in their voices when they talked with such appreciation of their own fathers' caring work, especially because this part of their history had obviously been severely ruptured.

The women were very eager to talk about their own learning and about the responsibility they had for the learning of their children. They talked about teaching their children how to respect others, manage money, interpret TV shows, stay away from guns, and, most prominently, how to face "reality out there." Teaching about this reality is one of the hardest and at times a seemingly impossible task. As Rose said, because children are scared of the outside world, "you have to get out there and show them what the world is like, prepare them for certain things that they can avoid." However, this primary task was fully embedded in all the other mothering activities: "As far as taking care of my children: doing what needs to be done for them, spending time with them, explaining what the world is like so they will be prepared for it. Being able to sit down and watch cartoons and live in a fantasy—but there is a reality out here that they should be prepared for."

Despite expressing their overwhelming fears and the need to protect their children, the women also talked a lot about how they themselves have to learn about mothering because "there ain't no real rules and regulations on really being a mother" (Rose). This was echoed by Jenna, who responded by saying that "no, because they don't teach you anything." Her words summarize the bleak social landscape regarding the offering of truly supportive educational contexts that would value mothering. Parenting classes are considered important only in the case of mothers who have been officially labeled as bad mothers, and who have fallen under the supervision of DCFS.

The women were very articulate about the tremendous learning required for becoming a good mother, especially in surroundings that pushed that responsibility to the very edge of individual capacities. They also openly talked about the fact that learning to be a mother includes consciously learning from mistakes, and learning from one's own ignorance. As Ruth said, "I learned I did some of the things I have because I didn't know better. But then you learn better." Rose added another vital dimension to this learning process. In a joking way she said that she suffered from the Peter Pan syndrome, that she will never grow up, and that she learned about having fun with children from her father. Her ability to get in tune with a child's world also made her learn from children. She pointed out that it is wonderful to "be able to grow with them [kids] and learn with them, because you can always learn something, even from a kid."

Finally, the women were very aware of the importance of formal education, and their comments covered a wide spectrum of reasons behind emphasizing this importance. Jenna, for instance, praised her father for making her do well in school, and she mentioned that "high school meant a lot" for the parents in her childhood neighborhood, and that "just getting out of high school was so great." She was tapping into a core aspect of African-American tradition: highly valuing education as one of the prime avenues for obtaining a certain measure of economic self-sufficiency and social pride.

At the same time, the Chicago public school system has a tradition of providing one of the bleakest pictures of formal education in the nation.[24] Combined with the economic devastation of Chicago's inner city where young people do not really have a sense of future,[25] the African-American tradition of valuing education has suffered severe damages. Ruth and Marge talked about children no longer appreciating education. Although she was quite conscious of the abysmal reality of the public school system, Ruby said that this would be the main advice she would give children: "Go to school! Get as much education as you can get so you will be able to support yourself, speak out, and be for real about it." Not surprisingly, Cora told me with pride that her children were all finishing school (except the boy who was killed), and that her oldest daughter waited until she was twenty-one to have a baby, which fact also allowed her to finish school. Rose really wanted her daughter to go to college.

In many ways, when talking about formal education, the women were also talking about themselves, as some of them did not finish high school. While this wish was at times expressed with passion as it was seen as the only way of bettering oneself, it was also caught in a tangle of conflicts. Not only was it difficult to stay motivated going to GED classes because they did not make any connection to people's life experiences, there were also all the endless responsibilities associated with grand/motherhood that made it next to impossible to find any time for oneself.[26] As described in chapter 4, it took the imagination, creativity, and dedication of a literacy coordinator to transform the formal institutional structures of a literacy center. The coordinator worked hard to make the literacy center a place where the women who prepared for a GED could establish direct, systematic connections with their own experiences, knowledge, and learning desires, and where a sense of continuity was built despite constant life interruptions.

CONCLUSIONS

The women I spoke with are imprisoned in racially and economically segregated "warehouses of the poor" (CHA). Public notions of good mothering are certainly wedded to the image of white middle-class rather than inner-city Black mothers. The work they do is not, however, fundamentally different from a lot of the work white middle-class mothers perform. For instance, modeling good behavior for one's children, being concerned about their education, teaching them about self-respect and respect for others, explaining the larger world, or the world depicted by television, spending time with them, having fun with them, clothing and sheltering them—which mother (or father) would not put these activities on a long list of ordinary things to do and expect? Moreover, what about the importance of taking some precious time for oneself, for resting, reflecting, reading, or traveling? What motivated me to do this study was more than affirmed by the women's narratives. While the above list of tasks and concerns may look quite ordinary, and may be almost automatically associated with the work of raising children in general, this list is not equally automatically associated with mothers living in public housing. This chapter is therefore meant to contribute to demolishing the general social stigmatization of mothers living in public housing as mothers who do not fulfill the good mother norm. This attempt to make poor Black mothers visible to the outside world is grounded in the conviction that their hopes, aspirations, worries, and concerns are not so fundamentally different from the ones held by other, non-Black, non-poor mothers, but that their extremely difficult life circumstances make these "ordinary" hopes and concerns particularly strong and demanding. In a social environment that not only taxes the emotional and spiritual strength of individual grand/mothers or othermothers to an overwhelming degree, but whose slim margins of support continue to be eroded, motherwork becomes a heroic endeavor. The next chapter describes how the new welfare laws enacted in August 1996 exacerbate the calls for heroism by withdrawing even more any remnants of public support for mothers on welfare by making employment a legal requirement.

NOTES

1. "Danger" could mean a number of things. According to Jenna, I was most likely being perceived as a rather naïve white person who wanted to buy drugs. I could also have run the danger of being caught in a gang-related cross-fire whose intermittent occurrences did not follow a clear schedule.

2. At the time of the interviews, the CHA (Chicago Housing Authority) was still managing and overseeing public housing, senior housing, scattered site City-State housing, and Section 8 vouchers, and the CHA police still existed as a separate police force. (The CHA police force was later dissolved) .

3. Rose, like several of the women I met, used to be part of a writing group that published some of its writing in a journal called *Journal of Ordinary Thought*. In order to

safeguard the women's anonymity I do not give any specific references to the issues in which their writings were published.

4. Ironically, the Robert Taylor Homes were named after the first African-American chairman of CHA's board who was strongly opposed to the building of large developments in poor Black areas (Popkin et al. 2000, 13).

5. Rubinowitz and Rosenbaum (2000) give a detailed analysis and critique of CHA's failure to commit to and carry out an effective scattered site program.

6. The Section 8 program is federally funded and administered by HUD, assisting low-income families, the elderly, and people with disabilities to obtain housing in the private market. Section 8 is practically the only alternative for people vacating public housing developments.

7. In their book *The Hidden War*, the authors (Popkin et al. 2000) give a detailed account of the city's various strategies, such as the Anti-Drug-Initiative, to combat and prevent crime in public housing developments. These strategies have had very little positive impact, if any at all. Not only has CHA been going through a tumultuous phase with respect to changing management practices as well as locations of managerial control, its strategies of crime prevention have also been based on assumptions that did not take into account the multilayered complexity of social life in the projects. Within a social world that is cut off from the rest of the city, and where the underground economy is the primary avenue for making good money, the "residents" (or "community") and "criminals" do not simply assume a clearly defined, oppositional stance.

8. However, in May 1999 HUD returned oversight of the CHA to Mayor Richard Daley, resulting in a *Plan for Transformation* (Chicago Housing Authority 2000). The CHA plans to reduce housing stock from more than 38,000 to a little more than 24,000 units, with a permanent loss of nearly 14,000 units of affordable housing. No mid-rises or high-rises will be rehabbed, and only 4,529 new units will be built, providing for more than 8,000 families currently living in mid-rises.

9. In October 1999, 10,000 Altgeld Gardens residents sued the CHA for exposing them to toxic landfills and for misleading them about health hazards. This action responded to the report from the federal Agency for Toxic Substances and Disease Registry that "no apparent public health hazard exists "(Peltz 1999, 1, 2). The EPA recommendation to simply cover the toxic soil was countered by a CHA environmental specialist who urged for relocation of the Altgeld Gardens residents (he has since been laid off).

10. The supply of affordable housing has declined, with a particularly tight market outside traditional Black areas. Moreover, once a Section 8 family moves, the landlord can rent the unit in the private market, thereby eliminating it from the stock of subsidized housing (Fischer 1999, 5). In addition, while within city limits a family cannot be rejected because they are using Section 8, in suburban Cook country (or any other of the six collar counties), landlords can refuse to rent to Section 8 families (25). When families cannot find an eligible unit within a certain time period (usually 60 days), the certificate or voucher is returned to the housing authority (9). Since CHAC, Inc. (a private for-profit agency that administers CHA's' Section 8 program) was created after HUD found CHA incapable of running its own Section 8 program) the placement success rate improved. As of September 1998, only 12 percent rather than the previous 50 percent of certificates and vouchers were returned (29).

11. Popkin et al. 2000, give a detailed account of the revitalization process at the Henry Horner Homes.

12. For an analysis of the decline of affordable housing for low-income and very low-income people, see the report to Congress by HUD on "worst case housing needs,"

Rental Housing Assistance—The Worsening Crisis (March 2000).

13. In conjunction with the Gautreaux decree, in the late 1980s the court appointed the Habitat Corporation as the receiver overseeing the construction of new public housing in areas that were less than 30 percent Black. Most of them were built in Latino neighborhoods since they were not considered "minority communities" (Popkin et al. 2000, 14).

14. See also Kotlowitz 1991; Pitts 1999; Popkin and Olson 1995; Popkin et al. 2000; and Wilson 1996.

15. See *Welfare Reform at Age One* 1998, and *From Welfare to Worse* 1998.

16. The theme of gangs providing protection to residents living on their turf was also mentioned by people whom Popkin et al. interviewed (2000). See also Venkatesh 2000.

17. See, for instance, Collins 1990, and Brown 1993.

18. These experiences are part of a growing trend of increasing numbers of grandmothers heading households and raising their grandchildren (Donovan 1999; see also DeParle, 1999a).

19. Collins 1990, 1993 1994; James 1993; Naples 1998a; Stack and Burton 1994.

20. For a detailed critique of DCFS, see Golden 1997.

21. On February 5, 2000, Mayor Daley and HUD representatives announced that they had reached an agreement on a plan that includes tearing down 51 high-rises. Some of the high-rises of other CHA projects such as the Cabrini-Green or Henry Horner Homes have already been sealed off to residents or demolished as part of the ongoing redevelopment plan; for details see the Chicago Housing Authority's *Plan for Transformation* (2000).

22. For a detailed account of Venkatesh's experiences and observations regarding the Robert Taylor Homes, see his *American Project* (2000).

23. Not surprisingly, women have been at the forefront of collective efforts to include resident voices in various redevelopment plans. Women comprise the majority of presidents of Local Advisory Councils, or, under a HUD decree, of leaders of resident management corporations. They speak at public rallies or events that protest the ease with which evictions jumped when revitalization efforts started, the uncertainty of where families who live in buildings targeted for closure will be relocated, or the shoddiness of replacement housing. In 1991 a group of women, the Horner Mothers Guild, sued CHA, charging that the agency had deliberately allowed their buildings to deteriorate to justify tearing them down. In 1995 an agreement was reached to redevelop Horner in five phases, including demolition, rehabilitation, and one-for-one replacement housing. No other public housing development in Chicago has received that guarantee (Popkin et al. 2000; Oldweiler 1998).

24. In 1988 the city adopted the Chicago School Reform Act, which was proposed by a number of reform groups. Under this act Local School Councils (LSCs), comprised of six parents, two community representatives, two teachers, and the principal (and, in high schools, a student representative), adopt a School Improvement Plan, enact a spending plan, and hire and fire the principal through four-year contracts. In 1995 the legislature turned the school system over to the mayor, mainly due to a financial crisis and "the perception that two-thirds of the elementary schools (and virtually all of the high schools) were not progressing" (Hess 1999, 1). One of the actions that ensued from restructuring reform efforts was placing over 100 schools on probation. Although in 1999 some progress was made in terms of elevating students' achievement scores, "Chicago Students are still some distance from matching national achievement levels" (2). In July 2001 the Illinois State Board of Education announced that it is going to issue a warning

list of academically troubled schools. While the 1998 list contained seventy-eight schools (fifty-eight in Chicago alone), the new list could name as many as 700 (*Chicago Tribune*, 8 July 2001).

25. As Elio DeArrudah who lived in a public housing area when I had conversations with him pointed out to me, Black teenage boys are particularly hard hit in that respect. The killings around them makes them rather sarcastic when asked about future plans as they can barely imagine surviving beyond their teens.

26. As discussed in the following chapter, various provisions of the new welfare law, the Personal Responsibility and Work Opportunity Reconciliation Act (PRWORA), seriously impede education and training.

— Chapter 3 —

Welfare Mothers:
Invisible Work Becoming Visible—
and Invisible Again

The new welfare law distinguishes poor single mothers as a separate caste, subject to a separate system of law. Poor single mothers are the only people in America forced by law to work outside the home. They are the only people in America whose decisions to bear children are punished by government. They are the only people in America of whom government may demand the details of intimate relationships. And they are the only mothers in America compelled by law to make room for biological fathers in their families.

—Gwendolyn Mink, *The Lady and the Tramp (II)*

Since beginning work on this book, I have been meeting and talking with women relying on public aid, but their dependency on what was then called Aid to Families with Dependent Children (AFDC) was not the focus of our conversations. My main concern was, and has been for a long time, how the theme and experience of motherhood weaves in and out of women's daily lives. It has always been clear to me that motherwork is inseparable from the overall social organization of the sexual division of labor. While conducting the interviews of women raising children in Chicago's public housing, however, and participating in a women's literacy group, also taking place in a public housing development, I realized that the women were caught in a tangle of stereotypical public images of Black welfare mothers.

It is tempting to lose track of the economic underside of public policy developments when studying the myriad of political and social institutional changes surrounding the development of the American welfare state and its particular legislation concerning aid to poor children and women. In all accounts of the

American welfare system, the sexual division of labor is a steady undercurrent, even where it is not articulated in those terms. For instance, the early twentieth-century discourse of white and Black women reformers focused on maternalism. While both groups had a notion of "social motherhood"—with the protective, nurturing mother as its central image—the groups related to each other in at times oppositional ways. How the notion of maternalism was understood, and how it guided political practice, therefore depended on which part of the female population proposed to act in accordance with its values. For instance, some white middle-class reformers identified with the plight of poor women, but most sought to impose their own notion of good mothering and a decent homelife on immigrant and working-class women whom they saw in need of a "transformative education" (Boris 1993, 232). On the other hand, the outspoken leaders of the Black mothers' clubs were members of the middle class as well, but as "race women" they emphasized cross-class associations. Since they knew how important Black women's income was for the survival of their families, they considered the employed mother to be as worthy as the unemployed one. The National Association of Colored Women therefore placed "the establishment of mothers' clubs—along with day nurseries and kindergartens—at the top of its priorities," accepting mothers' paid labor as a necessary reality (225). Consequently, as Gordon (1994b) describes in her history of welfare, the term maternalism could encompass quite different interpretations. Her careful analysis of historical shifts and developments, however, led her to identify three tenets that characterized most maternalists' views:

First, they regarded domestic and family responsibilities and identities as essential to the vast majority of women and to the social order, and strongly associated women's with children's interests. . . . Second, maternalists imagined themselves in a motherly role towards the poor. Viewing the poor as in need of moral and spiritual as well as economic help, middle-class women sometimes imagined giving that help as a mother to a child, combining sympathy with authority. Third, maternalists believed that it was their work, experience, and/or socialization as mothers that made women uniquely able to lead certain kinds of reform campaigns and made others deserving of help. (55)

In a way, these reformers reinforced one of the mainstays of the patriarchal notion of the feminine. Because Black women claimed a motherhood previously associated with white women, however, they redefined it in universal terms. Due to the history of slavery where women gave birth to labor power, and where their children could be sold in an instant, motherhood and "maternal instincts" therefore assumed an oppositional quality (Boris 1993, 221). Black women reformers did not consider the state as the appropriate arena for struggle. Instead, they fought a state that continued the history of slavery through many forms of social and economic discrimination, a history most violently expressed in lynching acts. White women reformers, on the other hand, considered the state the proper place for carrying out their struggles for reform (232). As "social housekeepers" white reformers fought for a variety of social programs, some of them aimed at protecting working women. These programs excluded, however, "immigrant mothers working in the home as industrial homeworkers or African American mothers working in other women's homes as domestic servants. Such home-based waged labor was invisible" (236). Thus, not only did white women's construct of motherhood remain within the orbit of a male-defined hegemonic culture, it also did not destabilize broader social-economic inequalities that were anchored in the sexual division of labor.

Regardless of the particular time period involved, however, race, ethnicity, nationality, age, and class have always been linked to various capitalist divisions of labor, simultaneously shaping variations of the sexual division. At the same time, as the history of welfare policies demonstrates, the feminine provides core ingredients for the gendered welfare state, regardless of its interplay with race or class. Both welfare policy and economic structures keep all women subordinated.[1] Writers who examine issues related to welfare within the parameters of a larger socioeconomic framework link today's neoliberal version of laissez-faire capitalism to the way the state perceives and treats poor women. This means that "when the forces of patriarchy and capitalism work in concert, the gender division of labor is enforced, to the advantage of both systems" (Abramovitz 1996, 105). All women are therefore affected, whether they are poor or well-off, white or Black, doing paid or unpaid work.

Despite the erosion of the inner and outer survival base of motherwork, children are still being born and need to be raised. As described in chapter 1, commodity production and, correspondingly, wage labor have always been fully dependent on subsistence work. This kind of work, however, is considered entirely useless when it remains outside the realm of profitability, and when it is oriented toward raising children whose combination of socioeconomic background and color makes them socially unwanted. These children have become superfluous for the megamachine of profitability. They are "disposable" (see Golden 1997). That's why we hear public, media-related outcries such as "Stop having babies!" "Get them to work!" As Williams (1995) put it, "Our present welfare war is pervaded with the assumption that black women have no business having any more children (its most common expression being the fiction, again, that women on welfare are having more children just to get more money)" (9).[2] Somebody has to benefit. Who benefits is the question that was the driving force behind the most recent reform of welfare, or, more precisely, the reform of bad mothers into good workers.

MORALLY STRENGTHENING SUB/MINIMUM WAGE JOBS

Moral justifications operate with the notions of good and bad. These notions are fully embedded in the capitalist system, thereby wedding them to public acknowledgment and financial support. Good or bad mothers therefore translate into worthy or unworthy mothers, that is, worthy or unworthy of support by the government or the state. Moral support is inseparable from financial support. It therefore translates into granting or withholding power and money. This gives moral justification to virtually everything that is necessary to fulfill the norm of getting or keeping money and power (von Werlhof 1996, 25). Welfare reform then becomes a reform of mothers—not to become good mothers but good workers who are finally earning their money rather than simply taking it. From that perspective, any kind of job is a good job. Because welfare is "not mainly an institution to regulate individual morality" but also, "more important, a labor market institution" (Piven 1999, 87), welfare agencies gear their efforts toward helping recipients enter the labor market as quickly as possible.

Most women on welfare have always been moving in an out of the labor market and have therefore been interchangeable with low-waged workers (Boris 1999, 53). Predictably, the institutional arrangements of the 1996 welfare policies "will affect large aggregates of people, and these cumulative effects will alter the terms of the labor market, especially the lower tiers of the labor market where poor and unskilled women compete for work"(Piven 1999, 88). By being clustered in low-paying jobs, primarily in food-service and retail trade, several studies of "welfare leavers"[3] report that about two-thirds of those who find employment remain poor, landing often further below the official poverty line than they were before they obtained a job. What intensifies the leavers' poverty is, however, not only the low pay of their jobs, but also the fact that many are engaged in part-time or intermittent jobs (Danziger 2000, 5).[4] Clearly, from being members of the "nonworking poor," these women joined the ranks of the "working poor," making about $8,000 to $9,500 a year (Cancian et al. 1999, 24).[5]

For women who find themselves at the bottom of the social and economic hierarchy, a good worker is therefore one who willingly, obediently, and without complaints does any kind of job for the lowest possible wage, and without any so-called "fringe" benefits. When "the invisible healing hand of the workplace" disappears, whatever problems these leavers encounter disappear as well (Grumman 1999, 11). For instance, in October 1999 the Office of the Governor presented numbers regarding the success of Illinois's "Work First" program. In its editorial section the *Chicago Reporter* (January 2000) tells its readers what underlies these numbers: "More than one-third of the people whose welfare cases closed were unemployed within a year and were not receiving assistance." Clearly, in Illinois as in other states, great numbers of leavers have become "America's Disappeared" (*The Nation*, 12 July, 5).

In August 1996 PRWORA, called the Personal Responsibility and Work Opportunity Reconciliation Act, was passed, dismantling sixty-one years of federal welfare legislation by abolishing AFDC. Most of the responsibility for attending to people in poverty was moved to the states.[6] They are now receiving block grants, and they are given a wide range of options for revising their welfare programs—now called Temporary Assistance for Needy Families (TANF)—to determine eligibility criteria for who is getting state support and for how long. Mothers who receive benefits have to find paid work within two years, and they have a five-year lifetime limit to receive any benefits.[7] In addition, food stamp benefits have been severely decreased. PRWORA has short-term provisions for health care and child care, but once these provisions are used up, few women will have found jobs that provide benefits. PRWORA has torn what for a large number of women was some kind of a safety net, no matter how fragile or temporary. In other words, new legislation cut "the lifeline, already only a slender thread" (Kittay 1998, 40).[8] What is a social right for others has now become a legal obligation for welfare recipients.

The corporate call for "Let Them Eat Ketchup" (Collins 1996) is now enhanced by the call "Let Them Sell Lemonade" (Pollitt 1999). Under PRWORA welfare recipients may be assigned to private employers who receive substantial tax credits or subsidies paid for by welfare "grant divisions" (Piven 1999, 90; see also Flynn 1999; Street 1998). For instance, a flyer from the Illinois Department of Human Services (IDHS) invites employers to cash in on the Welfare-To-Work and Work Opportunity Tax Credit by hiring welfare recipients. A Work Opportunity Tax Credit is calculated as covering 40 percent of the first $6,000 in wages if 400 hours are worked. Another example is given by a health-care corporation in Illinois that in 1998 paid its own workers $5.15 an hour (with no benefits), and that used workfare workers free of charge (Bleifuss 1998, 9). In addition, under the umbrella of new welfare regulations, states have, for instance, hired welfare recipients as work trainees, firing higher-paid city workers (Boris 1999, Greenhouse 1998, Mink 1998b).

Child-care work assumes a particularly prominent place in state attempts to put mothers to work. As reported by Michel (1998), PRWORA "specifies childcare as a promising occupation for former AFDC mothers—the *only* occupation singled out in this way"(50). Eighty percent of for-profit day-care chains, the fastest growing segment of the day-care industry, now hire welfare recipients who have no training and who receive the lowest pay—lower than the "regular" wages of child-care workers who are one of the lowest paid professions in the nation (Lewin 1998; Roberts 1999; *From Welfare to Worse?*). Child care is therefore provided "on the cheap" where welfare recipients are forced into this line of work instead of providing adequate funding and well-trained personnel for quality child care. In addition, the interplay of gender, race, and class perpetuates the trend of the late sixties that kept relegating poor Black mothers to domestic work as nannies, maids, or day-care providers. As Roberts (1999) writes, "during the 1960s, congressional debate over adding mandatory work provision to the welfare laws included white people's interest in keeping poor Black mothers available for cheap domestic service" (161; see also Glenn 1997). At the same time, child care on the cheap reveals how class and race divisions can be profitably utilized by keeping the raising of children ascribed to gender in general. A white middle-class mother is therefore at least responsible for finding a reliable but cheap nanny to do what is still considered *her*, that is, the white mother's job.

Welfare recipients can also be asked to perform one of the accepted work activities[9] that may very well be of a "make-work" type. The mandatory work rule allows for entirely unremunerated work in community service programs such as picking up litter on city streets or doing dishes in school cafeterias. While all these programs are small, New York City operates a large Community Work Experience Program (CWEP) where recipients "work alongside city workers doing such tasks as cleaning parks or helping with clerical tasks such as filing" (Pavetti 1998, 13). About 30,000 to 40,000 former AFDC recipients who perform menial tasks such as raking leaves or cleaning city streets are visibly marked as well: they are required to wear an orange vest (Piven 1999, 91).

The women's monthly cash benefits fall into the range of subminimum wage—when measured against minimum wage income. Consequently, by creating a "virtually indentured labor force of welfare recipients," these work activities fall outside the realm of the protections of current labor laws (Piven, 90–91). Clearly, "the seduction of cheap or 'free' labor, combined with the requirement that states enroll increasing numbers of welfare recipients in work, has produced gross exploitation and immiserated low-wage workers who have lost their jobs " (Mink 1998b, 111). Workfare therefore threatens the livelihoods of all low-wage workers.

Benefits can be reduced or terminated quickly, and for any kind of behavior deemed undesirable. The ease with which "sanctions" are dished out therefore gives women dependent on TANF even less leeway to weather any personal crisis without losing welfare benefits right away. States have a fairly free hand to erroneously deny benefits, something that critics have described as a form of lawlessness (Castern 2000). TANF regulations are so cumbersome and complex that caseworkers do not always give out all the right kinds of information to the women applying for or depending on public aid, thereby increasing the rate of sanctions. As Houppert (1999) writes, "The always lumbering and inefficient system has transformed itself from a bureaucratic behemoth into a whirling dervish, cutting people's benefits in a tangle of confusion that's nearly impossible to correct" (11). Welfare recipients can therefore easily lose their benefits, and often they have to wait months without any aid until the mistake is corrected. Administrators or caseworkers may themselves not always be fully informed about the difference between welfare, which is no longer an entitlement, and other benefits like Medicaid, which still is (12). For instance, in New York City's welfare offices (now called "job centers"), the receptionists routinely tell applicants that "there is no more welfare, that this office exists solely to see that they get a job, that if they miss any appointments their application will be denied, that emergency food stamps and cash grants don't exist, that there is a time limit on benefits—without explaining that they can apply for Medicaid or food stamps" (13).[10] Due to the legal pressure on welfare agencies to reduce the welfare rolls, sanctions are dished out as fast as possible, thereby creating a much desired downsizing effect.[11] The sanctions process has therefore "created a sizable churning of the rolls, in which thousands of people are dropped each month only to return later" (Toy 1998, 1).

Education and training opportunities have suffered tremendously through the enactment of PROWA. The new federal policy encourages states to place welfare recipients in jobs as quickly as possible, or to have them engage in work activities for increasing numbers of hours. The extent to which education and training can count as work activities is severely limited by this policy. Welfare offices are therefore transformed into job centers or "one-stop employment centers."[12] Whereas the former JOBS (Job Opportunities and Basic Skills) program focused on long-term education and training activities, under TANF only vocational educational training is considered an allowable work activity, aside from being limited to twelve months for any individual and 30 percent of those required to participate (Pavetti 1998, 9). Post-secondary education is therefore strongly discouraged in some states unless the recipient is spending the required number of hours working. What if the recipient is a single mother? How can she combine holding a job with going to college and raising a child (or children) on her own? As Bounds, Brubaker, and Hobgood (1999) write, "Although women might try to attend college on their own time, there is little time left after work requirements and family needs are fulfilled. Indeed, there has been a dramatic decrease in the numbers of welfare recipients enrolled in community college, university, and adult education programs" (10).

Many factors play into the often extremely restricted life and work opportunities for women workers in general, welfare recipients in particular. Numerous studies have shown that the majority of women on AFDC were desperately trying to get off the dole and find a job. Before the enactment of the new welfare legislation, about two-thirds of welfare recipients applied for assistance because of the birth of a child or a divorce. However, they left the rolls once their circumstances were stabilized. In other words, the women were often employed for certain periods of time until a family crisis threw them off the tightrope and they reapplied for public aid (Albelda and Tilly 1994; Amott 1993; Spalter-Roth and Hartman 1995). One of the reasons most welfare recipients have always been trying to find employment is also related to the wish for getting away from the humiliating treatment encountered at the public aid office. Above all, solo mothers have been trying to escape the social stigmatization of being nonpersons caught in a web of immorality by being without a husband or a job. As Williams wrote in 1995, one year before PROWA was passed, "We have ascended to the age of workfare and bridefare, with more and more programs containing regulations that require recipients to work or to marry in order to receive some measure of what they need. Women who have born the brunt of both failed marriages and a failing economy are now to be 'taught' the stabilizing, civilizing influences of hard work and a strong male hand around the house" (6). In other words, women can be dependent on a man or on the market, but not on the state. As mentioned above, the underlying morality is closely tied to market interests. What is good for the woman's character is good for the market because it is based on the premise that "*any* job outside the house, including caring for other people's children, is more socially productive than caring for one's own" (Mink 1998b, 26).

REAL JOBS VS. MOTHERWORK

A good worker is one who willingly takes a job that barely pays a livable wage and who keeps her private life (and the work associated with it) entirely out of the picture. By having to leave their involvement in child-raising responsibilities fully outside of the official world of work, women "are forced by law or by economic circumstances to choose wages over children" (Mink 1998a, 58). Their work as mothers interferes with their real job. A bad worker is therefore one who cannot keep the private world of the family (and all unpaid work associated with it) separate from the public world of paid work.

This is true—albeit in different forms—for women who are desperately poor and for women engaged in professional work. While there is a "dilemma" for professional women having children (Swiss and Walker 1993), for poor women the dilemma is turned into the brutality of requiring twenty-four hours of super-human heroism to stay employed in menial and low-paying jobs, and to somehow take care of their children without letting them interfere in the job. This means that poor mothers are caught in a tangle of many conflicting demands.

The well-documented desire to find paid work contradicts the myth that welfare mothers have no work ethic. What fuels this desire is the strongly felt need of being able to provide for the children. The authors of a study on welfare reform and the work-family tradeoff report that the women who were interviewed generally "considered work primarily in terms of how it would affect the lives of their children," hoping that their earnings would be high enough so they could better provide for them (Scott et al. 2000, 9). And this is where the women's concerns for the well-being of their children come in direct conflict with the fact that minimum-wage jobs do not carry health benefits and do not pay enough to be able to afford decent, reliable, and steady child care (see the contributions in Mink 1999). Due to the current changes in reimbursement rates for child-care providers, some lose money and reduce the slots available for children from poor households. In addition, required co-payments ("parents fees") are now too high for many women, and this has a negative impact on their participation in child-care programs. Mothers may feel forced to risk leaving their children unsupervised at home in order to not lose their jobs (see *Welfare Reform at Age One* 1998; *From Welfare to Worse?* 1998). Relatives, especially grandmothers, have already been more and more called upon to take care of these mothers' children, regardless of the hardship it may cause for these caretakers (DeParle 1999a). Or a child may be moved from one improvised child-care arrangement to another, certainly an emotionally troubling experience for the child involved.

Although the rhetoric of welfare reform does not publicly address the fact that women have been using the welfare system "as an alternative to dirty, dangerous, and low-paying jobs" (Abramovitz 1996, 29), it also does not address the fact that work schedules often do not match the hours of child-care provision. Work schedules may include nights, weekends, or rotating shifts (*Welfare Reform at Age One*; *From Welfare to Worse?*). Even more regular kinds of day shifts often require a tremendous amount of stamina—on the side of the mothers as well as the children—in order to start a long day early in the morning and finish it late at night.

DeParle (1994) gives a description of such a day in the life of Mary Ann Moore, a mother who left welfare and took a job as a cook in a Salvation Army homeless shelter. Her day starts at 3:30 a.m., and at 4:00 a.m. she has to wake her two-year-old twins and her other two children. She and her children have to leave the house before 5 a.m. and travel eleven miles to her mother's apartment in one of Chicago's public housing projects. While the children wait for their school day to begin, Mary Ann continues her journey of six more miles to her work site, where she begins work at 6:00 a.m. For the first five months she also had to work thirteen-hour shifts on Saturdays and Sundays.

It is not surprising that "most evaluations of welfare reform focus on adults, and successes are most often defined as reduced welfare caseloads, greater employment, or improved income" (Mistry et al. 2000, 6). Michel points out that "the reluctance to make adequate provisions for child-care is . . . symptomatic of a deeper aversion on the part of many legislators and public officials to helping poor and low-income women becoming truly economically independent" (51). While this is certainly true, this aversion has another dimension. Dismissing poor single mothers' caring work means to entirely disregard the lives of their children. It is ultimately the "spurning" of children (Mink) that unfolds into women's super-exploitation as motherworkers and job-holders.[13] A concern with the tremendous obstacles placed in the paths of women who are trying to gain at least a semblance of economic self-sufficiency has to include a concern for the well-being of young lives who need to be nurtured and cherished. Kittay, who discusses the social and political vagaries of the terms "dependency" or "independence," emphasizes that "having dependents to care for means that without additional support, you cannot—given the structure of our contemporary industrial life and its economy—simultaneously provide the *means* to take care of them and to do the caring for them" (1999, 199). And she continues the discussion by pointing out that

The demand that women on welfare "work" not only fails to value the unpaid dependency work of the women using welfare to support themselves and their children, but, by imposing on these women the model of the male breadwinner, it also fails to recognize the dependency work of mothering. In the name of fostering a fictive "independence," it refuses to acknowledge "the obligation of the social order to attend to the well-being of dependents *and* of their caretakers, and to the *relation* of caretaker and dependent upon which all other civic unions depend." (200).[14]

The sexist division of labor that underlies the model of the male breadwinner creates conflicting demands for women who need to be employed while simultaneously raising their children. It also, however, provides the man-the-provider model that is often acted out in rather ugly ways by unemployed husbands or boyfriends who begrudge women's attempts to become economically independent. This often makes it particularly difficult for women to escape an abusive relationship (Lloyd and Taluc 1999; Raphael 1995; Raphael and Tolman 1997). In a compilation of research that documents the relationship between domestic violence and welfare, Raphael and Tolman report that 30 to 60 percent of all women on welfare are current victims of abuse by their husbands or boyfriends. They are kept in isolation, or boyfriends sabotage their attempts to prepare for a GED test by keeping them up all night, hiding books, ripping up clothes, or beating them so they have visible bruises. Raphael also reports that boyfriends often stalk the women at their places of employment. While the new welfare laws include a Family Violence Amendment[15] that most states implemented as an option, very few women take advantage of it. They find it next to impossible to confide in the state, are trying to hide the existence of a man in their lives, and are afraid of losing their children to the state. In addition, in order for the states to collect child support, mothers are forced to name the fathers of their children, thereby also forcing many of them to name fathers they are trying to avoid. This difficult, complex situation does not get any public acknowledgment. It gets fogged up by the claim that women enjoy their dependency on welfare, and that they are therefore badly in need of moral reform in order to build the moral strength necessary to marry and sustain a two-parent household.[16]

Social and economic class divisions are major contributors to the particularly harsh and volatile conditions these conflicts create for poor mothers. It is poor and mostly racial-ethnic women who are not white who are taking care of middle-class women's children.[17] The availability of less privileged women to do low-wage jobs is now guaranteed by welfare policy (Roberts 1997, 203). As mentioned before, children should not interfere with the paid work performed by any woman, but women are divided here, and their children are differently affected. A wealthy woman can afford to pay another woman to take care of her children while she is working at her job. The poor (poorly paid) woman cannot afford the same. What is happening to her children? Clearly, the private and public are much more intertwined in the lives of "maids"—in reality, but also ideologically and normatively. The blurrier the lines of demarcation between the public (social) world of paid work and the private world of domesticity, the lower the value of work performed in these twilight zones. In the case of women, this means that the less divided these worlds are, the poorer the women because they have only poorly paid "dependency work" or cleaning kinds of jobs. Dependency workers, especially child-care workers, "are the most poorly paid workers relative to their level of education and skills" (Kittay 1998, 37).[18]

If welfare mothers want to adhere to what counts as a good worker and a good citizen, they have to learn to fully separate their private and public (economic) lives and let the work with their children sink into oblivion—a rather old phenomenon. If there is no connection to economic profitability, domesticity is unacceptable. The invisibility behind privatized motherwork can only be praised (and reinforced) if someone (the business owner, the income-earning husband or boyfriend) is profiting from it. Not surprisingly, a few days after PRWORA was signed and the care-giving work performed by poor single mothers was negated, Congress granted middle-class housewives rights to their own Independent Retirement Account (IRAs), thereby affirming these women's care-giving work. Because IRAs are an untaxed portion of *earned* income, this decision "formalized the distinction between poor single mothers' worthless *time* in the home and married, middle-class mothers' worthy *work* there" (Mink 1998b, 28, 29). When the usefulness or profitability for individual men and corporations is absent, the work done in the household ceases to be invisible and therefore good, and becomes highly visible and therefore bad. Thus, from being an expression of good moral conduct, motherhood becomes an expression of immoral sexuality.

OTHER PEOPLE'S WORKERS

The bad mother is the one whose invisible work becomes public by becoming dependent on public aid. The welfare mother's private life is open to public eyes, redefining the meanings of private sphere, motherhood, women, and work. The state, public administrators, and the media characterize in a highly moralistic tone mothers on welfare as incomplete, unworthy, or defective mothers, and as immoral, bad women.[19]

Until about a year after the new welfare laws started to take effect, the majority of welfare recipients, that is, about 65 percent, were non-Black.[20] Nevertheless, even before welfare reform took effect, the unworthy "welfare queen" was stereotyped as typically Black, lazy, and thus taking advantage of the state. As Williams succinctly stated, "Contemporary attacks on women have blended historical strains of racism, misogyny, and class bias into an unusually potent brew. Aimed particularly at black women, single women, and poor women on welfare, the attacks have handily condensed all three categories into the encompassing figure of 'the' black single mother on welfare" (1995, 7). This heavy strand of racism can only be exacerbated by the fact that white welfare recipients are leaving the rolls in larger numbers than Blacks, in large part due to "racism in employment decisions, the geography of jobs, and the effects of racially stratified educational opportunity" (Mink 1999, 2).[21]

It has been pointed out many times that the welfare system has a gendered and racialized history and structure (see, for instance, Gordon 1994a,b; Quadagno 1994; Roberts 1997, 1999). The private/public dualism so typical for Western societies has supported the entrenchment of motherhood as a vocation for white, middle-class women. As should be evident, this vocation, and the dualism underlying it, are played out differently in the case of welfare mothers

who are seen as typically Black. Black, poor solo mothers do not fit the normative assumption that underlie race, class, *and* gender regulations. Above all,
these mothers are not dependent on a male provider and their sexuality is not
controlled by a husband. They are therefore perceived as having a certain kind
of sexual freedom. The notion of an unbridled sexuality producing superfluous
children contradicts, of course, the equally strong public, media-driven portrayal
of welfare mothers as coldly calculating an increase in welfare benefits by deliberately producing more babies.

The caring work of racially or ethnically marginalized women has always
been ignored in favor of their roles as workers (Glenn 1994, 1997). If we place
this observation at the center of attention, we can see that the rhetoric of current
debates about welfare reform looks like a return to the role Black women have
always been expected to play, a continuation of the history of Black women as
"the mules of the world" (Walker 1983). In Mink's words, "Into the 1990s, the
racial mythology of welfare cast the welfare mother as Black, pinned the need
for reform on her character, and at least implicitly defined Black women as
other peoples' workers rather than their own families' mothers" (1998a, 59; see
also Boris 1999; Roberts 1999). Under slavery giving birth to a child, that is,
becoming a mother, was simply equivalent to producing labor power. Under
current conditions Black motherhood, and the work associated with, is likewise
without its own socially acknowledged space. Where the production of new
labor power has become superfluous, the mothers must make themselves, that is
their own labor power, available to the market.

Racial-ethnic women who are not white have always had to straddle the line
between their private, family world and the public world of a job. To some extent the very notion of separate spheres has always been an illusion, especially
for women of color for whom work and family have rarely functioned as separate. Mullings (1994) points out that

Throughout history African-American women have been forced to work outside their
homes, first by slaveholders and then by economic necessity. In a society in which the
dominant ideology has held that the woman's place is in the home, the African-American
woman's status as a worker becomes a point of departure for representations that function first to mobilize her labor and then to stigmatize the measure of independence
gained from her relationship to work. (266)

The convoluted meanings of public and private are part of this quagmire because for "racial-ethnic women . . . the notion of separate spheres served to reinforce their subordinate status" (166). This notion "became, in effect another
assault," because as women "increased their work outside the home, they were
forced into a productive labor sphere that was organized for men and 'desperate'
women who were so unfortunate or immoral that they could not confine their
work to the domestic sphere" (166). In Abramovitz's words, "When it comes to
African-American women, the welfare state enforces the work ethic, but *violates*
the family ethic." She points out that "social welfare policies either excluded

African-American women or forced them to work for low wages, even as it encouraged white middle-class women to stay at home" (1996, 100). Here racial and sexual exploitation combine in a particularly potent way. Consequently, a Black woman's desire to "make her family the most important priority" can be seen as "an act of resistance to a system which would define her place for her in terms of its own economic and racist needs" (Brown 1993, 81). This desire continues the tradition of subverting the social script of Black motherhood.

For Black women to lead a life that is devoted to the publicly financed work of raising children in private is intolerable in the eye of a public that is organized and funded by the corporate and political world. Certain social groups have always been considered less worthy of protection than others, and the state has its own corresponding history of pulling away from its traditional function of purposively intervening in the market economy in order to protect only the worthy citizens. Today's demonization of people dependent on welfare therefore repeats, or exacerbates, the shift that occurred in the sixties, a shift from "worthy" widowed white ADC beneficiaries to "unworthy" Black urban women who were accused of bearing children out-of-wedlock to avoid work (Axinn and Hirsch 1993, 570; Roberts 1997, 207). Today this demonization is aided by the general disappearance of political state control that used to set up protective barriers against market imperatives.

POVERTY IS A PRIVATE AFFAIR

It has now become an "industrial strength cliché" (Williams) that the poor themselves are to be blamed for their plight.[22] Today's "poverty talk" or "poverty discourse" does not acknowledge a failed public economy and a discriminatory public policy. Poverty is therefore "privatized," is seen as a private, individual affair, or an "ethnic problem." Current statistics that show that the majority of women left on the rolls are now African Americans or Latinas can easily feed into well-entrenched, racist blaming-the-victim attitudes. The political and economic structures behind the concentration of Black/Latina women in large inner cities can likewise easily be negated as major contributors to this racial-ethnic disparity. The disappearance of manufacturing jobs, and a geographical mismatch between the availability of most new jobs and the residential concentration of large numbers of the new jobless in central cities are issues that are left out of any public welfare debates. So is the growing disparity between rich and poor.[23] Instead, "over time AFDC has been slowly and perversely targeted as the *cause* of our large social problems, as if it were at fault for feeding people who without it would have just starved to death in peaceful oblivion instead of growing up greedy and infinitely more troublesome" (Williams 1995, 5). In other words, the poor are being reconstituted not to eradicate poverty but to reconstruct negative personality characteristics (Kingfisher 1999, 15).

In an article aptly entitled "Spinning the Poor into Gold," Ehrenreich (1997) reports on a conference on "welfare privatization" (with a registration fee of

$1,295) where Robert Rector of the Heritage Foundation had an important message to give to the corporate conference participants. He made it clear that it is welfare that makes people poor, "or at least what makes them demoralized and dependent, criminal and addicted, and, worst of all, pregnant" (46). Ehrenreich could only conclude from Rector's presentation that "welfare functions, semen-like, to impregnate the poor single-handedly"(46). Rector expresses in the most poignant form the moral justification for the current dramatic reductions of welfare payments, eligibility criteria, and lifetime limits for receiving public aid.

Although children represent only one-fourth of the total population, they presently account for nearly 40 percent of the country's poor population (Mistry et al. 2000, 6). The utter subordination of nonwaged subsistence to waged commodity work becomes most visible here. By pulling the rug from under millions of children who are still relying on public aid, hunger and homelessness will increase, and the subsistence work of mothering is becoming more and more survival work (see DeParle 1999a; Bounds, Brubaker, and Hobgood 1999, 8–9). By cloaking the work of raising children with the mantle of moral conduct, any public responsibility for the well-being of children is denied, as are the diminishing or entirely vanishing material resources the children's caretakers are faced with under existing economic conditions. Because poor children are the most vulnerable, they are "the walking wounded" (Sidel 1996,141; see also Edelman 1994).

PUBLIC OR PERSONAL RESPONSIBILITY?

Although PRWORA emphasizes "personal responsibility," what is society's public responsibility for the well-being of its most vulnerable members? At a point in history where the social has practically vanished as a separate realm by being entirely absorbed by economic imperatives, citizens are defined as consumers who contribute to corporate profits, or as workers who produce it (Gerschlager and Heintel 1993; Luttwak 1999; von Werlhof 1993a). This means that the state, and the wealthy, are relieved of the *burden* of social responsibility. In her discussion of neoliberalism's impact on welfare reform, de Goede (1996) points out that neoliberalism "is the champion . . . of individualism in which the wealthy and the business world do not need to feel public responsibility towards the poor and excluded" (351). Glazer therefore rightfully points out that "what is missing in public debates is the question why 'families' are responsible *for* their members, while workers are responsible *to* their employers," thus relieving employers from any responsibility *for* their employees. Consequently, "the family continues to appear as a unit outside the influence of the *private* ownership of capital and capital's domination of the *public* sphere" (1993, 13).

The terms "public" and "private" have multiple, historically, and culturally shifting meanings. Originally the terms implied a binary opposition between two spheres, where the public was directly associated with the political. The *polis* of the ancient Greek city-state, and the development of the European bourgeoisie in accordance with the rise of capitalism have both been considered the cradle of these distinctions, and of the Western democratic notion of the political (Arendt 1958, Habermas 1989). Public and private are therefore intricately linked to notions and concrete realities of democratic political arrangements, and to access to various political arenas where decisions are being made. Fraser (1995) gives an account of Habermas's sophisticated analysis of the relationship between public and private institutions, making complex distinctions between the private system of the economy and the private lifeworld of the family, and between the public state and public opinion institutions that shape the sphere of the public lifeworld. As these arenas have developed and changed over the past two centuries, they have become part of a "multiplicity of competing publics" (Fraser 1990b, 62). Irrespective of this multiplicity, however, the unholy marriage of sexist oppression with the originally binary opposition between public and private remains intact.

In her discussion of the gendered nature of modernity, Marshall states that "the 'modern' bourgeois family emerged not with some abstract separation of household and work-place, but with the entrenchment of motherhood as a vocation for white, middle class women" (1994, 55). This touches the core of the classical meaning of the private where the typical heterosexual nuclear family represents the original Western bourgeois ideal of the private sphere, or the private lifeworld of the family. This sphere has been considered sacrosanct because it is supposed to shield the family from governmental intrusion, that is, from intrusion from the political public *and* from interference by the private system of the market economy. In this context work equals waged work *outside* the private lifeworld of the family/household, which then becomes "a haven from the heartless world." The household is therefore the sphere where women's labor remains entirely invisible, is not considered work, thereby confining, controlling, and appropriating it in order to make it socially and economically useful to capital and individual men/husbands.

As argued in *Working and Educating for Life* (Hart 1992), from the perspective of female experience, this is an ideological achievement of the first order. And, as also discussed, not only did production in the form of subsistence production never cease to take place in the sphere of the private, it also never ceased to build the very foundation of "actual" social production. In addition, the old European boundaries between the social, the political, and the economic public, and what is ascribed to them or who has access to the private sphere, have over the past three centuries steadily become more fluid:

The distinction between a private and public sphere of life corresponds to the household and the political realms, which have existed as distinct, separate entities at least since the rise of the ancient city-state; but the emergence of the social realm, which is neither private nor public, strictly speaking, is a relative new phenomenon whose origin coincided with the emergence of the modern age and which found its political form in the nation-state. (Arendt 1958, 28)

Whereas the government is still the paradigm of the public and the family the paradigm of the private sphere, the world of business and activities occurring within its realm are sometimes considered private, and sometimes considered public (see Fraser 1990a). In addition, U.S. history has generally been complex, divided, or fragmented in many different aspects with respect to the public/private division. For instance, the very categories "women" and "men," and hence public and private, work and family, are interlaced with the divisions created by colonialism, slavery, and neocolonialism (which includes ethnocentric and ethnophobic perceptions of immigrants). Collins (1998) discusses in detail how race was deeply implicated in the nation-state's unique American version of the public-private division. From the very beginning the public had a bipartite structure, with local, state, and governmental units on the one hand, corporations, media, civic associations, and social institutions not attached to the state on the other, all of them constituting civil society (15). Age and gender were features that, together with one's property relations, determined white people's status with respect to citizenship rights. Blacks, however, not only lacked age and gender specificity, but they "remained *outside* of the public sphere— they were Black, enslaved, and judged by their group membership," therefore possessing "no property, not even themselves" (15). Since white citizenship rights rested on private property, and since slaves were part of that property, they also had no privacy rights. In addition, although for Blacks gender remained legally unrecognized, "Black women's reproductive capacities led to a unique place in their racialized system of property relations. Just as any offspring of an animal's owner became his property, Black women's children became the property of their mothers' owners. Under slavery, Black women's bodies produced property and labor" (17). Collins continues her analysis and eventually moves it into the twentieth century where residential segregation in the northern cities signifies the continued treatment of African Americans as a separate, derogated group, and where individuals are primarily identified by their group membership. However, racial segregation also led to the formation of a Black public sphere, a Black civil society (19). While residential housing segregation, and thus the notion of Black civil society, did not rely on gender, Black women's experience in the labor market did, especially since African-American women entered that social public sphere through exploitative work in private homes.[24]

The notion of public responsibility is a core ingredient of the meaning of the political. The federal state is the primary political body that gives shape to and oversees the execution of the practical imperatives of public responsibility. The public responsibility of the state to intervene when the market cannot sufficiently provide gradually developed with the advance of industrialization that left income, unemployment, or the health of its workers at the mercy of businesses. The federal state created a number of social welfare institutions (such as the 1935 Social Security Act) that aimed at preventing "the worst abuses of the labor market and to compensate for such catastrophes as the loss of a job or a work-related injury" (Abramovitz 1996, 91).[25] As Marshall states, "Taken broadly, the term 'welfare state' indicates a state form which embodies interventions into the market economy to take some responsibility for the well-being of its citizens" (1994, 132). Today's neoliberal renaissance of laissez-faire global capitalism has virtually abolished the moral-political principle of providing a counterweight to capitalism's *raison d'être*, that is, profit maximization. Soros (1998) captures the supremacy of market values over all other social or political values with the term "market fundamentalism." In a similar manner Luttwak (1999) speaks of "turbo-capitalism," a term that encompasses the various economic, political, social, and cultural implications of market fundamentalism. Although he points out that "what is new about turbo-capitalism is only a matter of degree, a mere acceleration in the pace of structural change at any given rate of economic growth," the mere speed of such structural change is "quite enough to make all the difference." Above all, "the most obvious cause of accelerated structural change (turbo-capitalism) is the worldwide retreat of the state from the market-place. There has been a wholesale abandonment of public ownership, central planning, administrative direction and most forms of regulatory control" (37).

As has been emphasized in this chapter, the sexual division of labor, the material-structural foundation of the classic public-private split, has been a common denominator for *all* women. The results of this labor have, however, been appropriated in different ways, creating sharp divisions between women, and creating complex, conflicting experiences with what is considered public or private. Social-economic developments and the emergence of a postindustrial social order have—on a surface level—caused a number of changes. One is the growing social acceptance of women combining their housewifely and motherly responsibilities with paid work, that is, entering the public world of private enterprise.

AUTHORITATIVE AND ENCLAVED SOCIAL PUBLICS

The work of raising children is a particularly good example for illustrating the shifting boundaries between public and private issues—depending on the power or powerlessness of the women involved. The most visible and omnipresent public of the media illustrates how dominant social norms are intertwined with or played out by corporate and political interests. In a hierarchically organized, stratified, and deeply divided or fragmented society, what is officially declared public and what lives as the public of private enterprise or of political representation is by nature not "of concern to everyone" (Fraser 1990a, 71). Thus it is only women with a certain measure of financial and class privileges who get publicly praised in the media when they decide to put their careers on hold in order to devote their time and energy to their children. Women who cannot afford this financial luxury, especially solo mothers, simply need to struggle day in and day out (and often throughout the night) to keep two full-time jobs, one paid and one unpaid. Where they cannot do both, media attention is focused on them as well. Welfare mothers are subjected to "public shaming rituals" (Williams 1995, 3) conducted by privately owned and controlled public media. The media therefore participate in general "status degradation ceremonies" (Garfinkel 1956) in which other members of the public, such as government officials or academic professionals, engage.

The media play a primary role in creating public images of welfare mothers, but their public function is inseparable from their powerful role in shaping our views of the world, and of all the people different from us, that is, the Others. As Kingfisher (1999) writes, degradation ceremonies "always construct the character of the denounced individual in opposition to an ideal character (e.g., needy vs. autonomous) and ritually remove them from legitimate order. The savage poor/poor solo mothers, then, serve a political function: they serve to define and support, symbolically and materially, the rest of us, the *normals,* the normative" (15).

The media constitute a unique kind of social public. Within their own, specific parameters, private power and profit interests merge a variety of social publics. Consequently, the media present images that are not coming out of nowhere. What is considered a public issue worth being turned into an electronic spectacle, paid for by political and corporate power, is also supported by other publics, such as the publishing industry, that participate in this process by supplying the necessary myths. However, while corporate and political publics are large and authoritative, others, such as the "discursive publics" of academe, constitute a smaller, more enclaved public that is generally "unable to make much of a mark beyond their own borders" (Fraser 1990b, 205).

The degrees of power various publics have "determines the outcome of struggles over the boundaries of the political" (205). These struggles deal with what issues should become or should remain depoliticized. They therefore do not become a matter of public discourse in the media but, instead, remain in the "privacy" of corresponding institutions. "Official-economic capitalist system institutions" are relying on *private* ownership prerogatives, or on allegedly impersonal market imperatives (206). Matters concerning unlivable wages, lack of basic "fringe" benefits, or unhealthy working conditions are not a matter of general public discourse, and they can be politicized only in a small, enclaved public of special, usually already committed audiences such as late night public TV or journals with specialized audiences.

"Specialized discursive arenas" (206) as constituted by academe are permeated by the same relations of dominance/subordination that structure society in general. Many academics or intellectuals therefore operate on the basis of established myths and ideologies and provide legitimate, "scientifically proven" fodder for electronic spectacles. These productions are examples of how the overall social-political power structure produces sophisticated forms of "thought-violence" (*Denkgewalt,* von Werlhof 1996, 57), inseparable from a "thought-disallowance" (*Denkverbot*). Such disallowance prevents certain politically charged issues from entering the arena of academic discourse and of the media public. It therefore prevents the fate of welfare leavers to become the focus of audible, effective "counternarratives that might temper administrative and individual reinforcement of the new law" (Mink 1998b, 10).

The helping professions (including associated researchers) have fully participated in the blaming or shaming of defective mothers. Within the framework of their thinking and acting, the fulfillment of women's "true calling" has turned into a behavioral and mental problem. By becoming wards of the state, mothers also became clients for helping professionals. "Client" is a term that came about with the "expert discourses" of medical/psychotherapeutic professions, where a "deep self" had to be "unravelled therapeutically" (Fraser 1990b, 212, 213). Fraser gives the example of battered women who later became clients, that is "victims with deep, complicated selves" (215). The "language game of therapy" and "neutral scientific language" ("spouse abuse") overtook the language of consciousness raising and the political talk of male violence against women (215). Ultimately, the client herself had to work on what had become *her* problem.

REFORMING OR EDUCATING MOTHERS ON WELFARE

In the preceding sections the dichotomy between private and public spheres and, correspondingly, visible and invisible work are placed into a larger analytical framework. An example is given here of how these oppositional divisions function in the actual encounters of welfare recipients and their caseworkers. Horowitz (1994) has written a study of a year-long program oriented toward teen mothers who had dropped out of high school. Although she describes a program that was in effect before PROWA was enacted, her detailed analysis of social service providers' work with young welfare mothers illustrates particularly well key aspects of this reform. Not only did the approach of some of the caseworkers reinforce the dominance of the official market economy that is dependent on the abstractions of a binary opposition between public and private, work and family, but their notion of reform was fully oriented toward teaching the women to keep these worlds strictly separated.

Although the welfare laws changed in 1996, underlying binary divisions did not. Rather, they were exacerbated by a further downgrading of the importance of the private realm, or the family, and of any work associated with it. By turning welfare offices into job centers and case workers into "financial planners" (Pollitt 1999, 11), and by being caught up in the "whirling dervish" of the welfare system, efforts to reform women clearly do not employ any notion of a deep, complicated self that needs to become therapeutically unraveled. Welfare reform has done away with any remnants of a therapeutic relationship between social worker and client. While Horowitz's descriptions illustrate how the trend to turn welfare offices into job centers was in existence before PROWA was enacted, she also points to possible avenues toward transforming the public/private dualism.[26]

Relations of power shape the process of imposing strict divisions between the public and private sphere for those without power, while at the same time scrutinizing the private lives of the powerless from the same position of public power. Horowitz's categorization of one group of social service personnel as "the arbiters" and the other as "the mediators" illustrates this phenomenon. While the arbiters reinforced a stereotypical notion of work and family where public and private worlds have to be strictly separated, the mediators acknowledged how these worlds overlapped in the lives of the young women. The arbiters worked against any attempts to "politicize" the needs located in the private sphere because that would have undermined the separation of private and public. They communicated to the women an image of the social world that was one of "stout, thick walls between the public and private areas of social life with narrow doors linking the rooms and through which no luggage can be taken" (228). Only those with power could build these walls. The arbiters therefore constructed a program with formal rules and strictly defined, hierarchically organized roles, thus developing "relationships of hierarchy, dominance, and dependency in which the young women were at the bottom of the hierarchy, subordinate to the demands of others, and dependent on others for help" (219). These relationships were based on "the daily rituals of deference and the requirement of petitioning for help" (219). The stigmatization of welfare mothers as morally inferior certainly influenced the arbiters' claim that as representatives of the social public they had to survey the morality of their clients (Horowitz 206; see also Pateman 1989).

To some extent the arbiters' adamant insistence on entirely leaving out what is associated with the lifeworld of the private family touched upon another layer of meaning associated with the division between public and private. Whereas the public sphere has traditionally been linked to reason, the private sphere, on the other hand, to the "irrationality" of feelings. For instance, by giving special prizes for cognitive skills, the arbiters illustrated their adherence to the conventional view of the public as being governed by "rational calculations," cognition, and "making money" (Horowitz, 213), not by feelings, emotions, or needs.

There are two dimensions to the arbiters' conventional view of the public. One is their identification of the public with the official economy, the other their interpretation of the needs located in the private worlds of the welfare mothers in a way that replicates the official power structure: The women's needs are reduced to the need to be employable. In other words, needs are predefined, seen from the outside, imposed from above, thus fully torn from the complexities of people's daily lives.

As Horowitz writes, "the arbiters want to 'fit in' and be perceived as belonging in the economic sphere" (219). Consequently, the arbiters considered the recipients of the program as the clients of a work site—and they would certainly have welcomed the current trend of turning welfare offices into job centers. Certain important symbols, "those of the public order," were associated with "important rules of the work world": competition, attendance, sticking to schedules, showing deference to the boss (218).[27] Relatedly, children's presence was considered entirely inappropriate. This created a conflict-ridden, contradictory situation for the young mothers. Their private lives, their private world of mothering, was not really private but "open to prying eyes; eyes with power" (175). At the same time the agency, especially the child agency, was feared because anything the women revealed about their lives as mothers would have been met with derision as it was not to be brought up on the programmatic work site. Moreover, any such revelations could also be used as a reason for taking the children away from the mothers—and all this under circumstances where being a mother was at the center of these young women's lives, creating a kind of unity among them.

A WORLD WITHOUT SOLID WALLS

The "mediators," another group of social workers, acknowledged the complexity and fluidity of the public and private worlds, their boundaries being "rarely clear, continually evolving, and intertwined" (232). These boundaries were, however, always overflowing, and they often got entirely conflated in the lives of the women. The mediators therefore also tried to teach them how to cope with existing boundaries, and how to set them up when that was necessary for their economic survival. They were also welcoming an overflowing of these boundaries by pointing toward the possibility (and ultimate necessity) of creating a social reality that would allow for "an alternative vision of the social worlds: one without solid walls" (224).

However, overflowing the traditional separation of the binary opposition between public and private implies a rather complex, multifaceted process. As Hernández (1997) points out, it requires one to "recognize links and overlapping interests and concerns such as how one sphere is constructed upon the other" (39). At the same time, this does not mean that one cannot keep a truly personal realm private. Although this realm does not have to be shared with others, what falls under its auspices would nevertheless "not be determined a priori as private" (39).

Horowitz describes different ways of resistance—on the part of the mediators and on the part of the clients. For instance, "the clients did not automatically accept the rules of the arbiters," even when they were threatened with suspension from the program. Some of the women conformed to the rules because they were very task-oriented and wanted to get their GED. The other participants of the program "revolted occasionally" and the "arbiters sometimes failed to generate conformity," thereby disappointing the arbiters' expectations of making the women feel dependent on their caseworkers. One of the signals for the "continual revolt of the young mothers" was their constant suspicion of the true intent behind the program's rules (166).

Horowitz describes other forms of resistance, especially around the issue of "the presentation and location of self" (220). She writes about the arbiters' inability to have the women subscribe to the way they reordered "identity priorities," and to have the women use

their public identities as clients, students, and future workers over their private identities as welfare recipients, girlfriends, and mothers. While the young women typically tried to interact in the program as clients, workers-to-be, and students, they did not always do so. Identities as clients and workers-to-be were too situational and risky an investment and "client" was degrading. They often left the program early for their children, boyfriends, and their checks on check day. (221)

The mediators, on the other hand, resisted the predominant needs interpretation of the arbiters' specialized "expert discourse." They assisted the women in addressing the often conflicting demands (for instance, taking care of sick children vs. showing up at work), and they helped them to make critical decisions, especially with respect to available or unavailable resources. For example, a job may keep a mother away from the child too much, but having a job will give her financial resources and a sense of being someone, of being treated with respect. The mediators acknowledged and worked with the women around the fact that "there are close relationships between disparate parts of one's life and they are and should not be totally separate" (223). They also knew that an individual has to learn under what conditions certain aspects of her life should remain in the background, however, and that this was a difficult task. The women had to learn that "at certain times, work must take priority over family, but not all of the time. Sometimes family must be treated as back region when the front region is work, but this is not always the case. While family life affects and is affected by work, they generally must remain in separate spheres." The mediators knew that is was important for the women "to know when and how to leave the children and social life in the back region and when they can be front stage "(223).[28]

"Real life" requires women to keep the boundaries clear and the spheres separate—and that's exactly what the arbiters were emphasizing. As discussed throughout this chapter, this official separation is part of the organization of power structure on the macrolevel. Horowitz writes about what we could or should do to restructure our world on that level, and she bases her suggestions on "an alternative vision of the social worlds: one without solid walls, structured roles, and rigid rules," where "curtains separate the various front and back stages through which one passes, often through rips and tears in the thin fabric in need of repair" (229).

CONCLUSIONS

As described in this chapter, where subsistence/motherwork has fallen out of the profit-producing cash-nexus altogether, it is dragged out of the shadows of the private sphere of the family. Motherwork gets publicly denounced as unwanted and superfluous by a political public that is comprised of government representatives, greatly assisted by the social public of the media and the public world of private enterprise. Corresponding maneuvers and strategies of these publics illustrate how the conditions for (unpaid) subsistence work get eroded or destroyed when this work loses its however fragile tie to (paid) market work in the private economy. Where this tie is established through the wages of a husband or boyfriend, the public affirmation of motherwork is expressed in the form of a benign mantle of silence spread over work that is conveniently and inconspicuously performed in the obscure but socially welcomed privacy of the nuclear family.

Where this tie is missing, and where motherwork is not privately financed but requires public assistance, motherworkers need to enter the public sector of private enterprise and thereby reestablish a connection to paid work—in whatever form. Caretaking work is therefore deemed acceptable only when it is done for someone else's children, and for minimum pay. The mantle of silence spread over the fate of the children whose mothers are now desperately chasing after employment possibilities is, however, no longer benign. It is a silence that deliberately muffles the cries of a particularly vulnerable population. There is no public space given to the children of the mothers who have been dropping off the welfare rolls in huge numbers, and who have become good for business by taking minimally paid, precarious, unstable, and financially insecure jobs. And, considering the dismal situation regarding affordable and acceptable child-care arrangements, there is also no sense of public responsibility for the well-being or fate of these mothers' children, which translates into the erosion or absence of primary conditions for motherwork.

As the previous chapter showed, despite this profound, multifaceted erosion of material and spiritual conditions for motherwork, many workers continue to salvage the utopian, life-affirming perspective of subsistence work, often encased in overwhelming fears about the future of their children. In a world where certain populations or groups of people are marginalized and kept outside the normative expectations of true, worthy citizens, the "consideration of the micro, the experiential, opens the possibility for a reading of dichotomies such as private/public, as partial texts for engagement and transformation" (Hernández 1997, 60). In other words, larger "texts" need to be read as well. These are the texts that acknowledge how the dichotomous relationship between public and private is still alive and well in the way women's works are valued or devalued. Reading these texts also means reading about other forms of oppression and exploitation, although the sexist division of labor remains the main axis where other vectors of oppression intersect.

The next chapter describes women's attempts to develop and nourish a sense of inner strength by coming together with mothers who are in similar situations, by trying to unlearn ways of thinking and acting that counteract this strength. These are attempts at taking small steps in the direction of changes on the micro- or experiential level. The women's official reason for attending the literacy center where this learning took place was to prepare for the GED, a first step toward finding employment, that is, entering the social public of the world of paid work. However, their learning desires drew a map of the private world where personal emotions and needs overlapped with concrete caretaking respon- sibilities. The private was not simply a separate sphere, but also a psychic space, and its contingent and changing connection to the social and political publics was always apparent. Thus, the literacy participants were also learning to take a reflective distance to their own experience by placing it into a larger social and political context, and by trying to understand how their private worlds, and their own inner space, were shaped by this context. This assisted them in trying to learn new ways of coping with, or even undoing, some of the devastations of an exploitative racist and sexist system, and of the violence that has seeped into the interior of a marginalized population.

NOTES

1. See, for instance, Abramovitz 1988, 1996; Gordon 1988; and Mink 1993, 1998a, 1998b, 1999.

2. Most women on welfare have only two children. See, for instance, Abramovitz 1996; Funiciello 1993a,1993b; and Sidel 1996.

3. The term "leavers" can refer to women who had just gotten off the rolls one, two, or six months before the study was conducted (Cancian et al. 1999). Moffitt and Roff (2000) are critical of the unreliability of data gathered within such a short time frame, and surveyed women who were on the rolls some time in the two years immediately prior to the interview and who left the rolls during that period.

4. Part of the intermittence is explained by the fact that the food-service and retail industries have high turnover rates.

5. Much of the dramatic decrease in caseload reduction has been attributed to a booming economy. This decline is only partly explained by changes in the labor market, however, as it counts women who were "sanctioned" out of benefits, women who were no longer considered eligible based on changes in administrative rules, or women who have been engaged in various state-regulated "work activities" such as community ser- vice work (Danziger 2000). In addition, some states are pursuing "diversion policies" that give applicants a onetime payment or require a period of job search prior to receiv- ing benefits (Danziger 2000; Moffitt and Roff 2000). Because the leavers are clustered at the bottom of low-paying industries with a high turnover rate, their jobs are most likely the ones that will disappear first when the economy weakens. Lopoo (2000) speculates that an economic downturn "could reduce the demand for welfare recipients by 25 % to 40 %" (16).

6. For a useful comparison of the now-abolished larger federal welfare program and the new system of state block grants, see Abramovitz 1996; for more recent discussions of its social, political, and economic repercussions see Mink 1999.

7. What counts as being on or off the rolls, and what therefore counts towards these five years, can differ from state to state.

8. Castern (2000) gives a summary of how this trend affects Illinois welfare leavers. *From Welfare to Worse?* (1998) reports similar tendencies in a particular region within the City of Chicago.

9. As reported by Pavetti (1998, 9), "Activities that can count towards a state's work participation rate include: (1) unsubsidized or subsidized private or public sector employment; (2) on-the-job training; (3) work experience; (4) job search and job readiness assistance for up to six weeks; (5) community service programs; (6) provision of child care services to an individual participating in a community services program, and; (7) vocational training (limited to 12 months for any individual and 30 percent of those required to participate)." States are allowed to specify these activities (see, for example, *Changes in Illinois Welfare Law: The Illinois TANF Program and Other Changes in Public Benefits,* October 1997). Although the states can define what counts as work activity, federal guidelines mandate that all adult nonexempt caretakers must engage in such an activity within twenty-four months, for at least twenty hours per week in 1997 and 1998, twenty-five hours in 1999, and thirty hours in 2000 and thereafter (Joseph 1999, 12). Pavetti makes a related, interesting point. While only a few states have developed "alternative work activities," that is, subsidized employment programs, "when it becomes more difficult to place recipients in unsubsidized jobs, few states or localities will have an infrastructure in place that will facilitate the placement of large numbers of recipients in alternative work activities" (13).

10. For similar problems in the City of Chicago, see *From Welfare to Worse?* (1998). In July 2001 a group of public aid recipients living in one of the poorest sections of Chicago marched outside the Illinois Department of Human Services' office to protest against "long waits for service, rude caseworkers, and a lack of bilingual staff" (*Chicago Tribune,* 25 July, 2001).

11. In order to receive their full TANF allocation, states are required to meet certain work participation rates: 25 percent of their caseload in 1997, 35 percent in 1999, and 50 percent by 2002 (Joseph 1999, 12).

12. This was reported in the fall 1998 issue of *COPC Central* (where COPC stands for Community Outreach Partnership Centers). This newsletter is produced by the Office of University Partnerships, a branch of the U.S. Department of Housing and Urban Development.

13. The disregard for the lives of poor children translates, among other things, into the disregard of their health. As reported by Houppert (1999, 11), in 1997 "an estimated 675,00 low-income people became uninsured as a result of welfare reform: the majority (62 percent) of these were children who in all likelihood never should have lost their insurance, according to a report by Families U.S.A."

14. The inserted quote is from Kittay's "Human Dependency and Rawlsian Equality" in *Feminists Rethink the Self,* Diana Tietjens Meyers, ed. (Boulder, CO: Westview Press, 1996), pp. 219–266.

15. The Family Violence Amendment gives state welfare departments the flexibility to provide battered women on welfare with specialized domestic violence services, thus giving them more time to remove the welfare-to-work barrier created by their husbands' or boyfriends' violent behavior. Individual states can decide whether to choose the Family Violence Option (Raphael and Tolman 1997, 2).

16. As reported in the *New York Times* (DeParle 1999b), many welfare recipients also suffer from the trauma of childhood violations such as sexual molestation or rape. This creates additional obstacles in the way of making a transition from welfare dependency to paid work. Many of the victims of these kinds of abuses suffer from anxiety and depression, and they are prone to seek refuge in alcohol or drugs.

17. For a historical overview and detailed discussion of the racial division of paid reproductive labor, see Glenn 1997.

18. See, for instance, *Who's Caring for the Kids?* (Krojec et al. 2001).

19. Numerous books and articles report on the character defamation of poor, single, and especially "non-white" mothers. See, for instance, Abramovitz 1996 and 1997; Mink 1998a, 1998b and 1999; Polakow 1993; Roberts 1997 and 1999; Schein 1995; and Sidel 1996.

20. In 1997 the majority were Black (61 percent) and Latina (10.7 percent). A higher percentage of white aid recipients leave the system with jobs than do Black women or Latinas, who are mostly removed because they fail to comply with state rules (Karp 2000, 7; see also DeParle 1998).

21. In his study of "Employer Demand for Welfare Recipients and the Business Cycle," Holzer (1998) makes a similar observation: "Given that most establishments and jobs are currently located in the suburbs, while long-term welfare recipients are disproportionately found in the poorest neighborhoods of central cities, the data suggest some potential 'mismatch' between the location of welfare recipients and the employers who would hire them" (9).

22. For a discussion of this view of poverty and a corresponding "poverty talk," see Gans 1991; Katz 1989; and Schwarz and Volgy 1992; for writers focusing explicitly on women and poverty see Amott 1993; Axinn and Hirsch 1993; Collins 1996; Dujon and Withorn 1996; Gelpi et al. 1986; de Goede 1996; Pearce 1990; Polakow 1993; Schein 1995; and Smith 1999.

23. In 1997 the top 10 percent of the population owned 73.2 percent of the nation's net worth. In 1995 the top 1 percent of American households owned about 35 percent of the nation's private wealth (*The Nation*, vol. 269, no. 19, 6 December 1999). While the latest census figures show that the poverty rate dropped to 12.7 percent in 1998, down from 13.3 percent in 1997, these figures hide two issues. One, the decrease in the overall poverty rate is primarily due to the sharp drop in the South. Everywhere else there was either no change, or the percentage of people in poverty increased, as in the West. Second, the gap between rich and poor has widened (*New York Times*, 19 January 2000, A21). Illinois provides a particularly telling example for the continuation as well as worsening of poverty levels despite the dramatic reduction of welfare rolls. The *2001 Report on Illinois Poverty*, issued by the Illinois Poverty Summit, reports that "despite the recent economic expansion, Illinois' poorest families remain economically stuck in the 1970s. Nearly one-fourth (23%) of all Illinois workers earned less than $17,000 in 1999, while Illinois' richest families saw their incomes go up the most" (21).

24. Collins summarizes with the following words how the multilayered, overlapping notions and spheres of private and public greatly affected Black women's lives:

As workers, Black women faced threats of sexual harassment and violence in their place of employment, the White-controlled private sphere. At the same time, because they had to travel through racially segregated public space to get to their jobs, African-American women also faced threats of violence in White- and Black-male-controlled public space in the public sphere. For many, family household offered little protection. . . . Overall, Black women moved from their private households, through the space of Black civil society, through White-male-controlled public space, into White-female-managed family space, and back again. (1998, 21–22)

25. There is not enough space to discuss the issue of a two-tiered welfare structure that was (and is) based on the public-private and male-female division (see, for instance, Nelson 1990).

26. I am here working with a notion of public that relies on the public surveillance

of private individuals and the lifeworld of the private family in the private system of the economy, or the world of paid work.

27.   The arbiters would also have been eager to seize the opportunity to dish out sanctions, since in order to cut the number of welfare recipients as fast as possible, missing an appointment can quickly be translated into denying an application for public aid (Houppert 1999, *From Welfare to Worse* 1998).

28.   Horowitz's use of the terms front and back regions is based on Erving Goffman's *The Presentation of Self in Everyday Life* (New York: Doubleday, 1959).

Chapter 4

Literacy and Motherwork

A family is still the basic unit and the oldest existing institution. Food, shelter, clothing and education are still the responsibility of the head of the family structure. However, in many of our families, the head means one who gives birth or the surrogate mother. Therefore, if and when basic needs are met, they are met by the woman. Usually, the woman who is victimized, traumatized and distressed has the man's greatest support during procreation, less during prenatal, and none postnatal. His presence is neither seen nor felt within the family infrastructure because he is not there! He, himself a victim of social injustices, spends more time incarcerated, on cloud nine, or making other sisters fruitful to multiply than nurturing, supporting, and educating his children. Thus, the woman is stuck with the difficult task of parenting, solo attempts to take on the challenge.

She does her best but because of her low literacy skills she is unable to effectively model and exhibit reading and writing habits that can strengthen and improve her life and the lives of her children, and thus the humiliation, oppression, and deprivation is trans-generational.

Nowhere is this situation more devastating than in low-income public housing. No offspring suffers more than the offspring of the powerless and impoverished solo parent lacking mainstream literacy skills. She has highs and lows. Her esteem is low and her stress is high. She feels betrayed by the school system, the political system, and the man she loves. This plethora of things overpowers and renders her disempowered.

Almetta, the coordinator of the women's literacy group at the ABLA Homes,[1] wrote these words as an introduction to a collection of essays written by members of the group. Her words summarize the social environment of the literacy participants. What Almetta writes is not very different from what the interviewed women who were not participants of the literacy group shared: over-whelming responsibilities placed on them, with very little or no support from the fathers of their children. However, Almetta explicitly adds the women's weak basic literacy skills to the list of things that render the women disempowered.

As described in chapter 2, where young people grow up with little or no sense of the future, with a disruptive, degrading public education system, with the danger of violence all around them, motherwork faces almost insurmount-able obstacles. It takes place in a context where housing conditions are dismal, where communities are neglected, where there is little hope for the future, and where children's lives are in constant danger. The last remnant of unwaged, life-supporting work, the work of raising children, is reduced to keeping one's ill-fed, traumatized children inside one's dismal apartment because their movement outside the doors endangers their lives. During the time I was attending a weekly session of a women's literacy group at the literacy center of the ABLA Homes, however, I observed that the women's hopes and learning desires were inseparable from the responsibilities and tasks associated with the work of rais-ing children.

HISTORY OF THE WOMEN'S LITERACY GROUP

During the time I was attending literacy sessions about 5,000 Black people lived in the ABLA Homes, then the third largest public housing project in the city. Less than 10 percent of the residents had regular jobs, and public aid was one of the main sources of income for solo mothers. While no official data ex-isted on the problem of illiteracy, its seriousness was not disputed by any of the city officials with whom I had contact.[2]

The ABLA Homes literacy center was open for women, men, and children, offering a number of services to assist people in obtaining official literacy skills. It was located right where the Chicago campus of the University of Illinois abruptly ends and where the Homes begin. It was housed in the Boys & Girls Club, a major social service provider for youth in the area. The center was al-lowed to occupy a small room on the second floor. Almetta, the literacy organ-izer, and graduate student assistants from the university put their energies into a number of different efforts, all of which directly drew on the expressed wishes of the participants. These efforts ranged from teaching the participants the use of books, remedial training in basic reading, writing and math skills, to more spe-cific job-related skills such as resume writing.

Every week there was a special weekly session of the women's literacy group, the Women Empowerment Hour (WEH). My contributions to a highly collaborative endeavor were regular participation in the WEH (from March 1994 till April 1995), GED-related volunteer work, and teaching a class that combined reading and writing assignments. Five to ten women usually attended the WEH. Some of the women came fairly regularly, others only once in a while. There were, of course, a number of different reasons behind their absences. These ranged from problems at home to finding a job (in one year about 50% of the participants got jobs or their GED diplomas and left the area). Almetta told me that rebuilding the group was an exhaustive task. Continuity of attendance increased from the time I first came to the WEH, however, which was only a few months after it was organized. I saw a strong connection between the growing regularity of participation and the spirit nourished at the literacy center, especially during the WEH. Because participation took time away from the urgent task of day-to-day survival, it greatly depended on the perseverance of the literacy coordinator to foster participation. She continuously offered help to develop self-esteem and a sense of empowerment in the participants themselves so they could share the task of mutual assistance. And this is precisely what the WEH was trying to accomplish.

While learning how to read and write is fully part of the preparation for obtaining a GED, and ultimately a job, the weekly sessions of the WEH were based on a rather complex vision of "success," a vision that was only tangentially related to finding a job. The organization of the class was based on the participants' own experience of daily life in the ABLA Homes, thus acknowledging extreme hardships but also drawing on and nurturing a sense of self in the midst of a number of social and individual onslaughts. Almetta captured this dual purpose of the WEH by stating that "the Women Empowerment Hour is a forum for traumatized, distressed, disempowered and powerless women whose goal is to improve reading and writing skills," and that power "is very useful, important, and can be fun. It is best when it is personal." More importantly, "The Women Empowerment Hour believes that power should be shared and works best when it is multiplied." She also wrote that Black women can "take part in planning THEIR future while improving personal relationships within the family structure."[3]

One of the participants I had observed over the months, and about whose life circumstances I had learned a number of devastating details, was generally either silent or talked a lot. Whatever the nature of her response, a mix of defiance, sorrow, and despair could always be seen in her eyes. When she and some of the other women worked on the rearrangement of materials and the beautification of the space, however, she was calm and focused, moving things back and forth in a clear, determined manner. This seemingly small detail was at the core of the learning environment: Not only did the literacy facilitator coordinate various efforts that were meeting different learning needs, but she also continuously worked on providing a structure that drew on and nourished the women's abilities and sources of strength. At the same time, it was also a structure that acknowledged the layers of pain in the women's lives and that provided a space for sharing the pain, reflecting on its multiple causes, and putting it into a larger context by interpreting its meaning from the different perspectives offered by the participants. This was the core meaning of developing a sense of power or empowerment. One of the participants wrote in her testimonial:

WEH is very exciting because you can talk about things that happen in your life and we can learn so much from each other. It also helps us express ourselves. I look forward to the WEH every Thursday. It helps me talk about things going on in my life. And those times when there is nothing to say or you don't feel like writing, you say nothing and you write nothing and that's o.k. too. All the time is not the time to do everything. But WEH capitalizes on the wit, the experience and the dynamics of the group.

Every week one of the women volunteered to facilitate the next WEH. She had to choose a reading, or create her own text, and develop a number of questions the participants had to answer. The WEH was formally opened with greetings from Almetta, and the women were given a few minutes to share with each other anything that happened during the past week and that they considered worth sharing. The facilitator then read her text and the questions, and the participants had about twenty minutes to respond in writing. They then shared their writings, often accompanied by lengthy discussions of the thoughts and ideas stimulated by the text or various responses to it. Time schedules were closely observed, and the discussions were always brought to closure at the end of the allotted time. After naming the volunteer for the next session, the women then randomly drew a name from a bowl and the winner received a small present (for instance, a notebook). No matter how difficult the topic, the WEH always ended with an appreciation of the participants' contributions and willingness to share. In addition, a variety of pleasantly arranged food and sometimes music or poetry all added to the comfort and stimulation of the participants.

ROLE AND PURPOSE OF THE MOTHER

The issue of mothers, and of mothering, was a recurring motif in the participants' own writing and in a variety of topics presented for discussion. Here are the voices of some of the participants:

I thank God for blessing me with a mother who loves her children. If my mother didn't care about me, I would probably be on drugs, in sin or in jail or dead by now.

My plans for my children are to help them when they need help and to learn all that I can learn so that way when they need me I can help them. I like reading books with my children and helping them with their home work. My children look at me and tell me that they are proud of me and that they love me very much.

I am now the mother of seven, four boys and three girls. It is much easier to raise boys than girls because girls mature faster and get their own minds. You can tell boys no and they obey, whereas girls will disobey. I brought my children up in church. I have been a church-goer since age 23. It helps them to learn responsibility and how to be responsible adults. It teaches them morals, values, manners and how to respect others and work to take care of the family.

In one of the WEH hours, the women reported on their own mothers' hard-working lives. One woman told the group about her mother, and how even when she was ill and lying in bed, she instructed her daughter how to make corn bread. In other words, she kept on caring for her family when she should have (and could have) taken care of herself.

The never-ending demand for providing care, a responsibility placed on all mothers, was the overriding theme during the WEH, as it was in the conversations held with the women at other public housing developments. While their own mothers epitomized this caring tradition, it also seemed to hit these mothers' daughters in the face. What had the caring task accomplished? The outside world had not improved. Instead it had worsened, and talking about caring opened the vault to one of the extremely difficult contradictions working in the women's lives: How the caring of their mothers has been a tremendous support for themselves and their children, and how absent, dead, neglectful, and abusive mothers have torn apart their children's souls. What is left? This is the area where the particularly troublesome, multilayered nature of caring is shown to be highly intertwined with social exploitation and self-oppression, often flipping over into the refusal (or inability) to care for one's own children.

The WEH's emphasis on empowerment started with an emphasis on *caring for one's self first,* of attaining *a sense of power from within.* Caring is an essential dimension of the spiritual, psychological, and physical survival of the individual woman *and* the children. As indicated by one of the participants' remark about her mother's failings, women have to learn to care for themselves first. Without recognizing the importance of their own selves, they will not gain the strength and power needed to move on with the overwhelming tasks that confront them. They would fall into drug addiction or passivity. In her essay "Empowerment Matters: Understanding Power," Townsend states quite poignantly that "'power from within' arises from a recognition that one is not helpless, not the source of all one's own problems, that one is restricted in part by structures outside" (1999, 30).

In order to increase their own self-reliance, women also have to learn to feel powerful by themselves, regardless of the presence or absence of the men in their lives. Almetta took great pains to politely but firmly tell the men who often accompanied the women to respect the all-women's group. Regardless of the fact that this group met only once a week for about two hours, the women were relying on Almetta's initiative since they had a hard time telling the men to leave. Sometimes a few men were sitting downstairs, waiting for the women in the WEH, and they also had to be told to leave. Almetta worked particularly hard to make the literacy participants understand that only by obtaining a sense of power would they learn to be, and cherish being, on their own and not permit abuse of any kind. This issue came up whenever the story of a woman returning to her abusive male partner was told, which happened rather frequently.

The following is an example of the reading and the questions provided by one of the WEH facilitators. These suggestions were deliberately chosen because they touch on one of the most troublesome issues brought before the group. The text provided below is indicative of a dense web of pain, fear, anguish, and worries. Before one can see and understand the tremendous amount of work required on many levels in order to inspire sparks of hope, it is often necessary to go to the bottom of what causes such pain. The text that was written and provided by one of the participants is replete with numerous questions and concerns. It is also founded on an experience between the participant and her mother, an experience she had shared through another writing: "When I was 13 my mother had stopped drinking but became very abusive before I left home at age 14 to live with my father. She repeatedly beat me. She burned me with a very hot iron." Here is the written material she provided during the WEH:

I would like to talk about how young girls go around and walk the streets everyday and how nasty filthy "ole" men mess with them. For example, when girls are on their way to school old men as well as young men honk their horns, flirt and tempt young school age girls with promises, money, drugs and sometimes just simple rides in late model cars. Many times the parents, especially mothers have no idea of the everyday struggles and experiences of their young daughters. Sometimes I wonder if the reason that some mothers don't really, really understand their daughters have to do with lack of understanding of themselves. This is what I really believe about my own mother.

Questions:
1. Think about what you've read. Name five things you like about your mother.
2. Name five things you dislike about your mother.
3. What are some things you wish your mother would do for you?
4. What are some things you wish your mother would stop doing?
5. If you had one wish for your mother, what would that wish be?

The responses to these questions brought out an array of experiences. They covered the whole spectrum of motherwork under the harsh circumstances of racism and economic exploitation, from mothers who never stopped caring and working for their families even when they should have spent some time taking care of themselves, to those who let themselves be drowned by the devastation around them. In many ways all essential aspects of motherwork were brought up: constant love, protection, care, and attentiveness. What was not talked about were the tremendous physical and emotional demands placed upon women who care for children under extremely harsh circumstances. Although these demands may be too much taken for granted by the women themselves, they may also be absorbed by the all-encompassing worry about children's safety and future. The knowledge about what it takes to attend to a sick child, to take care of its food, health, sleep, rest, play, or development, was always inserted in "larger" anxieties about the children *and* about the mother's self, her partner or boyfriend, or her community.

Every week the women brought with them and talked about their overwhelming emotional burden. The temptation of watching soaps and sitting and drinking (or taking drugs) was likewise overwhelming. This was one of the many harsh contradictions in the women's lives. As reported by the facilitator, some of the women could not keep up the emotional strain of talking about what happened to them, such as sexual abuse, or violence. Sometimes they told her the truth, wanting her to write about it. Other times they could not face the hurt and painted a rosy picture of their childhood.

THE SEXUAL DIVISION OF LABOR

Although the women rarely directly addressed the topic of absent fathers, it was an ever-present theme. That is one of the reasons Almetta addressed it quite explicitly in her introduction to the essays written by members of the women's literacy group. In some ways the absence of fathers seemed to have become a "fact of life." Since caring is a "woman's job," the invisibility of men as fathers indicates that the sexual division of labor is showing in a glaring light what can be called the extreme version of the general conventional notion of a woman's job. Not only was this confirmed by many stories the mothers living and raising children in public housing shared in another context (see chapter 2), but also by the women's writings and discussions at the literacy center. For instance, in essays where the women describe their own lives, the children are very present. The fathers of the children are absent, however, sometimes not even mentioned, or mentioned as the man who sexually abused the woman:

I left school a freshman, 17 years old and pregnant.

At age 17, I went to a doctor after two missed periods and discovered that I was 3 months pregnant. I went home and told my mother. She said there was nothing she could do about it. Then she asked for the father's name. I told her it was her brother and my uncle. She said I was lying and not telling the truth. We scheduled a blood test and discovered that I was telling the truth. My maternal uncle was the father of my child. After that day my relationship with my mother deteriorated. She put me out of her home and I slept in cars, under houses and anywhere I could.

I left school due to teenage pregnancy. My mother worked in a factory and was unable to babysit. And my sister . . . was also pregnant and could not help me after the birth of my daughter.

Irrespective of racial-ethnic or class divisions among women as a group, motherwork, and the ongoing destruction of its outer and inner survival base, cannot be analyzed without looking at the way it is fully entrenched in the sexual division of labor. In the history of the United States it has been played out in a number of variations and it has taken on at times quite different forms for Black and for white women. As the histories of southern plantations and later of domestic work in the North so amply show, it pitted Black women against white women (Rollins 1985, Tucker 1988). At the same time, despite all the profound differences among women of different races or classes, as a primary mechanism for exploiting women, the sexual division of labor has never been absent. The erosion of its social and economic conditions can therefore not be expected to bring about fundamental changes with respect to equally fundamental social norms and mechanisms associated with sexual oppression, no matter how much these mechanisms interact with class and race and ethnicity. As Zinn (1992) points out, the sexual division of labor that expects women to nurture and men to provide is reiterated in a highly distorted way under conditions of disenfranchising large numbers of Black men. This disenfranchisement, indicated by the extremely high unemployment rate among Black men in the inner cities, "is a gender phenomenon of enormous magnitude. It affects the meanings and definitions of masculinity for Black men, and it reinforces the public patriarchy that controls Black women through their increased dependence on welfare" (87). It is an essential part of this definition of masculinity to "sire" children but not to feel responsible for nurturing and raising them on any consistent basis (Hacker 1992; Pitts 1999; Loury 2000a, b). African-American women are therefore moving in a "narrow historical space, caught between pressures of racial liberation and gender liberation" (Mullings 1994, 281; see also Collins 1998).

Many children are born to single teenage mothers who cannot count on support by the men who "sired" their children. As reported by the Alan Guttmacher Institute in *Teenage Pregnancy and the Welfare Reform Debate* (2000),

Out-of-wedlock births among teenagers have increased dramatically in the last several decades and now account for almost 70% of all teenage births. Yet, trends in teenage sexual activity and childbearing reflect broader trends in sexual and reproductive behavior among women of all ages and income levels. Women who are 20 and older, for example, account for more than three-quarters of the unintended pregnancies and abortions that occur each year in the United States. Moreover, despite the sharp increase in teenage out-of-wedlock births, the increase has been even greater among older women. As a result, teenagers account for a much smaller proportion of out-of-wedlock births today than they did in the 1970s.

Above all, there is a growing absence of marriage as a path toward personal or family stability, or the partnership with another adult who will help financially and emotionally, especially with the children. For inner-city African-American women, marriage is less and less an option, especially since job prospects are almost nonexistent for Black inner-city men, making marriage to a man who cannot fulfill his provider rule more than unlikely. This is important to note, as it stops putting all the blame simply on the young age of the mother. As two of the women participating in the literacy group reported, it was not extraordinary for girls to marry and have children at an early age, and the teenage pregnancy rates were therefore much higher in the seventies than they are now. Today, however, in the absence of any conditions for a financially secure marriage, teenage mothers are particularly vulnerable, socially and economically.

It is therefore not surprising that the women did not talk about "fatherhood" during the WEH. Had it become a taken-for-granted fact that fathers, especially teenage fathers, do not even think about their responsibility? As Pitts observed, "It has become so commonplace, as to be unremarkable, this phenomenon of children and mother on their own and Dad as an infrequent drop-in visitor" (1999, 58). LaVar Barnes, a sixteen-year-old, commented on the destructive equation of manliness with fathering a child, and unmanliness with taking care of the child afterwards. As he said, "It's the truth. . . . I got buddies that do their shorties wrong," although they are eager to get girls pregnant "just to say they got a shorty" (*Chicago Tribune*, 9 March 1994). And, as one of the adult men Pitts interviewed expressed it, "We want to have sex, enjoy sex, but don't want to assume the responsibility for having sex. We want to have children, but don't want to assume the responsibility for taking care of the children, training the children, that kind of thing. We want the prize without running the race" (27–28).

During one of the WEH sessions, someone pointed out that a large part of treating women as "stupid" is to make them pregnant and to leave them for the woman in the next house or block. This also brought up the whole issue of what sexual conquest means for women, and I could see that it was in full operation. Showing "success" in the sexual arena is one of the mainstays of a feminine identity, and therefore one of the main roots of women's sense of disempowerment. In another session the women talked about the difficulty of fostering friendships among women who are often ruled by fierce jealousy. As reported by one of the women: "I told a woman that I had problems with my man. She nodded, showing me support, and the next thing I knew was she was together with him, and now she has five babies by him."

Centuries of modern Western processes of socialization have not bypassed the groups or populations that have been at the center of violent exploitation, be it people in the European colonies, or slaves and their descendants in the United States. As it is a sign of manliness to make babies but not to do the hard work of daily care, it is also manly to be economically independent. To be financially dependent on a woman goes against the grain of what it means to be a man. Henry Hardee, who as a homeless person was officially labeled "illiterate" in terms of institutional definitions, has worked on the fringes of the Chicago economy and educated himself as a political writer. He writes plays, and during the time I had contact with the women at the center, he coordinated a family literacy program at one of the public housing complexes. It was part of his "unofficial" mission to get the fathers involved in these literacy efforts. In his play *It's Rough On a Po' Nigguh Like Me Out Heah* Chicken Noodle, one of the protagonists, says: "I do take care of my children (when I got the money)." But who is doing the work of taking care of them when he hasn't got the money? In his play Henry Hardee also describes in vivid terms how joblessness has become a fact of life, and how it cannot be separated from the need to survive which may mean to be financially dependent on a woman:

A Blackman could be unemployed for a lifetime,
spend a lifetime on corners
in front of Currency Exchanges
in front of Liquor Stores
askin' for change [as if somebody is going into the Liquor Store]
Say can you help me out with something
after you take care of your business.

It's bad to be with a woman
when you ain't got nothin' of your own.
a man has to be responsible
for getting his own shit.
when you busted and your woman
got something you become
her recipient and she decides
what benefits you can and can't get.

When you layin' up on a woman
she thinks you owe her and she
thinks she owns you.
When you layin' up on a woman
you can't think straight
cause you scared she gon' leave,
scared her money gonna
get up and walk.
.....

Don't nevah let no woman become
your only source of money
she'll fuck you over every time.

In *Becoming Dad* Pitts discusses the interplay of racial discrimination and rise in unemployment due to economic restructuring, and writes that it therefore "becomes harder for a man to provide. It's a failure that diminishes a man, that emasculates him and leaves him desperate and resentful" (78).[4] Within the context of enforced employment for welfare recipients, unemployed men who cannot provide may therefore feel even more burdened by having their role as breadwinners entirely usurped by the women. In addition, coercive policies that were enacted by many states in conjunction with regulations concerning Temporary Assistance to Needy Families (TANF) look at "deadbeat dads" solely in terms of providers, although many noncustodial fathers can find only low-wage, off-the-books jobs as day laborers or casual laborers, often having to "patch together spells of jobs to create continuous work" (Roy 2000, 16). As one of the low-income fathers said: "The government says 'We want Dad around.' Then the government turns around and says 'Dad pays child support or we lock him up.' Dad gets lost just trying to survive. It's like society is tearing itself up" (quoted in Roy, 18). Where the men are barely surviving, coercive child support requirements may foster feelings of hostility toward the mother of their children.

This was expressed by one of the low-income fathers Edin and authors (2000, 12) interviewed: "They push you into a wall by asking for things you can't really do . . . You can't even support yourself, how are you go going to support that person? What are they trying to do? And that's the anger we have embedded in us. But you know, society puts on us this 'deadbeat dads' label. We are not deadbeat dads. Dad is trying to survive."

Clearly, the Western social history of dividing women and men has been sharpened and intensified in the inner city. As discussed in chapter 2, women are aware of the burdens placed on unemployed men, and that they are considered failures by society because they cannot provide for their families (see also Boris 1999). However, the plight of Black men's inability to find employment in the inner city at the same time reinforces this division by making it especially hard for women to resist doing the extra work of serving the men and the children "sired" by them. This plight also reinforces sex as a prime avenue for men to show their power and superiority (Pitts 1999). During one of the sessions, the problem of men sometimes trying to prevent women from getting a job, or from attending to their education in order to be better prepared brought out a lot of anger and pain.[5]

Violence against women has had a long tradition, and it is fully part of asserting male power. It takes on additional dimensions when money, the material power base, is absent. The women at the literacy center talked a lot about male violence that included open access to sex or women's bodies. During one of the WEH sessions, a poem was discussed in which the theme of men being "against women" was particularly strong. The women talked about men feeling superior by beating women because violence gives men a sense of their power.

POWER, VIOLENCE, AND MASCULINE IDENTITY

Clearly, the centuries-old ideology of true manhood is not resolved when men are left in the cold of economic superfluousness. The opposite is more likely to happen. By being thrown to the bottom of the heap in a wealthy, consumption-oriented, and ultimately violent and destructive social order, inherent aspects of Western masculine identity are laid bare: power, money, and self-interest (von Werlhof 1993b). And, as von Werlhof points out, the socialization of men into considering the use of violence as a normal part of their upbringing and their lives as adults is the Western form of male domestication (18–19). This means to have power over somebody considered weaker or dependent, and to let someone else, someone who is recognized as a true male authority, have power over oneself. Pitts also addresses the lure of "exaggerated masculinity" or "hypermasculinity" as an integral part of laying on a "cool pose," a rational answer to the fact that the game is rigged against black men. "To be a black man in America is to wear masks and armor. This is the lesson a black boy quickly learns" (1999, 24; see also Loury 2000a).

Wearing masks and armor means that committing one's loyalty to a gang includes being ready to sacrifice one's own life for its benefits, or to dismiss the lives of rival members—and whoever else happens to end up in the cross-fire, often children on their way to school or to a friend's house. Belonging to a gang is often the only avenue available for boys to satisfy the need of belonging, especially when the boy's own family does not satisfy the need (see chapter 2). Gang loyalty can therefore take the form of a ten-year-old boy doing the required killing, and being killed in return by his own teenage gang members for fear of the police forcing information out of the child (Rodrigues 1994). Gang loyalty feeds off another component of masculine identity: money, in this case obtained through activities in the underground economy.

In terms of motherwork, there is, of course, the issue of raising children in the midst of social destruction and destructiveness. During the Women Empowerment Hour, women kept talking about the presence of gangs in their and their children's lives, and that they never knew who would be hit next. It was also quite clear that men (and boys) in gangs were not "out there," but were in various ways a more direct part of their lives. In addition to the violence associated with gang-related turf issues, random violence against and among children is spreading, for the most part committed by boys and men. There is also a nationwide rise in child abuse cases (involving beating, shaking, or burning the child severely enough to require hospitalization) across the nation, where the abuser "is usually a boyfriend or stepfather who is around when the mother is not home" (*New York Times,* 5 April 1994). The child of one of the participants of the women's literacy group was killed by a former boyfriend.

How can men who have no prospect for any decent employment, and who may be financially dependent on the mother of their children, keep their rage in check when they are asked to do the demanding work with children, a responsibility that supposedly is not theirs in the first place? Clearly, in order to understand the social, cultural, and economic context of child abuse, one needs to engage in a fundamental criticism of sexual divisions.

LITERACY AND WORK

In Chicago's inner city the notion of "work and literacy" has been stripped to its bare bones. On the one hand, the categorization of people as "literate" and "illiterate," "competent" or "deficient" tries to silence the screams of people who have been victimized by this society and who turn their own victimization into the victimization of others. The silence is also broken by the sobbing, laughter, and calm voices of people who are struggling to keep or make a connection with the strength of their own sense of ability, knowledge, and power to stem the tide of destruction. This means that educators—from the inside or the outside, with special roles assigned to them or simply participating in one of the literacy efforts—need to recognize and build upon invisible literacies, or see where they are missing and need to be learned. For instance, one of the women talked about the importance of "parenting classes" that were (from what I could see) required by the city's child welfare agency, the Department of Child and Family Services (DCFS). Aside from the expression of her own troubles, sorrow, and internal damage, she also brought out a dimension that was a running theme in many other WEH sessions but that was also expressed by the women later interviewed in another setting: Women with children (their own or those of others) can or need to learn what it means to raise children. This kind of literacy is essential for dignified survival and a sense of future. It also refers to important work that gets easily shunned or devalued by making it a "woman's issue" rather than an issue of general social (women's *and* men's) concern.

Most men, no matter where they live, need to undergo a tremendous unlearning and relearning process. They need to develop a liking for nurturing abilities, something that has been squelched by Western notions of masculinity and that, under the current circumstances of destruction and despair in the inner city have also destroyed the tradition of Black men fulfilling the role of nurturer, a role some of the interviewed women remembered their fathers had played with great dedication. Jenna, for instance, told me she was jealous of the neighborhood children flocking around her father because he gave as much attention to them as to her own. However, there are attempts by men to learn what it means to be a father, no matter how dismal the job situation. For instance, the Paternal Involvement Demonstration Project (funded by the Illinois Department of Public Aid and the Woods Charitable Fund, Inc.) assisted men who were eager to provide some level of care for their children.[6] One of the men in the program is reported emphasizing that "men—whether they are struggling as he is or not—should surround themselves with people who have positive attitudes about taking responsibility for themselves and their children. Discussing parenthood and life strategies with such people is invaluable for encouraging men to take responsibility . . . ; the 'friends' and the family members who demean and discourage aspirations do not fit into the goal for healthy relationships" (Parker 1993, 4).

PIP was a voluntary program. The men ranged in age from eighteen to thirty-five and were recipients of some form of public aid or welfare benefits. Most had sporadic work histories, some had criminal records, and all regarded "the ability to find and hold down a job as a prerequisite to being a successful parent" (3). Likewise, Roy, who followed the project over a period of four years, reports that the fathers' "participation in family life mirrored their experience in the labor market," and because they "could rely less and less on the labor market to direct their life course," they "found it increasingly difficult to play a role in their family as a result" (2000, 17).

Raising children is not considered real work, not only because it does not provide a livable wage, but also because the skills, competencies, and kinds of knowledge required to do this kind of work are not recognized, either by society in general or by individual men. It is work that is made invisible by placing it under the rubric of "family literacy," a category that does not wrench itself away from traditional notions of femininity and masculinity. On a more general level, any redefinition of literacy also needs to take into account the traditions of Black people's knowledge and abilities that are entirely disregarded or dismissed by white corporate society. Smith (1994), for instance, studied the connection between a strong oral tradition of passing on and acquiring knowledge and skills and the abundance of "micro-businesses" in the Black South Side of Chicago. Those micro-businesses constitute different forms of self-employment, be it in the form of street vendors, yard and garage vendors, or direct sales vendors (12). Some of these micro-businesses are "hustles," that is, intermittent, informal business transactions (39). Smith points out that these self-employed people are labeled as "the disadvantaged, indigent, undereducated, and illiterate" although they are "educated about their environment and themselves," and they are "intelligent, insightful and displayed empathy for others" (37). In other words, they have useful skills and knowledge resources required for *daily life* (47). Smith also writes that "although overlooked by scholars, educators and African Americans, this group composed of self-employed adults may provide some of the best economic role models for adults with low skills" (49). The results of Smith's study make it clear that people would attend and stay in literacy programs that would take into account the extensive knowledge and skills that have been preserved or developed outside the official labor market *and* outside corresponding work and literacy training approaches. Smith therefore strongly suggests a fundamental reframing of the notion of literacy. By leaving the conventional framework of predesigned, technical, and measurable skills, vital forms of literacies and how they or the need for their development have been neglected are revealed. To reframe the notion of literacy also means to struggle against equally invisible illiteracies, and to directly connect them with their social and economic ramifications.

Within the WEH sessions I was struck again and again by the women's seemingly effortless and poetic use of language, an ability that was expressed in a number of ways. Some of the women struggled to put words on paper not only because of their low writing skills, but also because they had to forgo the ability to speak fluently and often poetically about complex issues—an ability that could at least be expressed during the following discussions. The WEH was organized in a way that led the participants to practice putting their words on paper but also gave them the space to indulge in their highly developed speaking ability. The importance of acknowledging this ability was brought home when I asked one of the women what she meant by the short sentences she had produced as part of her homework assignment. She immediately became apologetic and gave a number of reasons why they were so short. After I pointed out that I simply wanted to hear all of her thoughts on the questions she had tried to answer, and that I knew she had many important thoughts to share even when they were not put down in writing, she first looked puzzled, then relaxed, expressed pride in her own ability, and was highly motivated to put more effort into her homework assignment. In the words of the WEH, she clearly felt "empowered." Again, this small incident speaks volumes about the importance of breaking through the barriers of the conventional education systems. Instead of operating with the usual deficit model, which only recognizes certain kinds of "cognitive processes and modes of communication" (Brunetière, Metay, and Sylvestre 1990), space needs to be provided for acknowledging existing but unrecognized experiences and forms of knowledge that are closely linked to learning desires and abilities, a point addressed in the following chapter.

PERSONAL STORIES AND REFLECTIVE DISTANCE

The work of the women's literacy group was taking place under particularly harsh circumstance as they lived in a world that seems to have been pushed to the very margin of a society. At the same time it is precisely at the margins where the essence of the problems with "our" system are unveiled, where the social and moral bankruptcy of the "center" becomes most visible. In the absence of essential material and immaterial cushions, the center has seeped into the very interior of the margin. The need for fundamental social change therefore has to be juxtaposed with a description of the tremendous effort that goes into the making of small, multilayered changes affecting day-to-day living, changes that only indirectly affect immediate economic survival needs.

As the primary motif of the WEH has shown, the notion of change is closely linked to finding or nurturing a sense of power in one's self, that is, focusing on the individual without reducing change to that level, as is the tradition of conventional literacy programs. Although a personal sense of empowerment must be at the core of self-help, it cannot take place without collective support. In other words, the power within must be self-generated, "and it is the fundamental power on which women must build." It must, however, be connected to the "'power with,' the capacity to achieve with others what one could not achieve alone" (Townsend 1999, 30, 31). One of the main ingredients of the women's literacy initiative was to provide space for learning lessons from women whose life circumstances were not different from the ones of the women living at the ABLA Homes, who themselves lived in one of the public housing projects, but who also served as role models for strength, courage, and perseverance; for caring for one's community and for the children of one's community. These examples go against the grain of falling victim to the despondency all around. This is one of the hardest tasks confronting these women. Although their sense of self, and their self-esteem are constantly being battered, thereby draining the reservoir of strength needed to raise their children in the midst of destruction, they have to teach survival methods that do not come at the expense of self-esteem (Collins 1994, 57).

Among the women at the literacy center, collective support not only took the form of listening to and reading about outside/inside examples, but it also came from the participants themselves. Their many discussions on the relationships among women and men, among women and women, and among women and

children involved a cluster of themes that show the intricate interplay of connections and contradictions between the personal and the social-cultural, the ideological and the economic. Correspondingly, discussions that took place during
the WEH also show an interplay of personal stories, anecdotes, and the development of a general perspective that moves these stories into a larger framework
of understanding. This method often reminded me of my own experiences in the
consciousness-raising groups of the seventies where the personal and the general
were highly interrelated (Hart 1990). In addition, among the women' s literacy
group, the process of *conscientization* (Paolo Freire) was directly connected
with the "craft" of reading and writing (Bhola 1994, 47).

This method takes on a new dimension in a context permeated by outer and
inner destitution. Where economic survival is hardly an inch away from personal survival, it takes on a new importance. And this brings up another contra-
diction with which Chicago's public housing residents must wrestle. To raise
one's consciousness is a slow process, dependent on a lot of consistent support—on the building of trust and on the courage required to look at the misery
or brutality that is part of one's life. Raising consciousness, or conscientization,
also requires the inner strength needed to criticize oneself or one's failures,
shortcomings, or (self-)destructive coping mechanisms. In other words, it requires the ability to shed light on one's own personal life by acknowledging not
only its pain but also one's own responsibility in perpetuating parts of the pain.

As observed on many occasions, this was only possible when the participants managed to gain a reflective distance from their own personal horizon.
Sometimes it happened, sometimes the discussions got stuck in the personal,
and the group assumed a (however needed) therapeutic rather than consciousness-raising function. Consciousness-raising is one of the hardest tasks in a context where fear, pain, anguish, and rage are fed by a multitude of social and individual sources, all laced into each other and often impossible to disentangle
because of their overwhelming emotional power. Again, this is one of the many
contradictions with which people living in the ABLA Homes have to wrestle.
They are around their own people, and no matter how difficult, problematic, and
violent the environment is, they know each other, the conditions of their lives,
their own language, their culture. Almetta once told me about the women's fear
of the "outside world" although they desperately tried to escape from their own
familiar world. This posed a rather difficult question: Are there ways of learning, and wanting to learn, the language of the outside world as a second language, and in a way that does not just promise an escape from the neighborhood
but other possibilities as well?

As shown by the lives of the women participating in the WEH, and as shown
by the lives of the most marginalized people in this country (and everywhere
else), there is an intimate connection between "the economy" and "the super-
structure of values" (Bhola 1994, 43). However, we cannot simply envision a
change of values without also changing the material structures that have been
supported or created by current values. As should have become clear in this and

the preceding chapters, the issue of motherwork shows particularly well how the ideological and the material (or "economic") are closely aligned. "The economy" and "economic activities" can no longer be considered a separate or central concern only economists can address. Instead, "everything belongs fundamentally together and we can speak only from the perspective of this connection" (von Werlhof 1993a, 1051). Or, as Luttwak (1999) summarizes in his analysis of the most recent state of neoliberal global capitalism, or "turbo-capitalism," society becomes modeling clay to be shaped in accordance with economic imperatives. Thus, what is summarized under the rubric of "the economy" affects every aspect of daily life and living.

Motherwork does require a holistic mindset and a holistic practical approach. It is contextual, situational, collaborative, and intergenerational work, and it incorporates the physical, psychological, emotional, and spiritual dimensions of life. In whatever truncated or tentative form, all of these aspects were present in the women's literacy group. Its participants showed that there are (still) gaps in the system, and that life-sustaining desires and hopes are alive, in whatever beleaguered form. When one looks at work that is mainly performed by women, the usual ban on asking any critical or radical questions concerning work literacy becomes especially visible (see Hautecoeur 1990, 1996). Vital abilities, forms of knowledge, and skills are disregarded and thereby turned into "hidden literacies." The importance of learning new literacies and unlearning old ones in precisely those areas of knowledge and experience are disregarded as well. The words of the participants quoted earlier tell only part of the story about the work that has become an inordinate task in Chicago's public housing environment. It is the work of hope and care, and of building and sustaining the knowledge, skills, and abilities required to do it well. The women's words echo what has been described by one of Chicago's community organizations, Women for Economic Justice, as the meaning of work: "Work is raising and educating children. Work is providing a comfortable, cultured life for us all. Work is teaching youth, healing and caring for the sick, rebuilding neighborhoods, harvesting and distributing the food. Work is organizing for social justice" (A Call for Social Justice, quoted in *off our backs*, October 1994, 6).

The notion of work proposed in this quote clearly breaks through the entrenched dichotomy between a job in the labor market and work that is not only taking place "somewhere else" but is also directly oriented toward supporting and sustaining life itself. This includes some basic conditions related to life: food, shelter, community, a health-producing and health-maintaining environment, and hope for the future.

NOTES

1. As noted in the Introduction, "ABLA" stands for a cluster of four public housing projects.

2. Elio DeArrudah, the director of the Public Housing Literacy Project, provided a

lot of useful background information for this chapter.

3. All direct quotes are taken from of several printed handouts Almetta gave to the literacy participants.

4. The various contributions to the March–April 2000 issue of *Poverty Research News* give summaries of "important new streams of fatherhood research" (Roy 2000) as well as detailed analyses of the general life circumstances of fathers who find themselves on the margins of work and family, and how the inability to financially provide for their children makes many fathers withdraw from other paternal responsibilities.

5. These stories confirmed the findings of Raphael and Tolman's (1997) study in which they report that boyfriends or husbands sometimes keep women from staying in jobs by threatening or abusing them.

6. Kevin Roy reports that "a pilot demonstration was conducted in three sites in Chicago. Over 250 men ages 17–45 years enrolled in the project. Almost all were low-income, single, African American fathers of children who received Aid to Families with Dependent Children (AFDC) benefits. PIP was a voluntary program, and men found out about the program through word of mouth, friends or family, or presentations to community groups. At the end of its demonstration phase, the program consolidated its three sites into one, located at Kennedy King College on the South Side. In the subsequent two years (1996–98), PIP enrolled 397 fathers" (2000, 15).

Chapter 5

Teaching and Learning
as a Political Ally

As described in the previous chapter, the literacy center is located at the border-line between a major state university and one of the public housing complexes of Chicago's Near South Side. It is located directly across the street from a mostly white middle-class area, offering pleasant restaurants, bookstores, and other university facilities. One simply has to cross one street to leave the university surroundings and enter a quite different world. There is therefore a geographically visible disjuncture between an institution of higher education and people living in a racially and economically segregated area. Most of my educational work takes place at a private university, with my college located in Chicago's downtown area. It offers an interdisciplinary liberal arts degree for working adults. Part of its mission is to provide a structural acknowledgment of the fact that all human knowledge is inherently transdisciplinary, and that knowledge can be gained and constructed in many different ways.

Aside from teaching some of the staple courses about documenting prior learning or about research methods, the college encourages faculty to develop transdisciplinary topics courses. Whereas the university provides the larger institutional framework for teaching and learning, the content of my courses, the materials provided (such as readings and guest speakers), the life experiences of the adult students, and an emphasis on experiential learning modes provide the space for telling and listening to stories about a world that is both "out there" and that some of the students nevertheless bring with them to class. In that sense the semipublic enclave of academia is rather permeable. One of the courses I teach is called "Motherwork." It builds upon my interests in the different meanings and realities of the notion of work, and it addresses social, economic, and philosophical-ethical issues associated with welfare, and with the work of raising children in poverty. By teaching Motherwork I try to connect different worlds and make room for discovering points of connection as well as sharp divisions. Above all I try to structure my educational work in a way that assists students in learning from people who have been "othered" by this society.

This makes learning a rather multifaceted event. It involves learning about larger social-economic hierarchies and divisions, and it involves learning *about* the Other, learning *with* the Other, and seeing parts of the Other in oneself and parts of oneself in the Other. Ultimately, it means being able to engage in cultural and epistemological border-crossings. Practically speaking, not only do I bring to bear what I learned from visiting a world that is very different from the one I inhabit, but, equally importantly, these visits have also sensitized me in terms of students' own border-crossings, the different worlds they inhabit, and, consequently, their multiple identities. My own experiences with such border-crossings have therefore assisted me in becoming more aware of students' different social, cultural, and epistemological groundings. Not only is my work in the college classroom strongly influenced by what I myself learned from the women I had conversations with or observed at the literacy center, but also by what I learned about the complex and challenging process of learning from and about the Other.

By using the very term Other I am, however, already participating in a construction of difference that can easily bypass the fact that it is fully embedded in social-political hierarchies. Learning about and from the Other always includes an acute awareness of how various social divisions not only attach official identity labels to different groups of people, but also how some of these identities are placed at the lower rungs of the ladder of social esteem. Educational work must therefore include a recognition of how many students are confronted with the "difficult task of managing several stigmatized identities" (Hurtado 1996, 375). In addition, faculty who have to deal with the "situated dynamics of being of color and teaching in what remains predominantly white institutions of higher learning" face challenges that are quite different from the ones encountered by someone whose skin privilege as well as class membership translate into comfortable, automatically taken-for-granted entitlements and sources of institutional and personal power (Jackson and Jordán 1999, 6).

How the complexly interwoven strands of power determine limiting but also potentially liberating moments in the educational endeavor is the focus of this chapter. "Liberating" here means a number of things. Above all, it means seeing oneself and the other in a way that bursts through the confines of power-based identity labels, and opening one's heart and mind to listen to stories with a desire to understand and learn from them. This desire to learn has to overcome a number of obstacles. It may, for instance, be quite painful to hear these stories because they may throw light on how one's social membership is implicated in the injustices that caused this pain.

BREAKING SILENCE

It is one of my college teacher responsibilities to help create a space for students to break their silence on experiences that are generally stigmatized or devalued by society at large, to let subjugated knowledge be heard, and to assist everyone in the construction of more complete, truthful knowledge. I also need to recognize that no matter how hard I work to create a progressive, nonstigmatizing classroom situation, I am still representing the "academic power" of the university (Michelson 1996a, 646), and the power relations I have to struggle with inside my classroom are fully inserted in the overall hierarchical structure of the university.

Despite representing the dominant group in more ways than one, I nevertheless try to think and act as an ally. In Winkler's definition teaching as an ally means to "approach authority and the creation of classroom community as a condition for the production of knowledge and transformation of consciousness" (1996, 48). She adds also that to translate this concept into practical activities means "to describe what faculty from dominant groups can do to share power, build trust, and create an atmosphere of mutual respect in which to create knowledge with students from nondominant groups" (48).

To make the experience of previously excluded groups central does indeed have the epistemological dimension of knowledge construction and reconstruction. This intellectual dimension, however, is fully interwoven with the emotional tasks of circumventing or bursting through the confines of power hierarchies. These tasks include breaking one's silence; speaking against the grain of entrenched normative assumptions; expressing fear or anger in however muted ways to an audience that may not want to hear about it because this would shatter its own assumptions, or would stir up the fear and guilt members of the dominant group carry around. Fear and guilt are experiences that may block new learning for all involved, students and teacher alike, or rather block a kind of unlearning that requires "a conceptual reordering of whole areas" of one's existence, and being open to see new realities (Brew 1993, 91). Being given or creating the right kind of discursive and emotional conditions for such reordering of one's reality has to start with unclogging one's ears in order to hear the experiences of people whose realities have been devalued or silenced.

In my college classes where Black students are the numerical minority, I have noticed many times how they are silencing a knowledge rooted in their own experience of pain and anger. This is especially evident when we discuss Alice Walker's essay "In Search of Our Mothers' Gardens" (1983). At the beginning Black students always remain silent, and white students start out with politely expressing their admiration of Black women's creative spirit, and of the fact that Walker's mother could create an artistically designed garden despite her other overwhelming work responsibilities. After a while I usually have to ask some probing questions concerning the first half of the essay, because it is there where Walker writes about how women's creative spirit was so squelched during slavery that they became "insane." White students either become silent or, more typically, complain about Walker's fury at "something which is a thing of the past." In other words, they avoid the term slavery.

Black students remain silent because they have learned to "bridle" their anger, and they have learned that "to 'know' logically necessitates, temporarily, through an enormous amount of discipline and grit, the strategic suspension of anger" (Hurtado 1996, 378). While Hurtado's discussion focuses on women of color, it is not only race-ethnicity or gender that turns silence into a form of muteness, a loss of voice (Belenky at al. 1986), or into a powerful survival strategy. Class membership is another reality that gets shrouded in silence. Jensen calls on teachers in middle-class institutions to "strain to hear silences inside silences, a cacophony of silences, all the white space and ground beneath the middle- and upper-class figures that fill up the picture that society paints" (Jensen 1998, 203). The cacophony of silence includes the silence of social invisibility, of being regarded "with contempt and pity," a silencing of spirit because economic injustice is "felt deep inside as resignation" (204).

By trying to understand and respect Black students' silence as regards white students' complaints about Walker's rage, I am leaving the territory of political neutrality expected of a college teacher. As an ally I am taking sides by trying to explain why Walker's rage is well-founded, giving examples of the continuation of often blatant but also more insidious, structural forms of racism, and thus of the heritage of slavery. Not only do I have to understand the pain and anger that is part of the knowledge of suffering, but I also have to feel it myself as much as it is possible for an outsider, a white European person. While I cannot feel the pain of daily reminders that I am of a "lesser race," I can become outraged at what has been done to nonwhite people. In other words, I can speak "from an ethical oppositional stance" (Peterson 1996, 34). Using the example of my own collective history, I point out that as a German I have to try to understand the unspeakable Nazi horrors committed in the name of Aryan supremacy, that this history is far from being over, and that as a German I am responsible to keep the knowledge of this history alive. I am using my Germanness in a tactical way to give an example of how a non-Jew can take the side of Jews, like non-Black people can take the side of Black people. In other words, I try to show that it is possible to identify with the Other, and to see how this otherness is produced or treated by the dominant social group that claims my membership. I believe that a direct expression of rage at the injustices of a system that places me in a privileged position does create at times a very necessary emotional space in my classroom. After I express my disagreement with the white students' complaints, Black students do start speaking about their own anger and about the fact that slavery is by no means a thing of the past.

Seeing evidence that white students have at least begun a process of reordering areas of their reality is another matter because they are faced with quite different challenges. In one of my Motherwork classes, a white student had first been silenced by other students' unfavorable response to her rather stereotypical and indirectly quite racist comments about welfare mothers. A few weeks later she found the courage to speak again because, despite fundamental disagreements, she could count on some shared knowledge and experience. This gave her the courage to risk being judged and to break her silence by explaining to the class that she had based her views on her own experience. She was once very poor and without resources but managed to stay away from public aid by working extremely hard. She ended her statement by saying that she now understands how conditions can sometimes be so harsh that welfare is the only option. That's what she learned in class by listening to other people's stories and opinions.

It was not only from teaching my Motherwork class that I learned about the importance of discovering some common experiential ground, but also from my own experience of visiting mothers living in public housing. Such common ground—no matter how small or fragile—clearly assists in building bridges over racial-ethnic or class divisions. During the interviews my being a mother and grandmother clearly helped build some of these bridges, as did the fact that I extended my concern for the well-being of my own grand/child to the well-being of all children, especially the ones whose lives were confronted with so many dangers and hardships. My own class background also helped. Having grown up in poverty made me feel more connected to the mothers living in public housing, and to offer that sense of connection as an invitation to speak. Despite the quite visible racial differences between us, despite the fact that I had crossed class lines by becoming a member of the middle class, and despite tremendous cultural differences, I still preserved a "gut understanding" of what it means to live in poverty, and how caring for one's children or family entailed a lot of hard subsistence labor.

The cultural and historical context of my own experience of poverty was certainly fundamentally different from that of a solo mother in the inner city of Chicago, as it is for a Mexican migrant worker in California. Both would tell different stories about what it means to be poor, and how poverty is not only related to the work they do, but also to the fact that they are female, or African American, or Mexican. In other words, poverty is linked to different forms of social discrimination, all tightly woven into a system of economic inequality. In my own case poverty was partly related to the fact that I was born after World War II when Germany was a heap of rubble. My father's class and family background, however, tied him to a generally poor rural area in Southern Germany, contributing to the nature and duration of my family's state of poverty.[1] Seen from that angle, the poverty of a baker or factory worker in Germany bears similarity to the poverty of a migrant worker, or of an inner-city jobless poor person in America. They are all related to class inequality, although the cultural experience of these inequalities may be dramatically different.

THE LIVED EXPERIENCE OF CLASS

Poverty touches upon an extremely sensitive spot in people's sense of economic or financial success. As previously discussed, not only is poverty considered a sign of personal failure—especially when the poor person is white and able-bodied—but since it is strongly associated with certain group memberships, it is also a sign of collective deficiencies and moral failings. As discussed in chapter 3, the Black teenage mother on welfare is portrayed as the prototype of such personal-cultural failures.

While in my college classroom it has always been easier to address the visible (and often audible) difference of race, ethnicity, culture, or gender, it has also always been much more difficult to discuss these differences in relation to structures of economic inequality. Class is a troublesome category as it has a social-cultural and an economic dimension that makes it even less definable than ethnicity or race. As an educator who has come to see the necessity of providing space for critical attention to this term and to corresponding experiences, to make class a specific issue of analysis and story-telling means struggling on several levels simultaneously. How can class be addressed as a specific category (and experience) while seeing it through the lenses of race, ethnicity, culture, gender, or able-bodiedness? How can we overcome the conceptual void the notion of class always seems to fall into? How can we draw on texts that display the descriptive power of the term and that portray various forms and corresponding experiences of economic inequality? How can a more accessible analytical language be developed that avoids the dangers of a highly abstract theory, that does not provide any space for making a connection to the concrete, lived experience of class, and that is therefore understandable only to members of a specialized academic enclave? Finally, how can space be provided for voicing and criticizing the overall social, "deep-seated contempt for working-class people" (Helmbold 1998, 15), thus overcoming the silence of at least some of the students in my courses regarding class membership?[2]

As discussed in chapter 1, class *is* analytically distinct, and the fact that it combines in different ways with other social locations such as ethnicity or sexual difference means it is grounded in a reality of its own making. To understand this reality is particularly important, not only because class is interlaced with other social categories, but because each of these categories also "leads to its own insights which then require a reconceptualization of each in relation to the others" (Breitbart and Pader 1995, 11). How is it possible to disentangle class from categories such as sex or race, and to tell stories about the everyday experience of class?

When I teach my Motherwork course, it usually doesn't take much for students of all racial-ethnic or cultural backgrounds to examine the notion of subsistence/motherwork, and to relate it to their own experiences. These experiences address a multitude of problems and questions that are tucked away in the notion of unpaid, unwaged, socially neglected or devalued subsistence work.

Women students talk about the joys and hardship of bottomless care. Men students at times voice their surprise at their own ignorance of what it takes in terms of effort, energy, knowledge and skills to carry out the responsibilities associated with the work of raising children. Students often express gratitude for having learned a language that names their personal experiences. This language taps into an already existing elaborate vocabulary with respect to minute details of the daily care for children, but it also captures the general or nonpersonal dimensions of this work. Some of the students also appreciate the opportunity to share with each other experiences centering around the conflictual relationship of their dual roles as mothers and students, roles that are in most cases added on to full-time jobs. Since many of my students have been going to school on and off for sometimes many years, it also gives them an opportunity to talk about the way family responsibilities hardly ever give them the space and time they need—especially after a long day at their jobs—in order to be able to give full attention to their student life. By examining how their multiple roles "keep them rooted in their home culture despite their long-term exposure to campus life," they also see that class is gendered and has a direct impact on their upward mobility (Ferretti 1999, 71). Thus, when individual experiences are placed in a larger analytical framework that shows how they are being shaped by various divisions of labor—particularly, but not only by the sexual division—and by ideological legitimations of these general, structurally rooted hierarchies and injustices, the language describing these experiences is enriched, enlarged, or at times politically transformed.

It is much more difficult for students to frame their experiences, or their understanding of the experiences of others, in terms of class per se. This would mean being able to look at class as an analytically distinct concept and to relate it to experiences that are shaped by class or class divisions. To relate poverty to class (in whatever combination with race or sexual difference) seems to run up against a particularly strong social and emotional wall, set up by public opinion institutions such as the media. Not only do the poor get quasi-automatically associated with "minority," that is, with Black or Hispanic, but poverty is also portrayed as falling outside of the ideological scheme of the bipolar divisions between working and middle class. In other words, it is not associated with working class, but rather with "welfare recipient" or "dirt poor" (Pari 1999, 138). The media-driven cultural stereotype of the "underclass" certainly contributes to this entrenched association of poverty with dirt and nonworking takers of public assistance. As Williams so vividly describes, not only do the mainstream media portray poor whites in "insulting and dehumanizing depictions," they are also guilty of a "blanket elimination from collective consciousness of the black working class" (1995, 72, 60). She describes how the media have created a dualistic image of Black people where a small number somehow rose to the middle class. It is there where they "end up being figured only as those who were *given* what they enjoy," whereas the majority of Black people belong to the underclass "whose sole life activity is *taking*" (61). Collins sees a similar process at work when Black women are either portrayed as middle-class "Black Lady Overarchievers" or as part of a growing, seemingly permanent black underclass (1998).

How this view is an expression of classism was painfully illustrated in one of my Motherwork classes. Some students were clearly confronted with the task of admitting their own ignorance about welfare mothers' true reality, and of relating this ignorance to their own class position. One white woman, a single mother who had a well-paying corporate job, was in tears when she confessed to other students that until she took this class she had no idea about the social and financial struggles her own sister, a welfare mother, had to face on a daily basis. She had found some safety behind her own deliberate, stereotypical misunderstanding of her sister's reality because she adhered to the official belief that welfare mothers "do not have to work" and have "plenty of money." In other words, they are just taking. Reading about and listening to other poor mothers' stories had crumbled that carefully maintained ignorance.

When students discussed the ideological justifications for paying nannies or maids minimum wage for work that is otherwise glorified as a woman's true calling, one of the white students rather courageously told the class that her family had hired an "Hispanic maid." She also emphatically stated that the maid "was treated very well." Some of the students responded in emotionally quite charged ways, insinuating that this could not be entirely true. Their counter-arguments, however, were couched in the terms of economic analyses we had read in class. Judging from the passion with which the disagreements were expressed, however, I guessed that these counter-arguments were based on some experiential grounds, probably related to their own, their mothers' or female relatives' experience. Whereas the racial and ethnic dimension of a high concentration of women of color in domestic work could be expressed in analytical-structural terms, students were obviously not willing to talk about personal experiences that not only touched upon racist and class-biased treatments of domestic workers but also upon a socially denigrated occupation, or a low social status. In my experience as a teacher, something resembling working-class pride was rarely expressed, and then only by students who were active in unions.

The social dimension of class clearly predominates in these experiences. In other words, class is here experienced more as "cultural capital" one may or may not own rather than as a particular economic position. Reay (1997), who researched how class is experienced by working-class or middle-class mothers with respect to their children's education, gives an example of how this notion of cultural capital[3] is played out in these mothers' sense of self or self-confidence. The middle-class women displayed core ingredients of cultural capital: "Confidence, a sense of entitlement, knowledge of the educational system, useful social networks, and a feeling of being capable of seizing the initiative" (229). These ingredients were absent in Christine's, a working-class mother's, account, a woman who generally felt "incapable" or "powerless." As Reay observed, to bring a working-class past into the "middle-class field of education generates a sense of inadequacy and feelings of negative self-esteem" (229). Luttrell (1997), who was a teacher-researcher in two adult education programs, one in Philadelphia and one in North Carolina, makes a similar observation. While teaching, developing curriculum materials, and performing administrative duties, she collected the lifestories of white (Philadelphia) and Black (North Carolina) working-class women, especially with respect to their experiences in formal education. She writes about how these stories "support a view of schools as trading posts where students bring different sorts of 'cultural capital,' i.e., different kinds of knowledge, dispositions, linguistic codes, problem-solving skills, attitudes, and tastes, only some of which get rewarded or valued by school authorities" (5). Although the women's experiences of schools took place in quite different contexts, one rural and one urban, all the women were treated as "unworthy" traders of cultural capital.

The fact that class is such a theoretically extremely complex concept is certainly one of the reasons that "class differences are particularly ignored in the classrooms" (hooks 1994, 177). If they are addressed at all, then only in the rather theoretical, abstract terms of the capitalist system, or of the post-work society (Aronowitz and Cutler 1998). Thus, when hooks writes that "most progressive professors are more comfortable striving to challenge class biases through the material studied than they are with interrogating how class biases shape conduct in the classroom and transforming their pedagogical practices" (187), she addresses a rather dense knot of class-related issues.[4]

Within the enclaved public of the academy discussions of class as a highly theoretical concept are part of the middle-class university professor's cultural capital. In that respect, academic discourse about class, or class struggles, are part and parcel of general divisions of classes. Above all, institutions of higher education directly feed off the division between manual and mental labor, a core dimension of class divisions. Michelson points to the "implicit classism that ignores the social interestedness of distinctions between manual and intellectual labor," a class bias she correctly links up with the "masculinist dismissal of life-maintenance activity" (1996a, 640). In Harding's words such classism is, for instance, behind the fact that it is "women, poor people, and racially marginalized groups whose bodily activities in households, offices, restaurants, and other places where biologists sleep, work, and live are the precondition for biologists' having the leisure to pursue their studies" (1998, 160). The intellectual work of analyzing class structures therefore relies on others doing the manual work that builds and maintains the university that accords value to this analysis. As Kadi (1996) put it, "Workers at the university. We've built every university that has ever existed, yet we're shunned and despised within academia's hallowed halls. Explicitly and implicitly, we've been taught our place—and it's not in a student's desk or the professor's lounge. We're needed to construct the university, maintain, clean and repair it. Oh, we're welcome here, as long as we stay where we're supposed to" (39).

In her book *Thinking Class* Kadi addresses the interplay of clearly marked, quite visible divisions between mental and manual laborers, and how such divisions are concretely experienced by people whose labor occupies the lower ranks of the social hierarchy. She vehemently criticizes the fact that working-class people are used to provide the stories, or the "raw material of bare facts" which are then transformed into theory by middle- and upper-middle class academics. She calls on working-class people to theorize about their own experiences (40).

Kadi's book is a rare example of a personal narrative of the everyday experience of working class, and how this experience relates to her being an Arab-American woman, and thus to the intersectionality of classism, sexism, and racism. What she does not address, however, is the fact that the very notion of manual labor engenders its own hierarchy within the working-class community itself. In Luttrell's study the women's discussions of what counts as "real intelligence" affirmed a common-sense type or "really useful knowledge." As one of the respondents expressed it, this kind of knowledge needed to "deal with life and make the best of it"(26). In the white women's stories, "real intelligence" was, however, strongly gender coded by being applied to men's, not women's, manual labor. One of the women, for example, praised her brother who was "self-educated, not school-educated" as being "very intelligent" (29). Such praise was absent with respect to the women's self-taught skills, such as helping children with homework, sewing, baking, or gardening. As Luttrell put it, "The common sense associated with women's work, family life, child rearing, and other caregiving tasks counted less (if at all) than the common sense association with men's work activities" (1997, 36). Luttrell's descriptions echo Jenna's complaints that her husband did not think her work counted as work because it did not require hard physical labor (see p. 65). As an African-American woman, Jenna, like the Black women in Luttrells' study, did not "associate 'real intelligence' with skilled manual labor, partly because black men have historically had limited access to the 'crafts.' Instead, they viewed common sense, most often referred to as 'motherwit,' as all-encompassing, mentioning abilities to 'make ends meet': solve family, work, or community disputes; overcome natural disasters (e.g., droughts and hurricanes); and avoid racial conflict" (32). Clearly, the women's hard work was central to their family's and community's survival. Jenna's husband nevertheless represented a male perspective on motherwit, most likely shared by the men in the lives of the women whose stories Luttrell recorded. The sexual division of labor clearly interlaces with the manual/mental distinction, although in ways that show marked racialized distinctions.

As illustrated by student responses to employing a domestic worker, in cases where students gain enough courage to speak about economic inequality, they often incite rather vehemently expressed disagreements. The students therefore illustrate that class is not simply an abstract economic term but a lived, emotionally taxing experience as well. Learning from experience is a staple in educational literature, particularly in adult education where it has been treated as a foundation of knowledge, or as a "foundational concept" (Stone-Mediatore 1998, 118). Experience has also been "a keyword in social history, particularly the histories of subjugated or invisible groups, since the 1960s" (Canning 1994, 374). Dorothy Smith, who has been writing about knowledge embedded in the everyday world for some time, considers experience a place to start seeing and analyzing "the local contours of people's lives" (1997, 397). Learning therefore requires one at least to begin seeing how personal experiences are shaped by "the oppressive routine organization, the persistence, the repetition, of capitalist forms of exploitation, of patriarchy, of racial subordination" (397). Learning from experience also requires being able to name the experience, however, and to have a language at one's disposal that is capable of telling about and understanding core elements of this experience.

As Helmbold points out, not only are "narratives that analyze class by looking at daily life" quite rare (1998, 15), but they are also rather difficult to construct.[5] She correctly states that "we need theory that enables us to make sense of the complexity and to act on that understanding," and that "we need vocabulary and theory that transcends personal narratives." She continues by emphasizing that she does not "mean to dismiss story-telling, for it gives voice to the unheard and stimulates others to speak. But how do we make the leap from story-telling to theory?" (16). This leap becomes even more challenging when the theory of class spans the international dimension of the global capitalist system. Raffo (1997, 3) summarizes this difficulty quite clearly in the following quote:

I don't believe we currently have the political vocabulary to talk about class systems in a way that automatically includes issues of economic inequality, cultural difference, race and ethnicity, internationalism, imperialism, and historical change. We err in sometimes using class to mean a specific group of people or a specific identity, saying things like "working-class/poor/middle-class/rich people tend to think/vote/act/survive this way . . ." At other times, class is discussed only as a social system and a function of institutions, with little attention paid to its actual effect on individual lives and individual methods of survival and interpretation.

In *The Feminist Classroom* Maher and Tetreault (1994) state that class is a concept that is much more difficult to talk about in experiential terms than race or gender because it is an inherently *social* category. In other words, it cannot be associated with "natural" or biological characteristics such as sex or skin color that give them a certain constancy. Such biological differences between white and dark skin color, or male and female genitals makes Hurtado remark that "children know that they will *remain* boys or girls, Black and White."[6] Although biological differences are lodged in some physical realities, they are, of course, also social constructs that determine how they are perceived or interpreted, and what kind of cultural differences they signal that place them on different rungs on the ladder of social worthiness or esteem. Brodkin (1998) investigated how different groups of immigrants to the United States underwent various stages of a whitening process, and she describes the complex interplay of cultural, ethnic, and economic dimensions that determine the degree of whiteness different groups could reach. Because of the historically changing possibilities for becoming whiter, not-yet white, almost white, or fully white, corresponding ethnic identities are slower to develop, and it will therefore take children a bit longer to know "that they will *remain* Chicano or Asian regardless of the situation" (Hurtado 1996, 377). Black people, on the other hand, have always been excluded from the very possibility of becoming whiter, and being Black is therefore a predominant marker of Black people's individual and collective identity. Esposito (1999) makes an observation that illustrates this predominance of race. When he discusses the notion of culture in his college class, his primarily African-American students define culture as equivalent to race. Class, on the other hand, cannot be linked with such unequivocal differences, and it is therefore a rather confusing and ambiguous notion for the students taking his course on intercultural communication.

Folbre underscores the confusion and ambiguity associated with class when she writes that "class is more difficult to define than other categories of group membership. While people can generally categorize their own gender and race, they often use vague and contradictory terms when they describe themselves as middle class or working class" (1994, 57). Griffin (1996), who studied how people experience a sense of power depending on where they are located in the power matrix of class, race, and gender, also observed people's difficulty in describing their class position. For the mostly white, middle-class university students in her study, class remained a rather "fluid construct," defined primarily in cultural terms, whereas race was understood more as a biologically founded category (189). The term "biological" refers, however, to what Franz Fanon calls "racial epidermal schema." Within the parameters of the racial epidermal schema, race provides an integrated image that is woven "out of a thousand details, anecdotes, stories" (1967, 111). Together they make up the social-cultural meanings associated with skin color, or what Holloway calls "the color of our character" (1995). "Biological" therefore only touches upon the "corporeal schema" (Fanon) where a body experiences its particular position in space, in relation to other bodies or objects.

The confusion and ambiguity students experience with respect to class has an ideological but also material-structural dimension. As Raffo points out, "Class experience is . . . contextual and ever changing. Your class position and status at one point in your life might appear different in another" (5). As discussed in chapter 1, writers who come from the Marxist tradition—the source of the notion of a dual-oppositional class structure—have criticized the reduction of class analysis to the bourgeoisie, or capitalist owners of production, and the proletariat, or working-class. Wright (1997), for instance, discusses the multiple, often contradictory, dual, temporary or ambiguous class locations people inhabit under current capitalist conditions, and he pays special attention to the middle class, a conceptual construct absent in original Marxist writings. He focuses on the middle class such as managers or professional "credential holders," because he tries to disentangle the "conceptual knots generated by conceptualizing the middle class within the Marxist tradition" (60), and because this is the class that is the most ambiguous, temporary, or contradictory.

Raffo translates Wright's theory into experiential terms: "Most of the time you know if you are rich. Most of the time you know if you are poor. It is the vast middle ground that brings uncertainty" (4). She also writes that "people in the United States are confused about how to talk about class and about how to place themselves. Or, just as likely, that people in the U.S. have had Horatio Alger's rags-to-riches story drummed into their souls to a point where admitting less than middle-classness means admitting to laziness and sloth" (5).

Although this myth contributes to the indeterminacy of a middle-class position or identity, it also directly depends on and reinforces the notion of middle class itself as it derives most of its commonsense meaning from its oppositional stance toward working class. Any explicit acknowledgment of class therefore usually "operates with a dichotomy between 'working' and 'middle' class," and it is rooted in one's paid employment status (Reay 1997, 25). At the same time, class divisions are cloaked in silence, and being working-class is associated with shame. Not surprisingly, the students in Pari's class were reluctant to define working class, or identify with it, but they "furiously clamored to describe the middle class: suburban homes, cars, college degrees, professions, savings accounts, material possessions, and above-average incomes" (1999, 137).

Willow (1997) tells the story of how this dichotomy is played out in real life, and how it leaves out a number of things:

In my own experience, on those rare occasions when the topic of class has come up in conversation, the focus has always been on "middle class." From time to time, I've heard references to the "upper class," but few of the people I know have direct experience with that. So we drop it. Sometimes other terms, like the "underclass" and the "working poor," crop up. But for the most part, our speculations revolve around what it means to be "working-class" or "middle-class." In any of these conversations and any of these class terms, my own origins are simply left out. We are an invisible class, we are working farm folk. (108)

Willow here puts into personal-experiential terms what is a larger social problem: If the notion of class comes up at all, it is quasi-automatically tied to the idea that only two classes exist, if any at all. People who do not fit into either category are therefore seriously deviating from the norm. They are either referred to as "underclass," or, as in the case of people running a family farm, their work and their economic contributions become entirely invisible.

The middle class is meant to be "the buffer between the tiny number of truly wealthy people—i.e., those who don't have to work—and millions who do. And who are defined, then, by what they are not" (Vanderbosch 1997, 92). Vanderbosch here articulates the undercurrent of middle-class anxiety, of being "a paycheck away from oppression." Although she was educated into middle-class values, she nevertheless continues to experience the "pain of what it means to be near but not in the center" (91). Thus, "the essence of what it means to be 'working-class' . . . isn't simply the work I do or how much I get paid. It isn't the extent of my status, wealth, or power. It's the knowledge that I *am* the bottom of the barrel. That my job is to feel inferior" (91). She writes: "I suspect the middle class needs us—the stiffs at the bottom—to know who they are and where they stand. (Much the same way men need women.) The middle class needs a bunch of people to look at, to point to and say: "See, we're not like *them*. We're better. Not quite the top, but nowhere—nowhere—near the bottom" (91).

Clearly people who belong to the working class have to muster an inordinate amount of courage in order to be able to write about their experiences. Kadi, for instance, had to "deconstruct" the entrenched myth that the working class is unworthy or stupid:

We know the monster that presents itself if we dare step out of place. *Stupid. We are too stupid to study, learn, think, analyze, critique. Because working-class people are stupid.* So much energy goes into the social lie that poor people are stupid; capitalism needs a basic rationalization to explain why things happen the way they do. So we hear, over and over, that our lousy jobs and living situations result from our lack of smarts. I internalized this lie. (39–40; emphasis in the original)

Feeling powerless, or being made to feel stupid, is only one of the forces behind the silence surrounding notions of class, and one of the factors that contributes to an absence of public discussion of the economic underside of class relations. In Reay's (1997) study Christine, one of the working-class mothers, preferred to describe herself as "classless" because she did not want to be stigmatized as working class. Christine was therefore hiding behind the facade of the entrenched myth that we all are one big middle class. Kadi writes about how she had to uproot the myth of classlessness in her attempt to give a voice to working-class experience. And, as Christine's story tells us, it is also a myth that simultaneously covers up and reinforces the characterization of people who did not make it into the middle class as suffering from personal deficiencies. Likewise, the African-American students in Esposito's class defined themselves as African American from a race perspective, but "when class was the focus, they began to distinguish themselves from others who they felt were lower on the status chart." Despite the fact that most of the students were from lower-working-class backgrounds, "class was not an overt component of their total persona" (Esposito 1999, 229; see also Pari 1999). The working-class women whose stories Luttrell collected transposed class relations onto the level of certain types of intelligence which the women believed divides people and sustains social inequality. People who are "making it" into the middle class have the ambition and the will to achieve, whereas those who "make do" are mainly focusing on survival (1997, 28).

Not only is class an almost taboo subject, it is also "fraught with rage, grief, and confusion," making people avoid talking about it (Willow 1997, 106). In an institution of higher learning, this means students have to cross class lines and be silent about what went on in their lives before they entered that institution. To talk about class in experiential terms therefore means being courageous enough to come out of the "class closet" (Brownworth 1997, 67). However, the silence of people who remain in the closet, or, rather the "cacophony of silences" Jensen describes does not only speak of muted voice, pain, or resignation. It is also built "on shared implicit shades of meaning. No vehicle is provided, or allowed, for universal understanding. It is an intimate language for members only" (1998, 205). Beneath the shroud of silence working-class culture "has a psychology and an integrity of its own" (205). Writings such as Kadi's *Thinking Class* may provide an opening for discussing class in a way that builds on this integrity. Her narrative is replete with examples of pernicious stigmatizations of working-class culture. At the same time it also points toward possibilities for creating openings in educational situations that do not start or end with a description of oppression or exploitation, but that provide spaces for acknowledging and naming "hidden literacies," that is, skills, knowledge, and abilities:

Many different kinds of intelligence exist, and these cross class lines. Universities revere the type of intelligence that can synthesize information rapidly and understand abstract concepts. Equally valid types of intelligence enable a child to design and build a bird house, a mother to balance a budget with no money, and an "uneducated" man to enthrall listeners with stories, a young woman who hasn't had music lessons to compose a piano tune, a girl to write a poem, a homeless person to comprehend a poem, a neighborhood to devise a plan to stop a company from dumping toxic waste, three young women to invent scathing responses to catcalls and whistles. These types of intelligence require creativity, humor, ability to ask questions, care, a good memory, compassion, belief in solidarity, ability to project an image of something that doesn't physically exist. (1996, 51)

Kadi puts into concrete terms what can be used as building blocks for the appreciation of knowledge, abilities, and styles of communication and thinking that are developed in the nonacademic, working-class world (or worlds), and that counteract the general social categorization of the working class as stupid—in the most blatant expression of social contempt—or, in the milder version of such a perception, academically unprepared. By entering a world that is based on middle-class assumptions and that exudes class privilege, working-class students are expected to disown any previous knowledges or ways of knowing. They have to internalize a corresponding worldview before they can join a culture "that is fundamentally different and that replaces the assumptions of their own," making them feel "torn between opposing cultural expectations" (Jensen 1998, 204, 208).[7]

The knowledges they are asked to leave behind are part and parcel of a culture with its own language or "communication signals" that belong to "members only," and that are strongly attached to a sense of belonging and loyalty. In her college classes Jensen provides avenues for working-class students to demonstrate the way they learn and think in a positive, affirming, way while at the same time giving traditional middle-class assignments such as a term paper with references.[8] She therefore practices what Busman recommends as a process to undermine the cacophony of silence with which working-class students must battle: "The thinking abilities of oppressed peoples must be fostered rather than disparaged and discredited. The knowledge and memory of working-class lives and experiences must not be erased and silenced but, rather, insisted on and continually reintroduced as 'story,' 'history,' and social and political analysis. Institutions of 'learning' that represent only the 'knowledge' of the privileged can only replicate systems of oppression" (1998, 91).

EXPERIENCE AND KNOWLEDGE

As Busman writes with respect to working-class students entering the privileged domain of academia, "the 'trusted knowledge' of experience (at least the experience of the oppressed) doesn't count at the university level. Because what is valued at institutions of 'higher learning' is a disembodied theorizing about something other than the thing itself, working-class students are often placed in the absurd and crazy-making position of being silenced while a middle-class academic lectures to them about class issue in America" (82–82). Working-class culture is a colonized culture, a "culture boxed within another one" (Jensen 1998, 208), and the shaming and demeaning visited upon members of the non-middle class certainly takes its toll on their sense of self, their identity. As Zandy writes, "working-class identity *is* discernible in the context of U.S. capitalism: if you're expected to dispose of it—you're probably working-class" (1998, 235).

Claiming an identity which people "were taught to despise" is, however, rooted in experience (Harding 1991, 273). Learning, that is, garnering knowledge from experience, therefore has to grapple with "the problem of dominant experience and the issue of partiality" (Young and Dickerson 1994, 2). Nonthreatening opportunities have to be provided for members of the dominant group to look at their experience critically and to see to what extent they, or the knowledge they gained from it, originate from a location of socially granted power and privilege. At the same time discursive and emotional spaces also have to be opened up for members of nondominant groups to articulate their experiences. This allows everyone participating in an educational situation to validate this experience and to learn from it—although the actual content of learning may appeal quite differently to different students, depending on their group membership or collective identity.

"Women's experience" was a central theme in early feminist writings, and narrating that experience was a core strategy in feminist consciousness-raising. Feminist writers have not only expressed concern about uncritical appeals to the authority of experience "as uncontestable evidence" (J. Scott 1991, 777), however, but they also criticized the corresponding essentialist treatment of the category "woman." In response to this criticism, some feminist writers such as Stone-Meditatore (1998) have developed an alternative account of experience that addresses the issue of multiple identities, and of a hierarchical ordering of categories that shape individual and collective identities: "When experience-rooted rewritings of identity challenge discursive colonization and suggest cross-border, cross-cultural solidarities, these narratives affirm the power to name, embrace, and shift between social positions strategically. In so doing, they not only renarrate the past but identify a historical location from which to imagine a different future" (128; see also Mohanty 1991). Thus, experiences can become resources "for confronting and renarrating the complex forces that constitute experience," and they can become resources "for 'seeing' differently" (Stone-Mediatore 1998, 127, 128).

The stories the mothers living in public housing told are full of questions and concerns excluded in the narratives of dominant ideologies. The pain and fear that accompanied most of the stories were derived from a number of injustices that are sustained by these ideologies, and it therefore required strength and courage to narrate corresponding experiences.

Thinking about ways of tapping the power of personal narratives in the learning process requires a number of things. Above all, it means acknowledging that individual experience is structured by personal autobiography *and* by society at large, and that there is "a complex and sometimes contradictory relationship between personal biography and social history, between the nature of experience and social structure" (Brah and Hoy 1989, 71). Learning processes have to be structured in accordance with this realization. Social and cultural conditions shape any individual's understanding and interpretation of her or his experience, and everybody therefore has to *learn* how one's experience and one's way of seeing the world is embedded in and influenced by a multitude of factors. One's unique autobiographical circumstances and one's position in a particular society are the two major strands in this complex matrix of influences. Learning about and understanding what makes up this matrix, and how the particularities of one's personal life are embedded in larger social issues can follow many different paths. There is no pedagogical recipe.

Within the educational context of my college, in one of my Motherwork classes I tried to give students more emotional space to interact with each other and to *verbally* articulate their personal experiences and personal responses to class material. Their writing assignments were more focused on the readings themselves. Furthermore, I selected readings that covered a broad spectrum of approaches. They ranged from mainly theoretical analyses of the sexual division of labor to personal stories about some aspect of this larger social-economic structure. My purpose behind providing space for the telling of personal stories and for requiring a careful reading of different kinds of material was threefold: I wanted students to be able to tell their own stories, learn from the stories of others, *and* see all stories in connection with larger social issues.

In their final paper a number of students talked about rather disturbing personal issues, but they investigated their range of meanings from the larger perspective they had gained through their readings and through listening to other students' contributions. One of the women wrote a paper where she combined the analytical and the experiential in a way that drew on African-American traditions of story-telling. The paper was constructed in the form of a personal narrative, and the decisions behind what parts of the story to put on paper were clearly following the main outline of issues discussed in class. The student demonstrated how "the passion of experience" (hooks 1994, 90) could be the primary foundation for telling a story in a way that clearly represented larger theoretical issues.

The importance of learning about and acknowledging the value of different kinds of theorizing was also brought home to me in a different educational context. The coordinator of the literacy center pointed out that looking at things from a larger perspective, or seeing the big picture, would assist the participants in the group to understand their struggles better, to be able to sort out the individual, the collective, and the more general social contributions to the devastations in their lives. She asked me to teach a reading-writing class where this larger perspective was nourished. She believed that my being an outsider would make the participants more willing to work on gaining a larger perspective. The coordinator thought that it could be precisely this clear, visible, and audible difference between me and the participants of the literacy group that would enable the women to gain their own personal distance to their daily troubles, and therefore also gain insights into possibilities of dealing with them.

In order to connect the personal and the more general, I carefully chose texts based on personal accounts, written or told by Black women, and that together gave an overview of the larger story of race, sexual difference, and class (Summers 1989). I gave homework assignments that asked the participants to write about the main points of the text, but that also asked them to answer one or two questions regarding their own personal experiences. Some of the texts were quite clear about issues such as racism or sexism. Looking at these texts individually, but also referring to the ones we had already read, assisted the participants in piecing together a complex portrayal of Black womanhood in white society. The women therefore learned about the history of Black people from perspectives that were quite diverse.

In addition, the stories were told by women who occupied or represented a multitude of different roles, telling about a large variety of experiences. These experiences sometimes covered a lifetime, sometimes only an episode in the narrator's life, illustrating a characteristic of women's autobiographies. Michelson (1996a, 645) reports on scholars who studied women's autobiographies and who remarked that they "do not typically show formal cohesion and completeness; they use discontinuous, fragmentary forms and circuitous narrative patterns." I believe that reading such pastiches assisted the literacy participants to make a connection to their own lives that were marked by many ruptures and discontinuities.

To see how one's own experience is placed in a larger, more encompassing context enriches one's understanding of this experience. It means drawing on *and* critically reflecting upon experience and perspective from the foundation (or standpoint) of one's ethical-political commitment to creating a better world. Within an explicit educational context, sharing knowledge therefore requires a kind of interaction that can be pedagogically (or politically) successful only when it goes beyond the formality of politely expressing opinions, or simply shouting at each other. Instead, such interaction would have to move in the direction of identifying with the Other, and seeing where the Other is part of one's own sense of self and therefore one's life (Harding 1991, 271). Conversely, it would mean being able to look at one's own experience, and the knowledges or ignorances contained in it, "from the outside" by looking at oneself as being different, the Other.

This is not to be understood, however, as another version of falling into the trap of what Rich (1979) called "white solipsism" where the Other, in this case Black people, are seen from a white perspective that omits "that group-based conflicts and . . . hierarchical power relations generate differences in group voice standpoint," power hierarchies are solidified rather than challenged (Collins 1997, 375). Seeing race as part of a relational framework therefore means seeing where whiteness and Otherness are placed within the social hierarchy. Race would not be looked at "from the viewpoint of the marginalized, but rather from a perspective that looks at the *relationship* of margin and center" (Maher and Tetreault 1996), without losing sight, however, of the divisions between margin and center. Clearly, for people who are members of the dominant group, the attainment of a "view from below" (Hart 1992), or a view that recognizes how whiteness defines Blackness as inferior Otherness, requires tremendous struggle. Moreover, such a view represents a substantial intellectual and emotional achievement.

Such an achievement requires a structural and political move, a "shifting of consciousness" (Hurtado 1996, 385). For a member of the centered group, this means assuming a view from the vantage point of people who are pushed to the margins of society. For people who have been marginalized, it means finding ways of expressing "subjugated forms of knowledge," that is, knowledge that is not "the central aspect of our language, emotion, or social structures" (385). Hurtado describes subjugated knowledge not in terms of knowledge that white people cannot or don't want to hear. Rather, she describes it in terms of a general absence of conceptual instruments for articulating this knowledge to a general public. By contrast, these instruments are in ample supply for articulating knowledge that emanates from and cements the dominant culture. Smith addresses this absence of a formally recognized language when she writes about experience being "through and through saturated with social relations, including the social relations of discourse" that determine the categories people use when describing their experiences, but also "what they cannot talk about" (394). Similarly, Hurtado states that the absence of officially given conceptual instruments creates the task of finding ways of naming the nameless, of "dismantling the webs that have previously constrained . . . consciousness" (385).

In light of the reality of multiple identities, however, and, correspondingly, multiple audiences, several different languages or "multiple voices (or multiple *lenguas* [tongues])" have to be developed that make it possible "to talk to different audiences without losing a sense of coherence" (385). That this is a struggle was demonstrated in one of my classes by a Black woman from Puerto Rico. She told the class how she is treated by white and Black Americans, but also by Latina/os or Puerto Ricans: All of them categorize her first as an African American, then as African when people detect a slight accent. Only when she starts speaking Spanish to Puerto Ricans is she recognized as a Puerto Rican of African descent (see also Hart 2001).

To discover and cherish thus-far unrecognized abilities is a multilayered, far-from-easy process. During my conversations with mothers living in public housing I once expressed concern about the fact that some of the women started crying when they talked about particularly troublesome aspects of their lives. One woman told me that this is part of the process of being able to talk about their own hardship to someone from outside their world. She also pointed out that talking about it helped the women to recognize and name their own strength, abilities, and knowledge as regards their caring labor, and to admire the intelligence, creativity, and stamina they had to muster on a daily and nightly basis.

CONSTRUCTIVE CONVERSATIONS

The women's stories, the affirmation they experienced by telling them, and the tremendous contribution these stories made to my own knowledge about motherwork were part of a constructive conversation. It was constructive because it provided the opportunity for articulating, building on, and thereby reconstructing existing knowledge. Although this process of constructing knowledge through conversation may differ, depending on the context and on who participates, it is a collaborative one, and the knowledge it produces is itself "more participatory and collective" (Hurtado 1996, 386).

It is through speech, through listening and talking to each other across divisions that a more complex and complete knowledge of the world can be created. This opens the question concerning what kinds of interaction would assist students in making different knowledge claims, and in telling stories from their lives in a way that would also be an invitation to respond, to agree, or to disagree.

In feminist/critical pedagogy the issue of dialogue has been discussed quite extensively, both as a condition and also as a goal.[9] Tarule describes dialogue as "making knowledge in conversation," as a form of group conversation where "ideas bounce around," where "all ideas are included, debated, contested, expanded" (1996, 280–81). Knowledge is therefore constructed through interaction, through "language-constituted relations." In other words, "learning occurs through conversation" (283). I want to use the concept of conversation. To some extent it seems to overlap with the notion of dialogue, but it also gives dialogue a broader, less structured, and less restrictive meaning. In addition, my practical use of the term is based on the recognition that "not all dialogues, discourses, or interpretations . . . are created equal. If 'we think because we can talk'. . ., then the kind of thinking possible is constrained or enhanced by the nature of the community" (285).

Alcoff (1991) criticizes a "discursive practice" where "more privileged persons" engage in an "imperialist speaking ritual," that is, they speak *for* rather than *with* others, thereby relying on or expanding their "own authority and privilege." She points out that "the problem with speaking for others exists in the very structure of discursive practice, no matter its context, and therefore it is this structure itself that needs alteration" (23). In formal educational settings these discursive practices clearly predominate. Not only is the teacher officially given the authority and privilege to speak for others, such as for "the oppressed," but students who are members of the dominant group also occupy a place in the nexus of social hierarchies, a place that guarantees or fosters a sense of entitlement to speak for others, especially for people from marginalized groups. For instance, when a white student claims that racism is a thing of the past, she or he clearly speaks for "non-white" people who may have a completely different perspective on the issue. Schutte therefore correctly points out that "unless exceptional measures are taken to promote good dialogue . . . the culture of the subaltern group will hardly be understood in its importance of complexity by those belonging to the culturally dominant group" (1998, 56).

A learning group can be considered a however transitional kind of community that mirrors larger social relations, manifested in who can speak and who is silenced or wants to remain silent, or what can and cannot be talked about. My understanding of conversation is therefore strongly influenced by Patricia Williams' use of the term in *The Rooster's Egg* (1995). Within the context of this book, the meaning of "conversation" is rooted in a vehement critique of social and political power relations, and it is an expression of her hope that the divisions created by these relations could be bridged through conversations. Her writings also make clear that conversation is not simply a process of exchanging different viewpoints but takes place only when people do indeed listen to each other. They may not, however, engage in a *reasoned* dialogue (Noddings 1991) where people explicitly justify the content of their contribution, or where they engage in a predictable, controlled, and continuous process of reflecting on, that is, mirroring, each other's viewpoints. As Ellsworth so aptly put it, this kind of communicative dialogue is an embodiment of pedagogical practices and rules that have been written about extensively. Communicative dialogue is based on the core question, "Do you understand?" and the expected answer is "Yes, I have stood under, I have taken your perspective upon myself, I can reflect it to you now in a way that you will recognize and expect—no surprises" (1997, 92). Engaging in a conversation would therefore allow for such surprises, for insights or responses that would bubble up from people's hearts or souls. Where a conversation becomes a form of political action, it allows for voices to be heard that are otherwise silenced or struck from public consciousness. It allows for an overflowing of reason and emotion, for understanding oneself and the other, *and* for giving space to the unknowable, incommensurable in oneself and in the other.

In a classroom this means creating the conditions for conversation where people truly speak and listen to each other. In an environment in which people are sensitive to each other's viewpoints without being confined to the pedagogical rules of showing that they "stand under" the other's perspective, divisions, and conflicts that are anchored in externally given and internalized power hierarchies would be allowed to emerge. Internalized oppression or oppressiveness may therefore also bubble up, turning the classroom into an emotionally taxing place. At the same time, commonalities may surface at different times during classroom interaction. They at least temporarily would take away the sting of emotionally rather risky maneuvers such as sharing deeply held beliefs or allowing others to see one's contribution to various forms of (self-)oppression. For instance, one of the commonalities students in my Motherwork class found was their having been in contact with the work of raising children, whether they were biological mothers or not. Such commonalities, however, did not obfuscate sharp divisions that clearly could not be bridged by engaging in a good communicative dialogue.

Listening is a core dimension of the relational matrix of constructive conversations. What Dorothy Smith says with respect to taking people's experience as a starting point for knowledge construction is true for the political act of listening as well: "People's tacit knowledge of what they know as a matter of daily/nightly practices surfaces as people speak and as what they speak of is taken seriously, undistilled, untranslated" (1997, 396). In educational situations where I am first of all a learner, an acknowledgment of power relations is essential, but it is only a small part. During my interviews of mothers living in public housing, I became a "listening partner" (Belenky, Bond, and Weinstock 1997). The authors of *A Tradition That Has No Name* engaged in a project whose explicit purpose was to "enable isolated mothers to gain a voice, claim the power of their good minds, and break out of their seclusion" (4). In their case, as in mine, this could only happen when listening had the strong ethical dimension of caring for the people who spoke and for what they were speaking about. In Schweickart's words, "the receptive agency of listening, like that of reading, is structurally analogous to the role Noddings attributes to one caring in a caring relation. Like one caring, the listener must care for the utterance of her interlocutor" (1996, 319).

I had the privilege of listening to stories that were often told with the "passion of experience" (hooks 1994). I assume this passion was behind the relative ease and at times amazing abundance with which the women talked. What certainly also attributed to their feeling relatively comfortable about telling me stories was the fact that they were in their own environment, and that they were surrounded by women they knew well. In addition, my greeting them with profound respect, and my expression of a sincere interest in their stories probably facilitated the crumbling of the general social wall of entrenched disinterest or misrepresentation. At the same time, although I listened quite attentively to the women and often felt the tremendous pain and anguish in their voices or saw it in their faces, I also knew—and I knew that they knew—I could only get a glimpse of the complexity of their experiences. While the women's lives had important yet incommensurable elements, I tried to recognize and acknowledge those elements. As Schutte points out, such a recognition "is fundamental to acquiring an understanding, even if only a partial understanding of the culturally differentiated 'other'" (63).

In retrospect, I can only guess the women accepted my listening as a kind of "gift," as "an enabling attention" given to their speech (Schweickart 1996, 320), but a gift they gave back to me by speaking about their lives. I was the one who wanted to learn, and this desire to learn was anchored in my profound interest in documenting their stories as an outsider, as someone representing the dominant social group. The work I had to do as an ally learner was to convey my commitment, and to listen. Clearly, my listening to people's stories about their lives in a way that let their tacit knowledge emerge meant keeping a constant check on my interpretations and staying critical of my perspective and of the preconceptualized knowledge I brought with me. Listening is undoubtedly a form of intense, "interpretive agency" (Schweickart 1996, 319) rather than a form of silent passivity. Nevertheless, the process of interpretation cannot bypass the critical dimension of scrutinizing the material with which one weaves one's interpretations.

EMBODIED KNOWING

Interviewing mothers living in public housing contained an element of mutual appreciation for what each side could bring to the conversation. It helped enlarge all our worlds. I believe that the explicit purpose of my interviews to document the strength and courage required to raise children in a public housing environment created an opening for our talking and listening to each other. But the women were certainly also enticed to talk because someone from the outside wanted to listen to people who were either entirely invisible to the outside public, or who were portrayed in derogatory terms by the media. In addition, they could talk about work that is otherwise socially unacknowledged or stigmatized, especially when it relates to children in whom this society has no interest. Corresponding skills and knowledges that are lodged in or generated by the experience of doing this kind of labor have no official name, or they are "concealed" by this society (see Michelson 1996a, 640 for making a similar point). In the lifestories Luttrell collected, the women grouped these knowledges under the names of "housewifewise" or "motherwise" (1997, 13). By contrasting these terms with "schoolwise," the women revealed a split in their own evaluation of their abilities. On the one hand they emphasized the usefulness of this common-sense type of knowledge as it represented their ability to problem-solve, and to "balance a lot of things, if that counts." On the other hand, they did not classify this knowledge in terms of "real intelligence" (30).

Knowing in more analytical ways, that is, being able to name the nameless and share it with others therefore means developing a language. What Helmbold says with respect to documenting the experiences of working-class women has general validity: In order to articulate the knowledge garnered from experience, and in order to be able to share it with others, people have to "make the leap from story-telling to theory" (1998, 16). Theorizing does not, however, leave behind the embodied social subject. A critical analysis of experience has to include an understanding of the way experience is embedded in the power nexus of social relations *and* that experience has a material, corporeal underside.

The women's story-telling often had a strong visceral dimension, especially when accompanied by pain and fear, or when it tapped into a body memory of physical violence. This visceral dimension is fully woven into the bodily dimension of people's identities, and into the way information about social/cultural hierarchies is stamped into body memory (Kadi 1996, 74). The body therefore signifies a primary although "enigmatic place . . . in the making of subjectivity or identity" (Canning 1994, 373).

Embodied forms of knowledge are lodged in the lived experience, or "in the local particularities of the everyday/everynight worlds in which our bodily being anchors us" (Smith 1997, 393). These knowledges are therefore embedded in "a way of knowing that is often expressed through the body, what it knows, what has been deeply inscribed on it through experience. This complexity of experience can rarely be voiced and named from a distance. It is a privileged location from which one can know" (hooks 1994, 91). An epistemology that values this kind of knowing therefore does not set body and mind into an oppositional, hierarchical relationship. It is fundamentally different from typical Western masculinist epistemologies that rest on the dualism of "reflection/experience, knowledge/skill, and theory/practice," a dualism which underlies "all versions of the mind/body split and the privileging of mind over body" (Michelson 1998, 218). The opposites between mind and body, or rationality and matter, "originate in a twofold concealment: of the woman's body and of labor power" (Michelson 1996a, 640). This is an extremely important point because it implies an epistemology that entails a two-tiered dismissal of the body, and of work related to or directly affecting the body.

First, Michelson's quote includes a reference to a dichotomous split that underlies all economic relations, and that influences one's position in the payment structure: the split between manual and mental labor. Kadi vividly describes how this split can easily be excluded from analyses of other, related dichotomies: "In the years I spent in Women's Studies, we spent hours and hours analyzing the superficial nature of dualistic thinking around men/women, white/black, and thinking/feeling, and reflected on more complicated and realistic understandings. But we never touched on the smart/stupid, rich/poor breakdown" (1996, 51). She breaks through the "classist myth" by stating that "capitalism relies on rich people having uninterrupted access to poor people's bodies. Otherwise, how would work get done?" (78). Thus, ways of knowing and knowledge construction that do away with the mind/body split cannot ignore how social-economic arrangements affect the laboring body, or *"bodies in and of labor"* (Ebert 1996, 236). It is difficult to valorize the body where working conditions are not only exhausting, but often, especially in global factories of transnational capital, pushing people to the limits of survival. Second, Michelson describes how the hierarchical opposites between mind and body, or nature and culture originate in the dual concealment of the woman's body and of labor power. In Mohanty's words women's bodies and labor are therefore used to "consolidate global dreams, desires, and ideologies of success and the good life" (1997, 10).

An "economic epistemology" that underlies the classist myth excludes and marginalizes women's experience, thus replicating a masculinist hierarchy of meanings and value. This masculinist hierarchy includes assigning work to women "that men do not want to do for themselves, especially the care of everyone's bodies—the bodies of men, of babies and children, of old people, of the sick, and of their own bodies. And they are assigned responsibilities for the local places where those bodies exist as they clean and maintain their own and others' houses and workplaces" (Harding 1998, 152). Subsistence/motherworkers are concerned with sustaining life, and they are therefore bound up with our corporeal foundation, our bodies. As Harding writes:

As professional healers, midwives, and nurses, women have been repositories for and developers of knowledge about everybody else's bodies. Women's knowledge of our own bodies often has proved more reliable than modern biomedicine's diagnoses. Women today, as in the past, perform much of the daily care of sick and aging relatives and develop distinctive patterns of knowledge that often enable them to diagnose what ails their elderly kin more accurately than can physicians and other health care workers. (106)

Harding continues her account of the production and sustenance of different patterns of knowledge (and ignorance) by linking them to mothering activities where women—or men—need to develop such patterns "in order to address the challenges such responsibilities entail" (106). These responsibilities tie us to material necessities such as food and shelter, necessities that make us dependent on the work that provides them.

Educational practices that are based on a "sexual epistemology of economics" (Beasley 1994) are oriented toward healing the mind/body split. These practices are therefore grounded in actual and transformational ways of living and working. It is a pedagogical challenge par excellence to include the bodily dimension of knowing, the fact that vital knowledge is not disembodied, into one's educational endeavors, especially in an institution of higher education where "mind" is automatically accorded privilege. Thus, although people's bodily presence and the different categorical markings their bodies carry influence all educational interactions, this is either ignored or explicitly denied.

In many educational situations people still share a space, and their interactions with each other are not (yet?) technologically mediated. They are therefore physically present. Bodily appearance, degree of able-bodiedness, skin color and "phenotype" (Hurtado 1996, 377), voice, shape, or age play into how one is seen or approached, how one is identified or which identity one gives to oneself. Although all these identities are social constructs, they have a bodily, visible dimension that goes beyond or underlies the social in a very concrete, material, or "natural" way. Dibernard, for example, discusses how the definition of "a person with a disability" contains a number of social constructs, but that it is an identity with a strong physical component (1996, 137). The bodily or physical dimension of people's identities is always present in our educational endeavors, even if it does not have an explicit name. Michelson makes this point very clear in an essay called "Re-membering: The Return of the Body to Experiential Learning" (1998). She analyzes how the "long-standing Western contempt for the body" directly structures the adult education staple of experiential learning, and she describes how the infamous mind/body split legitimizes the hierarchical ordering of knowledge and corresponding kinds of knowledge-practices (218). As she points out, this split underlies the nonbodily construction of officially valid knowledge. It is therefore invisible. It takes the members of the most centered group, white men, out of the realm of corporeality. In an ironic but significant twist, Michelson not only calls for re-membering knowledge-practices but also demands a re-attaching, or re-"membering" of the male sexual organ "onto the body of a male" so that he can no longer "posture as the ungendered, universal human" (231).

EPISTEMOLOGICAL AND CULTURAL BORDER-CROSSINGS

My concern for life-affirming ways of living and working lies at the heart of my attempts to foster and develop a subsistence perspective. It is a perspective that affirms and nourishes life-sustaining desires and hopes, and that therefore undermines the division between reason and emotion that accompanies the mind/body split of masculinist epistemologies. Motherwork is a form of subsistence work, and it provides numerous parallels for educational work that is likewise life-oriented. The multifaceted, complex tasks that comprise motherwork intricately combine intellectual and emotional demands that cannot be neatly separated. In my classrooms I therefore try to create the discursive *and* emotional space needed for moving in the direction of "subsistence knowing" (Hart 1992), highlighting the ethical-political implications of this kind of knowing or knowledge construction.

As discussed in *Working and Educating for Life* (Hart 1992), knowledge, skills, and abilities which are shaped as well as presupposed by an education for life are varied and complex. They range from the intuition-based, noncognitive "feel" for and awareness of one's own as well as others' individual uniqueness and difference to a relentless critical scrutiny of individual and social phenomena. Intuitive knowing, based on the positive act of respect and affirmation, is therefore fully intertwined with the critical, evaluative stance of participating in the other's reality. It is such a stance that gives meaning to the requirement of taking the other seriously. Empathetic understanding of the other and critically evaluating aspects of her story are therefore not separate, but only different moments in a combined, dialectical process. Both are embedded in the overall concern for power-free forms of interaction and communication that likewise encompasses the motivational as well as cognitive-critical realm of acting and learning, requiring both a desire for such social relations as well as the ability to recognize and criticize existing structures of dominance (197). As previously discussed, lived experience is a key criterion for meaning, and symbolic representations of this experience are structured dialogically rather than monologically. That means that knowledge claims are inserted in an interactive knowledge validation process. It is part of the African-American cultural tradition that in order for ideas "to be tested and validated, everyone in the group must participate" (Collins 1990, 213).

In a chapter on Afrocentric feminist epistemology, Collins writes that "the narrative method requires that the story be told, not torn apart in analysis, and trusted as core belief, not 'admired as science'" (210). Many stories, narratives, and Bible tales are applicable to the lived experience of African Americans, and they are "often told for the wisdom they express about everyday life." And, as Collins emphasizes, "the distinction between knowledge and wisdom, and the use of experience as the cutting edge dividing them, has been key to Black women's survival" (208). However, a corresponding alternative epistemology is impossible without its direct link to an ethic of caring that suggests that "personal expressiveness, emotions, and empathy are central to the knowledge validation process" (215).

By listening to poor mothers' narratives, I have been learning more about variations and intricacies of the epistemology of subsistence knowing, and it has helped me in my own learning process of becoming a listener who is more attuned to the often subtle or intricate ways students demonstrate such ways of knowing in my college classes. Some of the women—and Jenna more than anybody else—were doing theory in a non-Western way. As Christian points out, "people of color know about a kind of theorizing which is different from 'the Western form of abstract logic'" (1990, 336). It can be expressed in "narrative form, in the stories we create, in riddles and proverbs, in the play with language, since dynamic rather than fixed ideas seem more to our liking." Due to my European intellectual training, it has been an ongoing learning process for me to see the making of theory in quite different ways and to see how the "epistemologies rooted in Africa construct a different relationship between 'theoretical' knowledge and embodied, emotional experience" (Michelson 1996b, 450). I quickly learned, however, to appreciate the opportunity of listening to Black mothers' stories about living and raising children in public housing. As a European American middle-class woman, I engaged in cultural *and* epistemological border-crossing by coming in contact with and learning to appreciate "culturally local discursive legacies" (Harding 1998, 151). The mothers told their stories in rather complex, dynamic ways, and they often played with language or with the way different audiences would interpret the meaning of their stories. This playfulness was nourished by a unique African American tradition of using language, or theorizing, and it was precisely this tradition that wonderfully captured the multitude and complexity of psychological, spiritual, physical, and intellectual tasks and responsibilities associated with motherwork.

Subsistence/motherwork is place-bound, and it relies on and generates local, embodied knowledges. Like all local or regional knowledges, it contains assumptions and theories that "have been generated within social experiences, relations, traditions, and historically and culturally specific ways of organizing social life" (Nelson 1993, 147). Social groups therefore constitute epistemological communities that are identified in terms of shared knowledge, standards, and practice (149).

Subsistence/motherworkers are, of course, not a monolithic social group or community, but rather a subcommunity within a larger group whose cultural and political identity may make all its members socially (and politically) strangers or outsiders to the dominant cultures and practices that structure their lives (Harding 1998, 155). However, all subsistence/motherworkers share the fact that the labor they perform is socially devalued or ignored, and this social invisibility is part and parcel of a general cultural and epistemological predominance of white, masculinist, and classist values and meanings. Aside from being local or place-bound, these knowledges are therefore situated within a larger, hierarchically organized, and power-driven social-political context. In other words they are *situated knowledges*, and they are conducive to the construction of a standpoint that seems to "promise more adequate, sustained, objective, transforming accounts of the world" than the one constructed from the perspective of the "conquering gaze from nowhere" (Haraway 1988, 584, 581).

In earlier writings I addressed the importance of assuming "the standpoint of the oppressed" in order to burst through the confines of the allegedly generally valid but actually partial and distorting "view from above" (Hart 1992).[10] The standpoint of the oppressed assumes a view from below, and "to see from below is neither easily learned or unproblematic, even if 'we' 'naturally' inhabit the great underground terrain of subjugated knowledges" (Haraway 1988, 584). As a learned, and therefore achieved, standpoint, it exposes the power-based injustice of social relations, and how our everyday worlds "are knitted into the extended social relations of a contemporary capitalist economy and society" (Smith 1987, 110).

Although a standpoint is situated in the particularities of the everyday world, extended social relations are not discoverable from within the experience of these particularities. Although standpoint theorists such as Nancy Hartsock, Dorothy Smith, and Alison Jaggar have been criticized for not sufficiently translating experience, or material reality, into an achieved political standpoint, they make clear that a standpoint is not reducible to experience because the webbed connections between experience and extended social relations are not discoverable within its boundaries. As Harding (1998) points out, the lives and experiences of marginalized groups offer an "epistemic privilege." They have a group interest in asking questions that dominant groups have a strong interest in avoiding, devaluing, and silencing; however, "the answers to such questions are never completely to be found in those experiences or lives" (151). Epistemic privilege can be realized if members of such groups, or people who belong to the dominant groups, recognize that the most critical questions arise from the everyday lives of nondominant groups, and that they only provide the starting point for larger critical, counterhegemonic analyses. Harding asserts that "for the answers, one must examine critically the dominant conceptual frameworks that reflect disproportionately the interests of dominant groups" (151). This is similar to Dorothy Smith's suggestion of constructing the everyday world as a problematic, directing "attention to a possible set of questions that have yet to be posed or of puzzles that are not yet formulated as such but are 'latent' in the actualities of our experienced worlds" (1987, 110).

In Collins's words, a standpoint is not reducive to having or interpreting experiences the same way. Instead, "standpoint theory posits a distinctive relationship among a group's position in hierarchical power relations, the experiences attached to differential group positionality, and the standpoint that a group constructs in interpreting these experiences" (1998, 193–94). Collins moves into one of the contested terrains of standpoint theory: its relationship to individual and group identity, and to the complexity of multiple identities and thus multilocality. Although Smith addressed the issue of relations among multiple everyday worlds more than a decade before Collins's discussion of standpoint theory, she did not extend her analysis to the crissccrossing of multiple identities within individuals or social groups. Collins calls for examining "how intersectionality might relate to situated standpoints" (210). She reminds the reader to go back to the origins of standpoint theory "in a more general theory of economic class relations," especially since it sheds light on race-class intersectionality (211). Not only does race create "immutable group identities" (204) that are enhanced by residential segregation, other exclusionary practices such as employment discrimination also characterize the race-class intersectionality in the United States (218). African-American women therefore find themselves in a shared but not uniform location in hierarchical power relations, a location marked by "heterogeneous commonality" (224). Because of the visible, spatial structure of African-American group identity, Collins finds standpoint theory more applicable to race-class intersectionality than to gender relations:

Because women are distributed across a range of race-class groups, all women confront the initial task of developing a shared understanding of their common interests as women. However, they must do so in close proximity to, and often in sexualized love relationships with, members of the group that allegedly oppresses them. Since women must first construct a self-definition as a member of a group, ideas may precede the building of actual group relations. Women certainly know other women within their own race, economic, ethnic, and/or citizenship groups, but most have difficulty seeing their shared interests across the vast differences that characterize women as a collectivity. The process of constructing a group standpoint for women differs dramatically from that confronting groups with histories of group-based segregated spaces. Women come to know themselves as members of a political collectivity through ideas that construct them as such. (221–22)

Collins certainly lays bare a key aspect of the difficulty women encounter when constructing their own group identity across this vast range of differences that are inserted differently in a variety of power relations. Although she emphasizes the origins of standpoint theory in Marxian economic analyses, she does not address the material grounding of Hartsock's feminist standpoint in the material reality of the sexual division of labor, that is, in the intersectionality of sex and class. Not does one's sexual anatomy contributing to a rather immutable group identity, and thereby to an affliction that follows every woman into the paid labor force, but one's sex also carries the heavy weight of doing the unpaid work of caring, or—in the case of middle- or upper-class mothers—of being responsible for contracting this work out to other women for minimal pay. A feminist standpoint would see how the sexual division of labor has the property of being systematic. Although Haraway refers to world history when she talks about "a centrally structured global system with deep filaments and tenacious tendrils into time, space, and consciousness" (1988, 588), her metaphors certainly fit a description of how the sexual division of labor likewise reaches into all women's lived experiences. As such, it can provide a common thread for developing a feminist standpoint that "picks out and amplifies the liberatory possibilities contained in . . . experience" (Hartsock 1983, 232).

Identifying epistemic privilege does not simply add to the stock of socially acknowledged, valid knowledge by pointing to cultural diversity or the existence of "ethnoknowledges" (Harding 1998, 159). Cultural differences crisscross with political ones, just as a standpoint is constructed out of the experiences of shared histories and shared location within power relations. Without cross-cultural understanding, and without border-crossings among vectors of oppression, "liberatory epistemologies" cannot be developed (Pryse 1998, 9). Liberatory epistemologies recognize "power differences within or between cultures [that] also create different opportunities for systematic knowledge and systematic ignorance" (Harding 1998, 151). Pryse talks about epistemological coalition-building as a means to develop liberatory epistemologies, and she places this endeavor within the framework of standpoint theories. As previously stated, assuming the standpoint of nondominant groups can lead to asking the most critical questions about the nature of social-political structures of dominance. Assuming the perspective of people whose social location offers epistemic privileges also means assuming the standpoint of everyday life and examining how one's social location is concretely experienced, and what knowledges and ignorances are generated by these experiences.

With respect to learning and experience, it is therefore particularly important to see that a standpoint is broader than an experience and broader than a perspective. It is broader because it does not "naturalize" experience by giving it the primary authority for locating and constructing knowledge, thereby separating people into autonomous, socially unrelated entities (Ebert 1996, 118). It is broader than a perspective since it may be critical of certain aspects of a particular perspective. While it is necessary to understand how this perspective is rooted in culturally sanctioned knowledge claims, it is also important to critically evaluate these local, cultural assumptions and interests in order to see whether some of them may not only *not* be contributing to creating a more just and livable world but may actually help to maintain an unjust world. Clearly, such a critique goes "beneath the appearances created by an unjust social order" and is therefore more than a process of "opening one's eyes" (Harding 1991, 127). Instead, it is strongly linked to actually struggling for the creation of a better world where hierarchical relations between inside and outside, margin and center are absent. In Haraway's words,

"Our" problem is how to have *simultaneously* an account of radical historical contingency for all knowledge claims and knowing subjects, a critical practice for recognizing our own 'semiotic technologies' for making meanings, *and* a no-nonsense commitment to faithful accounts of a "real" world, one that can be practically shared and that is friendly to earthwide projects of finite freedom, adequate material abundance, modest meaning in suffering, and limited happiness. (1988, 579)

To engage in epistemological coalition-building therefore includes the ethical commitment to creating a more just and livable world. This means connecting local, situated, embodied forms of knowledge with an awareness of the global and of how the multitude of cultural-regional differences are embedded in the global matrix of interdependence, especially as shaped by the global market, which hierarchically orders "sites of the production of worker and/or consumer subjectivities" (Code 1998, 80). Liberatory coalition-building therefore does not mean wandering around the Global Cultural Bazaar or the Global Shopping Mall but understanding how these webs are intersecting with the Global Workplace and the Global Financial Network[11] and how they feed on "racialized ideologies of masculinity, femininity, and sexuality" (Mohanty 1997, 10).

To create a multicultural classroom and a multicultural teaching/learning approach means looking at groups of people, such as mothers, or women, seeing how they form sub-groups within their own racial-ethnic or cultural communities, and seeing how they have commonalities based on fundamental similarities in the work they do. Examining the lives and experiences of disparate groups in terms of how their material-cultural location enables and constrains their own process of knowledge-creation is itself a knowledge-gleaning process. This process can "open up into informal comparison and critique, both epistemological and moral-political," and it can move across "links, affinities, and generalities that [are] never absolute but always negotiable," and therefore "also neither assmililative or divisive" (Code 1998, 78).

CONCLUSIONS

In many ways, the provisionality and ambiguity of knowledges that result from such a process are structurally similar to the knowledge that is shaped by the work of raising children. As I wrote in *Working and Educating for Life* (1992), because the mother is in contact with the continuously changing nature of her child, and, consequently of her task, the mother's knowledge can never be finished or absolute, but must remain tentative and provisional. It is constantly affirmed or disaffirmed, created and recreated. In *Schoolsmart and Motherwise* Luttrell makes similar observations. When the women she interviewed talked bout their common-sense knowledge they referred to knowledge that was "part of their caregiving activities and relationships with others." This knowledge is of a kind that "comes in flashes," that is "emotional, relational, individual, and particularized; it is geared towards meeting (individual) needs. The women themselves emphasized feelings and intuitions, not the thoughts that enabled them "to do what you have to do as a mother." Just like society at large, the women conflate the knowledge of care "with affect, feelings, and intuition, while the cognitive, learned, and thoughtful dimension of how women acquire this commonsense/motherwise knowledge gets masked" (1997, 31).

Furthermore, since children and adults live in different worlds, and adults can never fully know what it means to experience the world from a two-year-old's perspective, Lugones's (1990) concept of "playful 'world'-traveling" is useful here. Playful world-traveling can refer to the ability to travel to the world of the child and get a glimpse of it without imperialistically occupying or appropriating it. This danger is set up in advance due to the unequal power relations between adult and child. However, trying to be vigilant against falling into the traps set up by one's pregiven adult power can assist in being, or becoming equally vigilant against tendencies towards "cultural imperialism," and in listening to someone from a different, nondominant culture responsibly and vigilantly (Code 1998, 81).

As illustrated in this chapter, educational processes that are attuned to liberatory cultural and epistemological border-crossings do not confront learners with the completeness of certain predetermined or predefined knowledges. Instead, knowledges that are shaped by the learning situation itself, and that are constantly created and recreated, ambiguous and provisional, are allowed to emerge. These knowledges have multiple sources: subjective and objective, social and individual, about self and about others. Since in principle all learners contribute equally to the process of knowledge-creation, it cannot be determined from the outset who will learn from whom. Different sources of knowledge combine in an endless variety of ways, but they are embedded in the common medium of critically examining and revisioning this world. This calls for "stretching the limits of imagination(s) toward responsive and responsible local sensitivity, both close to and far from 'home'" (Code 1998, 74). It means to move in the direction of ecological thinking, or into holistic ways of knowing that do not place mind and body, Black and white, North and South into hierarchical opposition to each other.

NOTES

1. Although most people around me were poor, there was no stigma attached to poverty, a stigma that emanates from the cultural image of an intelligent, educated, and successful middle class. Poverty was not a theme in my childhood, and it was not measured against what it did not represent, as it is in the United States. Because of the absence of any contrasting images, especially since there was no television that portrayed the haves in contrast to the have-nots, and because of the mix of factory workers, crafts people, and farmers in my neighborhood, there was also no middle-class group membership temptingly waiting on the horizon of individual success—a trope of today's media-controlled American culture.

2. Linkon (1999) addresses the fact that the notion of class rarely comes up in conversations with colleagues at her college, although race and gender regularly do. When she is teaching, students greet the notion of class with silence, confusion, or downright resistance. The contributions to her anthology *Teaching Working Class* provide excellent examples of incorporating social class into course design and pedagogical approaches in a variety of different academic disciplines, but also in educational settings outside of a university. While the issues concerning working-class students and working-class academics differ with respect to local culture, "race, gender, sexuality, age, and so on," the working/middle-class polarity nevertheless underlies images of class membership that keep students silent. See also the special issue of *Women's Studies Quarterly*, titled *Working-Class Lives and Cultures* (1998), for discussions of teaching and learning about the multifocal reality of class, and of the growing trend of establishing working-class studies in universities.

3. Reay here utilizes Bourdieu's (1984) notion of cultural capital, a concept that has been used and interpreted in a variety of different contexts (see, for instance, Lamont and Lareau 1988).

4. Luttrell tells a story about how the academic disinterest in working-class stories and experiences is not absent in the arena of women's studies either. At a regional

women's studies conference, nobody showed up to listen to her presentation on working-class women learners except two students and two staff members of the Women's Program at which she worked (1997,17).

5. Various contributions to *Teaching Working Class* (Linkon 1999) address this issue, in particular Pari's essay on "Writing the Personal."

6. In some ways Hurtado here repeats the social bifurcation of male and female, or feminine and masculine. Not all children, or adults, automatically associate with one or the other sex.

7. Jensen and Zandy (both in *Working-Class Lives and Cultures*) write about the pain involved in crossing class lines. As Jensen writes, "Crossing classes means redrawing one's internal map so dramatically that the outer and inner landmarks will never again match up in a way that could lead one home for a visit" (1998, 213).

8. By acknowledging the knowledges and competencies that are rooted in local cultures outside of the academy, it is also possible to discover similarities between different working-class cultures and therefore bridge the race-ethnicity divide. Esposito, for instance, shows that similarities in speaking patterns demonstrate "similarities between black and white class systems" (1999, 230).

9. See, for instance, Ellsworth 1997; Kenway and Modra 1992; and Tarule 1996.

10. This view represents "the purportedly universal perspective which is in fact local, historical, and subjective: only members of the ruling groups are permitted to elevate the perspective from their lives to uniquely legitimate ones" (Harding 1991, 273). What I called the standpoint of the oppressed is based on a belief I share with Haraway (1988): "There is good reason to believe that vision is better from below the brilliant space platforms of the powerful." With Haraway I therefore argue against "various forms of unlocatable, and so irresponsible knowledge claims. Irresponsible means unable to be called into account"(581). This is not the place to go into a discussion of postmodernist or deconstructionist criticisms aimed at standpoint theory, especially those voiced by certain versions of these rather complex, far-from-uniform theories. Nevertheless, I agree with Haraway's observation that relativism is one of the results of extreme poles of postmodern and deconstructionist thinking, where everything is part of "the powerful art of rhetoric" and where "the 'equality' of positioning is a denial of responsibility and critical inquiry." In that sense "relativism is a way of being nowhere while claiming to be everywhere simultaneously" (577).

11. Mohanty here draws on Richard J. Barnet and John Cavanagh's *Global Dreams: Imperial Corporations and the New World Order* (1994, 114–15).

— Chapter 6 —

Creating and Sustaining Life and Community

A new generation of women leaders is carrying out an invisible revolution.
All over the globe women have been asserting collective rights to protect
their children against pollution, disease, and homelessness. Not content
merely to fight for improvement in the lives of their families and communities, many of these women justify their action by making broad claims about
human needs and rights according to an interpretation of justice that they
themselves are developing through their actions.

—Temma Kaplan, *Crazy for Democracy*

Individually and collectively, poor women are engaged in daily and nightly
struggles against the practical implications of social inequality, poverty, and
environmental devastation. Many of the issues the women address are therefore
related to basic survival, such as health, food, shelter, the availability of jobs
that offer a livable wage, and better educational opportunities for their children.

As described in chapters 2 and 4, in the case of African Americans in Chicago, decades of race-bound residential segregation are now fully enmeshed in
global and local economic restructuring processes. A general social-political
disinvestment in the postindustrial or "post-Fordist" city (Jezierski 1995) therefore disregards the basic human needs of many of its residents. This is true not
only for Chicago, but for other cities as well. For instance, the Anglo- and African-American women in Grand Rapids, Michigan, whose lives Peake (1997)
explored with respect to a "social geography of the city," spent all their financial
resources on rather elemental needs such as shelter, heating, and food, and
"nothing on items and services that are commonly seen as constituting basic
needs, such as education, health insurance, child care, and life insurance" (352).

Faced with the many repercussions of poverty, racism, and sexism, individual struggles often mean simply trying to stay afloat, making it from day to day,

or even being surprised at one's survival (Childers 1997, 98). Clearly, on a microlevel these struggles are in need of social or communal support by kin, friends, neighbors, a church, or other—however informal—community groups or organizations. While there is a strong tradition of collective struggles among poor working-class women, on a macrolevel there is also "a nexus of social, political, and economic forces that are sometimes regional, sometimes global and almost always serve the interests of others besides poor women" (Orleck 1997a, 105). It is this nexus that shapes the possibilities and limitations of collective struggles.

Middle-class researchers like myself can easily fall into the trap of disregarding the silent and invisible survival struggles of many poor women, focusing instead on organizational, collective efforts that are more visible to an outsider, and therefore easier to write about. As Childers (1997) observes,

Generalizing broadly about the lives of poor women like the women on welfare . . . makes it easy to transform them into a tableau for the historical imagination. Frozen in time, they represent what many of us yearn for: evidence of virtual collectives of poor women struggling and striving together. This tableau also pleases because it directly displaces the mirage so often offered in the media: the characterization of a group called "welfare mothers" as though they all have the same psychology and belong to some separate, lazy, dangerous species. (95)

Nevertheless, trying to examine what kind of life-affirming traditions, abilities, values, and life orientations have been in danger of being destroyed by the social-economic meltdown of central cities, and why, does not allow one to disregard these traditions and values. They are still carried out in ordinary women's ordinary everyday lives. It also does not allow one to neglect examining where they are sustained and acted upon in however beleaguered form. Peake, for instance, examined the racialized nature of women's everyday experiences with poverty in the social space of a city. She interviewed urban neighborhood organizers and reports that they "stressed the difficulty of finding individuals who were interested in community level change, saying: 'It's a very rare individual that sees beyond issues of their own street and wants to become involved.'" By probing further into the lives of Anglo- and African-American women, however, she also observed that

some of the women did have a vision of society in which people had control of their lives. A large proportion of women . . . belonged to organizations. . . . Overwhelmingly, it was African-American women who were most concerned about their neighborhood—they had to develop a resilience in the face of racialized deprivation, poverty, and discrimination and were concerned with their rights to a safe, secure, and economically sound existence for themselves and their households. (357)

The fact that African-American women expressed more concerns about their neighborhood than white women is certainly related, although not reducible, to the phenomenon of hypersegregation. Three-fourths of African Americans live in highly segregated areas in most metropolitan areas. Massey and Fischer (1998) point to the severe spatial segregation of poor African Americans, compounding a concentration of poverty that surpasses that of poor whites, Asians, or Latinos.

To be concerned with a safe, secure, and economically sound existence for one's household includes being concerned with the lives of one's present and future children, and thus with the future of one's community. As Krauss (1998) succinctly stated it, "Women's visions of environmental justice and social inequality are mediated by subjective experiences and interpretations and rooted in the political truths they construct out of their identities as mothers and members of specific communities" (149). Terms such as activist mothers (Naples), mother-activists (Jetter), or community othermothers (Collins) try to capture the interplay of concerns for the well-being of children—their own or those of others—and for a larger community. I want to link these terms, the concerns underlying them, and the work associated with or resulting from them, with the notion of subsistence work and, correspondingly, a subsistence orientation. As discussed throughout the book, these terms have broader, more encompassing meanings than those generally associated with the term "mother" or "mothering practices." While their meanings are primarily grounded in the experience of motherhood—whatever that means, depending on the cultural context in which it occurs—they do not have to be reduced to this experience. Instead, they can branch out in many different directions. At the same time the numerous kinds of poor mothers' political struggles are united in a profound way. Their concerns and activities are related to the experience of a kind of work that does not fall under the official rubric of profit-producing and therefore "productive" labor.[1] Instead, it is work that is oriented toward nourishing and affirming rather than extracting from life.

As described in various chapters of this book, motherwork is a form of subsistence work. When viewed through the lenses of a life-affirming perspective, motherwork is valued for embracing its dependence on the biological or "natural" dimensions of giving birth to a child, and of working and living with the child's many biological changes. By looking at motherwork as a form of subsistence work that is anchored in and transcends biology, or "nature," by seeing its interconnectedness with social and cultural forces, this fundamental material foundation of life is acknowledged and respected rather than denied or abhorred. The fact that we have bodies that are moving through a complex biological process from birth to death is therefore neither seen as a blemish or a burden, nor does it become prey for commercial and medical exploitation. In that sense motherwork, like any other kind of subsistence work, is "both burden and pleasure. It does not promise bread without sweat nor imply a life of toil and tears" (Mies and Shiva 1993, 320; see also Hart 1992).

Because motherwork can indeed not be done without sweat, it can easily be lumped together with other kinds of devalued work that administer to the body and its needs. A deep-seated abhorrence of this kind of work is so entrenched in the collective Western psyche that it is not uncommon to have child care listed with other "chores," such as cleaning or doing the laundry. There are several issues at work here. One is the fact that diminishing resources such as time and money magnify the burdensome aspect of motherwork by making it more and more all-absorbing. At the same time, while raising a growing human being is fundamentally different from doing the laundry, these "chores" are internally connected to the Western ideal of femininity, and therefore also to what is considered typical women's work. The low status of women's work is clearly indicated by the word chores, thereby reiterating the tradition of its social, cultural, and material devaluation.

To look at motherwork from the larger perspective of subsistence work helps to acknowledge the tremendous variety of mothering practices that differ according to class, race, ethnicity, cultural origin, or nationality, *and* to identify some core issues concerning the relationship of these practices to the richness, diversity, and nurturance of current as well as future life. Such acknowledgment also helps to examine how motherwork provides a springboard for political action and what aspects can serve as guides for a kind of political involvement that recognizes and works with all dimensions of life. If subsistence work is fundamental to survival, and to acknowledging and affirming the richness of life, so is political work emanating from it, connected with it, or branching out from it, because it takes up fundamental issues of life and death. It is political work that is embedded in the life-affirming work of mothering. It is therefore not surprising that "in the history of poor people's struggles for subsistence in the United States, mothers have always played a central role" (Orleck 1997b, 87).

This opens up many questions. Where and how is a life-affirming subsistence orientation still alive, under what however beleaguered conditions? What are some concrete examples of poor mothers being engaged in subsistence struggles? What are their chances of bringing about fundamental social change?

THE SPARK OF RADICAL CHANGE

The primary motivation of mother-activists or community othermothers for getting involved in political action is the well-being of the children, "the freshest link in the web of reciprocal obligation" (Lemke-Santangelo 1996, 146). To look at motherwork within the larger framework of a subsistence perspective that is oriented toward the fullness and richness of all life means to see how mother-activists make a leap from a concern for the well-being of their own children to that of all children in their community. Lois Gibbs, who has been a major organizer of the "Housewives at Love Canal," therefore states quite succinctly that

Mothers have a particular role to play because mothers are the ones who are most passionate about the future of our children. They're the ones who are willing to take those extra steps to protect the future of those children because they are the childbearers, because they are the nurturers, because they are the ones who think generation to generation. . . . And I think that they're critical to the environmental justice movement and to the environmental movement in general. (1997, 43)

Gilkes (1994) points out that this critical, all-encompassing perspective poses the "largest political threat to the dominant society" (242). With respect to some core principles of the capitalist political economy, a concern for one's own children that expands into a critique of an unjust society can be perceived as a violation of private property rights. The African American history is replete with manifestations of a strong communal tradition that includes the nurturing of children by extended family networks. Within that context, private property rights are unimportant, at least in the social-cultural meaning of the word. As Collins writes, "By seeing the larger community as responsible for children and by giving othermothers and other nonparents 'rights' in child rearing, African Americans challenge prevailing property relations. It is in this sense that traditional bloodmother/othermother relationships in women-centered networks are revolutionary" (1990,123). "Kitchen-table activism" therefore bears a radical seed. Where that seed is nurtured, mothers who work on behalf of their own children can and will then expand their work into "a broader political engagement on behalf of other children, moving beyond familiar concerns," addressing "pressing social and political issues of national import" (Orleck 1997c, 17, 4).

The larger social and cultural context in which motherwork takes place can structure its reality and experience in fundamentally different ways. Likewise, mother-led movements, both in the United Sates and in other parts of the world, employ a wide range of quite diverse strategies. In light of this tremendous diversity and complexity, Orleck asks an important question: "How does our sense both of politics and of motherhood change if we accept the idea that, for many women in cultures around the world, motherhood is a powerful political identity around which they have galvanized broad-based and influential movements for social change?"(7).

The anthology *The Politics of Motherhood* (Jetter, Orleck, and Taylor 1997) contains many descriptions of such politics in different social and cultural contexts. Not only do these different mothers have very little in common, but even within their very own societies they are sometimes divided by caste, class, race-ethnicity, or political ideology. Despite these differences, however, as an institution that is meant to support new life motherhood contains "a spark of radical change" (Orleck 1997c, 4). While political engagements assume a tremendous variety of forms of protests and organizing, what unites them as radical, or what comprises their commonality, can, in principle, logically unfold into radical action: the care and nurture of new life.

Caring for and nurturing new life can move in quite diverse, conflicting, or contradictory directions, that is, in ways that do not unfold the radical potential of these activities. For instance, new life can be nurtured for mainly profitable purposes where a child is "domesticated" into considering material success and social status as the primary goals in life. In other words, the ethics of care can be carried by the market-driven ethos of individual power and success. Mothers who perform this work may not be conscious of the exploitative, unethical implications of the ethos of individual success. They may simply do their work within the pregiven confines of their own world. As Ruddick (1997) writes, a feminist, critical assessment of their political work therefore requires "to consider realistically but generously the complex motives and worldly limits of mothers who act politically" (371).

Moreover, a "politics based on motherhood . . . can be invoked in the service of any political agenda," and "the tenets of a politics of motherhood—the care and nurture of children and the health of their physical and social environment—can serve divergent and contradictory political causes" (Hirsch 1997, 368). These tenets can be invoked by mothers fighting against environmental pollution, or by right-wing or Klan mothers (Koonz 1997; Blee 1991, 1997, 1998). As Blee (1998) writes in the introduction to a collection of essays on women engaged in radical protests, "Radicalism can exist on the right as well as on the left. Radicals are those who seek social, political, or economic changes meant to produce great equality within society, or those who seek changes meant to restructure society in a less egalitarian fashion" (3). Wrigley gives a particularly striking example of the latter by documenting Boston's right-wing antibusing movement. The white working-class women engaged in forms of political action that were "rowdy and disruptive" (1998, 254). They clearly violated the norms of femininity while legitimizing their actions by "stressing their maternal awareness of each child's needs and their jobs as their children's protectors" (261). Their tactics and concerns were, however, fully ensconced in a racist social-political world, visibly marked by Boston's history of racial and ethnic segregation (256). Blee's suggestion that goals rather than the tactics of political action should be scrutinized are especially valid here (3). While on the surface mother activists may employ similar tactics and may legitimize their actions by voicing concerns for their children, their goals may pose no threat to, or even reinforce, sexist or racist social relations.

Consequently, although there is no single definition of motherhood, mothers are inserted in a complex nexus of social, political, and economic power relations. They *always* play a political role. Although the spark of radical change is contained in the experience and work of caring for and nurturing new life, the power nexus within which this work takes place may, however, keep the spark from becoming the glow of a protective warmth, or from igniting into political fury over conditions that threaten or destroy life. In other words, although a "maternalist perspective" (Ruddick 1991) does contain the radical implications of a subsistence perspective, it does not automatically unfold its radical implications. This happens only when the power relations that try to muffle or extinguish it by eroding its material and cultural conditions are acknowledged, understood, and fought against.

Ruddick is correct when she writes that the transformative power of the experience of motherhood can be put to public use by "extending ways of thinking and acting that originate in the responsibility, care and love for children" (1997, 372). While she emphasizes the cultural dimension of this maternalist perspective, she fails to make a connection with its material and economic foundation. A maternalist perspective, just like a subsistence perspective, is rooted in concrete labor, a kind of work that is embedded in a long history of negation and super-exploitation. A fight against the erosion and destruction of its material and cultural conditions is therefore always a political-economic fight. Motherist politics that try to ignite the spark of radical change carry core aspects of this work into the arena of politics, and the tendrils of motherwork reach into the strategies, forms of organizations, as well as leadership styles of mother-activists who are not only engaged in subsistence work but also in subsistence struggles.

POLITICAL WORK

Woman-centered and woman-defined community work is a form of political activism that does not fit conventional notions of "doing politics." This is one of the reasons Naples (1998a) uses the term activist mothering in her studies of community workers active during the War on Poverty[2] because the term not only highlights political activism, but it also "captures the ways in which politics, mothering, and labor comprise(d) mutually constitutive spheres of social life" (111). Moreover, as an important sociological concept, the term also "serves to counter traditional constructions of politics as limited to electoral politics or membership in social movement organizations as well as constructions of motherwork and reproductive labor that neglect women's political activism on behalf of their families and communities" (111).

The nonrecognition of various forms of women-led political activism by official political organizations has been examined from a variety of perspectives and within a number of different social, cultural, and historical contexts. These analyses range from discussions of cultural politics to documentation of grassroots workplace organization.[3] In *Women Transforming Politics* (Cohen, Jones, and Tronto 1997a), a broad understanding of politics not only redefines "the range, intensity, modes, arenas, and purposes of political action" (7) but also illustrates that "what counts as politics to any one individual or to a particular class, sexual, or racial group may be at odds with mainstream definitions of the political, and is affected by histories and geographies that bind different groups to a political system in different ways" (3). These descriptions and analyses "highlight the intersections of discourses and structures of race, class, ethnicity, sexuality, nationality, and ability on women's political roles" (7).

Despite its multiple and multilayered intersections with many other categories, sexual difference, or gender, nevertheless remains central. Not only have women always been politically active, but the "traditional boundary markers that circumscribe the field of politics" thrive on the public/private dichotomy, making invisible not only the daily activities of women without which the system could not have run at all, which support male-defined, visible political activities, or which make enormous contributions to the meaning and quality of public life (5). Saeger (1996) discusses grassroots environmental organizations in the United States and gives an example of this invisibility. Although "women are the backbone of virtually all environmental organizations in the United States," their political work in grassroots, community-based organizations remains unacknowledged by male-dominated management and policy-making ranks of most mainstream environmental organizations (271). Blee (1998) makes a similar point in relation to definitions of "radical politics," where radical is either equivalent with male, especially in left-wing politics, or, if women are the focus of action or analysis, with organized feminism. In order to unwrap women radicals from the mantle of traditional invisibility, Blee suggests looking at goals rather than tactics, directing one's gaze to areas of life that are usually excluded by analysts of radical politics, and assuming an altogether different way of looking. When "informal networks of friendship, kinship, or neighborhood rather than elections, positions, and hierarchical organizations " as well as gender become the center of attention, political work becomes visible as such (4). Blee refers to Tilly and Gurin's term "protopolitical" as being useful here as it operates "outside formal political structures and [is] based on solidarities of everyday life" (4).

In order to recognize and acknowledge the political dimension of community caretaking or activist mothering, however, one has to start by recognizing and acknowledging the actual labor summarized by these terms. This kind of work is fully embedded in the dailiness of everyday life, and so are the social, economic, and political problems pervading it. As Gilkes writes with respect to the experience of African Americans, "Community work is a constant struggle and it consists of all tasks contained in strategies to combat racial oppression and to strengthen African American social, economic, and political institutions in order to foster group survival, growth and advancement" (1994, 213). How this work is organized, and how it is embedded in people's daily and nightly lives, has a strong cultural as well as political dimension. It is political work that attends to a localized context, that relies on everyday empirical or local knowledge, where mothers develop "a visceral sense of how large-scale political issues affect the lives of individual children" (Orleck 1997c, 4).

Lack of social acknowledgment and support of motherwork is mirrored by the fact that mother-activists or community othermothers also "labor in obscurity," assuming "responsibility for the mundane tasks that would foster social change" (James 1993, 48). In other words, political struggles that emanate from the values and concerns associated with subsistence work are subsistence struggles. And just as the term subsistence work connotes a positive, life-affirming orientation *and* a struggle for bare survival, so does the term subsistence struggle. Not only are activist mothers always struggling against external as well as internal forces that necessitate continuous, exhausting, never-ending work to maintain, repair, or build community structures and institutions, but their struggles are often struggles for bare physical survival. As Collins points out, this is a core theme of racial-ethnic women's motherwork (1994, 49). And "like all deep cultural themes," it has contradictory elements. While survival is essential, survival work extracts high personal costs. These often include a loss of individual autonomy and a "submersion of individual growth for the benefit of the group" (50). In addition, the magnitude of motherwork often produces a sense of defeat, a merciless anxiety, the stress of keeping children in school, children who are stigmatized as "at risk" (Polakow 1993, Funiciello 1990). In her book called *The Habits of Surviving,* Kesho Scott (1991) likewise explores the tremendous psychological and social costs paid by community workers engaged in daily struggles against sexism, racism, and poverty. Similarly, in reference to the women activists who fought against the pollution at Love Canal, Kaplan (1997) observed that they had to "face their husbands and children, who accuse them of withdrawing affection and attention while pursuing political goals. Guilt about not being home, stress over taking in extensive community work in addition to their many tasks as homemakers, and worry over the harm pollution has already done to their families cause personal pain" (41).

Not only does women's political work severely tax or drain their personal, emotional, or spiritual resources, the women also have "minimal access to the usual resources generally associated with traditional concepts of power such as control of the distribution of society's resources, and command of its wealth, armed forces and mass media" (James 1993, 50, 51). Moreover, not only do poor women lack access to these traditional insignia of power, they have little or no material resources to begin with. As Collins points out, Black women's community work "as mothers, wives, and churchwomen" often lacks adequate resources and support (1998, 29). Moreover, she points to an erosion of a social glue observed in Chicago's public housing ghettos as well, that is, "the erosion of long-standing organizational bases for Black women's community work [that] has led to decreasing numbers of African-American women who are able to engage in community work within segregated, self-contained Black neighborhoods" (31).

The power of the media and certain people's ability to strategically manipulate it play a particularly important role in a society that thrives on media spectacles. Breitbart and Pader (1995) give an example of how inaccessibility to a major social resource such as the mass media can result in a bundle of mistreatments. In their study of the political processes behind transforming the Columbia Point public housing project in Boston to Harbor Point, a multiethnic variable-income housing complex, they discovered that women engaged in political work are typically seen through "the categorical strait-jackets that guide the representation of race, gender, culture and class " (15). The vital political work of the women who were the main organizers and decision makers in the Harbor Point project was either ignored, or the mostly white reporters of major Boston newspapers depicted the women "as either passive, dependent products of a culture of poverty and/or potentially threatening and disruptive members of an urban underclass" (13). As the authors of this study point out, "Women's involvement in struggles for housing and urban organizing is often ignored, or its significance minimized, both because this work is viewed as an extension of their invisible work as home-makers and caretakers of the larger community, and because it contradicts popular expectations of low-income women" (14).[4]

Kaplan's study of the Homemakers of Love Canal reveals a very similar pattern. Because the women involved in this grassroots movement were working against living on a toxic waste dump, and because they were "mainly concerned with local issues, with what affects ordinary people every day," their actions did not meet the interest of the public media. As Kaplan observed, "the media and public opinion are preoccupied with the spectacular, with the activities of celebrities. What's more, the participants in grassroots movements are ordinary women attempting to accomplish necessary tasks, to provide services rather than to build power bases. Therefore, the work they do and the gains they make hardly seem politically significant" (1997, 6). However, Kaplan also documents how the women quickly learned to become "shrewd political operatives, adept at using the media to get their message across" (18).

The media are not the only public that takes note of, distorts, or ignores poor women's political struggles. Krauss (1997), who studied the activities of white working-class women in various toxic waste movements around the country, gives examples of how members of the official public such as policy makers and the media share core assumptions. They either slight or entirely ignore women's knowledge about vital issues related to their family's and community's health. In one case policy makers relied on "expert testimony" when addressing "numerous toxin-related health problems" that had already been uncovered by the women living in the respective area (133). They thereby not only trivialized the women's concerns, but they also discredited their everyday empirical knowledge of how the toxins directly affected the health of their children. Kaplan's description of the struggles of the women who formed the Love Canal Homeowners Association (later to become the Love Canal Medical Trust and the Citizens Clearinghouse for Hazardous Waste) confirms this official denial of the life-threatening (and for some deadly) chemical dump called Love Canal (1997). The group collected information about diseases and ailments and correlated these incidences with "small creeks and a veritable system of drainage ditches called swales carrying the toxic wastes far from the canal, seeping into outlying neighborhoods." The Department of Health that received these medical records denied, however, any danger by labeling the evidence as purely anecdotal (27).

Orleck (1997a) gives another example of how the official public destroyed the results of community work done by welfare mothers in Las Vegas. These women first "educated themselves about their rights and entitlements under county, state and federal law" (110). They then formed an organization called

Operation Life and developed a number of self-administered social service programs: a child-care center, a teen recreation program, a public swimming pool, and a community-run press (111). City and state worked together to close these programs by cutting off funding. As Orleck writes, "What pains and galls the veterans of Operation Life is that they pooled their talents and energies and built a genuinely workable system for delivering social services to poor families in their community, and then had to watch it torn apart piece by piece" (116).

Since these kinds of activities happen outside formal organizations and political institutions, it is not surprising, nor is it a coincidence, that the women themselves do not necessarily categorize their struggles and activities as political ones. Lemke-Santangelo (1996) described this self-evaluation of political work with respect to the women she interviewed in the East Bay area. These women "saw their community activities as an extension of their private caregiving" (153). Hardy-Fanta (1997) makes a strikingly similar observation, this time with respect to the stories of Latina women from a variety of backgrounds and countries of origin. They "revealed a vision of politics that is different from that of traditional political theorists, Latino and non-Latino alike. They seemed to emerge from their families with a view of politics imbued with what feminist theorists call an 'ethics of care' . . . Politics for them, consists of 'helping others,' 'fulfilling an obligation,' 'sharing and giving,' and providing support'" (226). Many of the community workers in Naples's study also did not interpret their activities as political ones, since they believed that "politics is not concerned about the needs of low-income people." As the women saw it, politics are designed to serve those in power (1998a, 21). Some of the women used the term "politics" as a clearly negative construct that was closely associated with unethical behavior and infighting. They therefore drew a line between their neighborhood or "civic" work and "political activities and politics" (110).

By adopting "maternal metaphors and language to describe themselves and their work," the founders and leaders of these women-led organizations are often ignored (Belenky, Bond, and Weinstock 1997). Or they are subjected to trivializing and disempowering stereotypes that characterize them as "stubborn, apolitical, unable to change," and as "sentimental apoliticos" (Ruddick 1997, 371). In even more stereotypical ways, women organizers may also be labeled "hysterical housewives" not only by officials, but also by supposed male allies (Kaplan 1997, 20; see also Saeger 1996).

However, women can also use their role and experience in the private sphere as a source of strength, knowledge, skills, and a sense of humor that they then translate into political strategies in the social and political public sphere.[5] Women who engaged in various political activities that are rooted in a life-affirming subsistence perspective have often directly employed these stereotypes by contradicting disempowering images. For instance, Marie Pozniak, a friend of Lois Gibbs, engaged in an act of sexual bawdiness by pinching a police officer on his backside, making everyone laugh. As Kaplan observes, "By acting as sexual aggressors, [the women] contradicted the image of asexuality and docility generally associated with motherhood in our society. By playing an uppity Carol Burnett instead of a victim in a soap opera, Pozniak and her supporters reversed stereotypes and took the upper hand" (37).

In the face of the mega-machine of economic, social, and political power and control, mother-activists' strategies have to be resourceful, imaginative, and creative. Rabrenovic (1995) gives an example of the creative use of motherhood's link to traditional gender roles. These roles were acted out in forms of protest against the plight of deteriorating neighborhoods affected by economic restructuring and residential segregation, including vanishing job opportunities, drug-related crimes, prostitution, and steadily worsening local services (81). As Rabrenovic writes, the women who engaged in different kinds of protests sometimes "gained attention and sympathy by using social stereotypes to challenge their opponents and symbols of their roles as wives and mothers, such as pots and pans, to publicize their demands and ridicule their opponents. With an imaginative use of familiar symbols and theatrical devices, women were often able to increase public visibility for their demands and win some state intervention" (83). In a similar manner, the mothers at Love Canal used situation comedies by willingly making spectacles of themselves. They chanted in front of TV cameras, they acted out the images of feisty female TV characters, and they set out for a demonstration carrying coffins as props (Kaplan 1997, 39, 29).

The use of emotions was another strategy that directly exploited women's stereotypical, ridiculing denigration. Krauss (1998) summarizes how white working-class women strategically used emotions during their struggles against environmental pollution, thereby appropriating and politically transforming public, derogatory labels:

Motherhood became a strategy to counter public power by reframing the terms of the debate. The labels "hysterical housewives" or "emotional women," used by policy makers to delegitimize the women's authority, became a language of critique and empowerment, one which exposed the limits of the public arena's ability to address the importance of family, health, community. These labels were appropriated as the women saw that their emotionalism, a valued trait in the private sphere, could be transformed into a powerful weapon in the public arena. (142)

Krauss's words touch one of the main arteries of subsistence work: the emotional work women perform, or are expected to perform, in all spheres of life, be it within the privacy of the family, in their daily interactions with neighbors, or in the social public of the corporate world. While this emotional work can therefore cement existing power relations, it also contains a radical potential. As one of the women engaged in toxic waste projects expressed it, emotions "may well be the quality that makes women so effective in this movement . . . They help us speak the truth" (142).

When mother-activists effectively use symbols and stereotypes closely associated with a denigrated feminine sphere, they blur the lines that are usually rather sharply drawn between a "female" and a "feminist consciousness." Kaplan observed that the women leading grassroots struggles "merely act according to what I have called 'female consciousness.' By female consciousness I mean that certain women, emphasizing roles they accept as wives and mothers, also demand the freedom to act as they think their obligations entail" (1997, 6). Thus, "Far from being a biological trait, female consciousness develops from cultural experiences of helping families and communities survive" (7; see also Kaplan 1995). Although a female consciousness is bound to traditional gender roles, it is also bound to the potentially revolutionary implications contained in those traditions—which may be employed in a way that cements *or* challenges underlying power hierarchies.

Women activists who stay fully within patriarchal gender relations, don't question them, and focus on motherhood as a core dimension, inevitably get tangled up in conflicting expectations when they engage in public political action. Defending their maternal rights or expertise when fighting for their children involves leaving the home front of their work responsibilities. Not surprisingly, many marriages of women involved in as different causes as racist antibusing or environmental protection end in divorce (Kaplan 1997; Naples 1998b; Wrigley 1998). While divorce in and of itself does not signify radical activism, the violation of a primary feminine norm, that is, staying at home and taking care of everyone's needs, does, however, bear a radical seed. When trying to acknowledge this radical potential, it is nevertheless important to keep in mind that the notion of "traditional gender roles" has many different, contradictory, that is, far-from-uniform meanings, depending on which social or cultural arena these roles are being played out. For instance, the "deeply embedded gender divisions of community work" performed by the West Harlem women who organized against a sewage treatment plant in their neighborhood provided the context "for a vibrant and committed movement working to preserve a decent quality of life in West Harlem" (Miller, Hallstein, and Quass 1996, 74). As the authors who studied women's community activism in West Harlem point out, the "pre-established, socially defined gender roles made it possible for women in West Harlem to unite against a common threat" (75).

While the whole structural-material and ideological system is set up to perpetuate its devaluation, devalued "nonwork" becomes threatening when it goes public, when it refuses to stay in the netherworld of the private. This is its radical potential and this is its threat. Not surprisingly, the effort of the West Harlem women to challenge the established gender roles by becoming active in a highly visible and politicized arena met strong disapproval by male political leaders. The women "moved out of the 'acceptable' realm of 'behind the scenes' advocacy into an expanding dialogue. As they engaged the city administration and elected officials in a citywide dialogue and began networking with organizations outside their community, the old mold began to break" (75). Women were obviously allowed to be active in community work as long as this work remained in the background, and as long as they did "nonthreatening" volunteer work and did not seek political power and visibility equal to men (76).

In order to summarize some key aspects discussed in this and the previous section, it is appropriate to look at a particularly extreme example of political motherwork, extreme because it took place under the auspices of a military dictatorship of terror, rape, and torture, of being "disappeared" or having one's own children disappear, in many cases forever. It is the political work of the Mothers of the Plaza de Mayo, originally a group of fourteen women that got together in 1977, taking to the Plaza de Mayo, the most public place in Buenos Aires, Argentina. They demanded information about the whereabouts of their missing children, and they wanted to do that by being as visible as possible. In a society where all opposition was annihilated by military force, they used their maternal role quite self-consciously. They strategically manipulated it in order to gain some security, deliberately drawing on the official Christian rhetoric of family values that the military dictatorship used to legitimize its reign of terror (Taylor 1997, 187). Hernández (1997) describes how the Mothers "took the rituals of the normative performativity games of being mothers, and pushed them to a point where they flooded the regulatory practices and became totally menacing to the intelligibility models held by the Military" (52). For instance, the Mothers "were mimicking the untiring woman that moves around the whole day and who has an established schedule for the laundry or shopping" (52). When walking on the plaza, the women also covered their heads with white handkerchiefs, a symbol that two decades earlier had demonstrated the modesty of women moving about in the public sphere. The women subverted the controlling aspects of the symbol of white handkerchiefs by publicly marking the presence of all those who had been made absent. Instead of marking modesty the women were therefore "making life and love political" (53).[6] By dismantling the public/private dichotomy they also turned one of the core insignia of patriarchal control of women upside down.

Their actions exemplify the conflict-ridden terrain of motherhood. Moments of radical protectiveness of life are inextricably intertwined with moments of patriarchal control, this time, however, pushed to its ultimate manifestation. The right-wing rhetoric of family values translated into forms of torture, specifically aimed at pregnant women, or, "if and when they gave birth, they were beaten, humiliated, and often killed" (Taylor 1997, 186). The Mothers protested against the horrors inflicted upon the population by a "threateningly sexualized, phallic body/machine" (184) that annihilated life, including life in its most vulnerable form. This is the political, the radical dimension of the Mothers' work, and it is rooted in their desire to protect or value life. By consciously manipulating their maternal role through theatrical self-presentation, that is, by using the images that had previously controlled them, they performed a public spectacle that inverted the focus of the military spectacle—remembering, *not* dismembering the disappeared (190). The Mothers were faced with and resisted the most brutal treatment, and they found ways of inspiring others to follow their lead:

When the military tried to force the women from the plaza, they marked their presence indelibly by painting white kerchiefs around the circle where they usually walked. Instead of the empty streets and public spaces mandated by the military curfew, the Mothers orchestrated the return of the repressed. Buenos Aires was once again filled with people: spectacular bodies, ghostly, looming figures who refused to stay invisible. The public spaces overflowed with demonstrators as the terrorized population gradually followed the Mothers' example and took to the streets. (190)

Motherhood had became a public-political rather than private-biological notion, just as the women "came to consider themselves the mothers of all the disappeared, not just their own offspring" (189). Their theatrical devices, and the way they played out the performative aspects of motherhood, highlighted *and* denounced the gendered stereotypes of mother, soldier, virgin, or "elderly, physically weak and sexually nonactive women" by projecting images opposed to the junta's image of "a lone, heroic male leaving family and community behind" (190). As Taylor writes, "The Mothers emphasized community and family ties. Instead of the military's performance of hierarchy, represented by means of rigid, straight rows, the Mothers' circular movements around the plaza, characterized by their informal talk and place, bespoke values based on egalitarianism and communication" (1997, 190). In other words, regardless of the fact that a restrictive patriarchal system remained basically unchallenged, and that mothers who had left the confines of their homes to engage in bold and dangerous political protest did not alter the politics of their homelife, the Mothers did extremely radical work.

The point made here is that any effort to value or validate the work of activist mothers cannot be reduced to examining to what extent their actions resulted in fundamental changes in the structure of the social world that surrounded them. Instead, one should focus on the ultimately radical implications of their courageously independent defiance of a phallic body/machine that violated and destroyed life, or signs of life, and how this defiance is integral to a communal sense of responsibility. While the Mothers of the Plaza de Mayo give an extreme example of this communal ethic, it manifests itself in many ways in the approach, strategies, and processes characterizing other mothers' movements that follow similarly the guiding light of social justice.

COMMUNITY AS FAMILY

A pronounced communal orientation is the thread that weaves through all mother-activists' political work. It is a core ingredient of subsistence struggles that are rooted in the spiritual and physical interconnectedness and interdependence of life in all its versions. By being fully embedded in cultural norms and practices, motherwork has a strong spiritual dimension. On the utopian, life-affirming side, motherwork requires a holistic mind-set and a holistic practical approach. This is precisely what makes motherwork an example of subsistence work. Bernice Reagon (1986) illustrates the vital interconnection of communal and spiritual orientations by describing "mothering" as the process of "looking at relationships between people in the community," and looking at them "in the larger, natural world, beyond and before, sometimes, the human family" (87). Thus, mothering is a metaphor that guides her in analyzing and understanding whether a community is already nurturing life, or has the potential to do so:

Among all living things in the universe, there is a nurturing process. It is the holding of life before birth, the care and feeding of the young until the young can care for itself. This process is called mothering. When applied to the examination and analysis of cultural data, it can reveal much within the historical picture of how culture evolved and how and why changes occur in order to maintain the existence of a people. It is important . . . to look for the nurturing space or ground. Look for where and how feeding takes place. Look for what is passed from the mothering generation to the younger generation. (87)

This quote illustrates the communal dimension of motherwork, and community is therefore a recurrent theme in the stories of mother-activisis. The women value their work because it benefits their community regardless of whether it is paid or unpaid. Acknowledging motherwork as a form of subsistence work provides a major entry point into the conventional framework that splits the worlds of work and family, and of the individual and the larger community, thereby crumbling some of its major assumptions. Notions of "community othermothers," "social motherhood," (Collins) or "socialized motherhood" (Hernández) signify highly permeable boundaries between the categories of work and family, and between corresponding experiences on the individual and collective level of existence. Actual, real-life women need to find, however, a language that expresses a communal ethic of care. "Family language" is often the only one that comes closest to this orientation, and it is also the only one that is directly available. When Brown (1993) writes that community and support networks are family, the term blurs the usually sharp delineation of family and community, public and private, work and love, production and reproduction.

The women who led protests against toxic waste dumps redefined their roles as mothers by making their concerns public, that is, by entering the public arena (Krauss 1998, 138). They used family language as the "movement language" (142) by exposing the contradictions between the official ideology allegedly espousing "family values," and policies that directly counteracted the well-being of families. As one of the women engaged in political protest activities said, "It appalled me that money could be more important than the health of my children" (137).

Family language is sometimes used because it most directly expresses the values that underlie political actions. The Mothers of East Angeles, an organization of Mexican-American women who were fighting against the city's decision to build a state prison in Eastside Lost Angeles, used "mother" as a metaphor for protecting their community. At the same time, they also understood that they engaged in their political struggle as "good citizens" (Pardo 1995, 360), thereby explicitly expressing the political dimension of their community motherwork. In a similar manner, Winona LaDuke objects to being called "a Native American activist, which I think is kind of ludicrous. I mostly consider myself a responsible parent" (1997, 77). LaDuke fulfills the role of a responsible parent as the leader of an organization that reclaims the Anishinabe people's original lands from federal, state, and county governments in Minnesota, cochairs the Indigenous Women's Network, and is the program director for an environmental program that works on issues related to environmental justice and community restoration. Clearly, African-American, Asian-American, Latina, and Native American women "find their historical role organized around the nurturance and defense and advancement of an *oppressed public family*" (Gilkes 1994, 241, my emphasis; see also Hardy-Fanta 1997).

Elsa Barkley Brown gives a particularly powerful example of how non-European, "Afrocentric" notions of family and community are fully embedded in the totality of paid and unpaid work, and how this work could be collectively organized and could build on and develop many organizational skills. The washerwomen of her childhood organized their work and daily activities in a way that demonstrates a profound communal subsistence orientation, one where community is considered family. They "collectively scrubbed, rinsed, starched, ironed, and folded the pounds of laundry as they also talked" (83). The washerwomen first "organized themselves in a more formal fashion—so that the woman with the largest kitchen actually contracted all of the work and hired many of the other women to work for her as laundresses" (83), and later they organized a mutual benefit society, a bank, and a department store (84). Brown describes how she not only realized that the washerwomen provided economic resources, but "that those mornings spent scrubbing were also spent organizing." It was therefore "with clear planning and organizational skills that they had developed over the washtub—it was with a commitment to each other which had been born in the mounds of suds" (83). The roles of washerwomen therefore "went far beyond economic resources" as they performed the "roles as organizers, planners, policy makers, leaders, and developers of the community and its institutions" (84). In a similar manner, the oral narratives of women who found temporary employment as residential and non-residential community workers during the War on Poverty show "community caretaking" as one of their consistent themes. As Naples writes, "The term captures the ways in which politics, mothering, and labor comprised mutually constitutive spheres of social life for the community workers" (1998a, 111).

In *Black Feminist Thought* (1990) Collins lists the three settings where Black women have been engaged in as "everyday political activists"(148): "political and economic institutions, Black extended families, and the African-American community as 'family'" (146). As she writes, "By placing family, children, education, and community at the center of our political activism, African-American women draw on an Afrocentric conceptualization of mothering, family, community, and empowerment" (151). It is the "community othermothers" who simultaneously work in all settings, and whose daily expression of their obligation as such mothers often "developed into full-fledged actions as community leaders" (131).

Cooperative forms of interaction influence or shape the organizational and leadership style of mother-activists. This can take on a variety of forms. Naples, for instance, observed that the women community activists, "more than men, were concerned with nurturing the leadership skills and political empowerment of other community members" (1998b, 132). This approach to organizational style is, of course, related to the fact that community activism is often seen as an extension of private caregiving that, quite logically, translates into the importance of shared experience. It is this sharing of experience that gave the activist migrant women of Lemke-Santangelo's study "recognition and credibility," and that gained them the admiration, trust, and respect of the communities in which they lived or worked. The women therefore "refused the titles and recognition of formal leadership. These, they maintained, would remove them from the very communities they were part of" (1996, 153). Instead, they practiced the kind of leadership they had "learned from their mothers and other female role models," exhibiting "a black, southern female-centered leadership style which was based on non-hierarchical, nonegocentric forms of organizing" (154). Rich makes a very similar observation when she calls the leadership of women of color "teachership" (1986, 165). Barnett (1995) provides links to a common feature of African-American history where "a collectivist orientation and lack of self-promotion . . . are persistent themes in Black women's activism from slavery to modern times" (108). She describes the Club from Nowhere, an organization comprised of mainly poor and working-class Black women who engaged in fundraising activities in support of the Montgomery boycott. Although one of its core members "was referred to as the 'head,' authority and decision-making were vested in the group as a whole. Professionalism and expertise were not the basis of leadership" (213). Kaplan used the metaphor of an orchestra to illustrate the uniqueness of this leadership style: "All can play most of the instruments, but what they usually do is put the notes together to create an ensemble whose power surpasses those of the individual tones. A synergy of sound" (1997, 5)[7]

While the metaphor of synergy of sound captures a fairly typical way of social interaction in various poor, working-class women's movements, it obscures, or entirely leaves out, the reality of conflict or of fundamental social divisions that not only occur within these movements but that also structure parts of the entire network of social relations of the community within which the activists live and work. Collins is therefore critical of the danger of naturalizing hierarchical male-female relationships by leaving the family metaphor unexamined:

Because actual family relations are rarely fair and just, using family as metaphor for constructing and understanding of group processes can duplicate inequalities that are embedded in the very definition of what constitutes a well-functioning group. This has profound implications for any group that understands its internal dynamics through the lens of "family." Since the 1970s, increasing numbers of African-American women have recognized how this notion of naturalized hierarchy within a family constitutes a problematic organizing principle for the organization of actual Black families. (1998, 225–26)

Collins places this concern within the specific historical and social context of racial segregation that is, of course, closely linked to economic disadvantage. She describes how the vital importance of racial solidarity and a communal ethics did not allow women to speak or lobby on their own behalf, or to confront issues dealing with unequal power relations among women and men (26–28). She therefore challenges "conceptions of Black civil society that naturalize hierarchy among African-American men and women," a recognition that "requires questioning long-standing norms that simultaneously have used family language to define African-Americans as a race and have often conceptualized Black political struggle via the rhetoric of family" (225–26).

Regardless of intragroup conflicts or hierarchical relationships, where community othermothers rely on social support networks, they "do occupy political space within a community" (James 1993, 48). Extended families, "fictive kin," or "friends who assume the responsibility of kinsmen and are given fictive kin terms" (44)[8] are an important social resource base. So are friends and neighbors. Norms and values grounded in a belief in collective responsibilities and an established web of reciprocal obligations all carry the work of social motherhood or community caretaking. Ultimately, these values are based on an ethic of care that can be expressed by a general commitment to caring for whoever is being perceived as needing it, and by the act of caring for the most vulnerable or helpless members of a community. Just like all community othermothers, the washerwomen Brown wrote about combined unpaid and paid labor at home and in the community in order to improve, build, or transform community institutions. Community work therefore crosses the boundaries between "personal troubles" and the economics and politics that are behind troubles, such as water leaks, rats, roaches, and lack of heat. When opening up one's house for those in need, the lines between community work and family-based labor become blurred.

The sharing of resources is an essential part of activist mothering, giving "caretaking" a broad meaning. Traditionally, community-based values defined community as "anyone in need" (Naples 1998a, 17). The East Bay migrant women, for instance, clearly blurred the distinction between public and private by "providing economically vulnerable migrants with room, board, and advice on where to find employment and permanent housing," and they also "extended hospitality to family and friends who 'ran out of luck' after settling in the East Bay" (Lemke-Santangelo 1996, 147). Naples (1992) lists some of the activities that comprise "mothers' activist mothering" in her study of Latinas and African-American women in low-income neighborhoods. These activities included "taking neighbors to the hospital, helping to care for the elderly, advocating for increased child-care programs, fighting school officials to improve the educational opportunities for young people, struggling with landlords and police officials to improve the housing and safety conditions in their community, and interpreting for non-English-speaking residents" (452). Gilkes (1994), who studied African-American women's community work and social change, lists issues related to job training, drug addiction, welfare rights, and education as some of the primary concerns behind women's organizational efforts.

Churches have been another major social resource. Especially in African-American communities, churches "have been central in supporting a variety of social, economic, political, and ethical actions essential to Black community development" (Collins 1990, 151). Black Christian churches, the fundamental organizations of Black civil society, have traditionally been the site of struggles for social justice, and they have provided the institutional foundation for Black women's community work (Collins 1998, 27). [9] Not surprisingly, "church values and norms are those of female-centered kin networks" (Scott and Black, quoted in Lemke-Santangelo 1996, 156). Churches have therefore often assumed the role of extended family, thereby serving "an overworking kinship service," and they brought "individuals into a mutual aid association that used the talents and skills of its constituent members to benefit the whole" (Lemke-Santangelo 1996, 156). As Lemke-Santangelo writes with respect to the experiences of migrant women,

The church, like home and neighborhood, was a center of the African American community, transmitting traditions and values and providing its members with spiritual and material resources. As such, even the most conservative parishes functioned as temporal sites of spiritual resistance, preserving life and meaning under the most dehumanizing conditions. Thus, women's efforts to establish and maintain churches reflected their desire for permanence and stability in the face of chronic hardships imposed by deeply rooted structures or racial and class discrimination. (158)

Local churches have therefore been an institutional home for African-American women where they could "cultivate and formally exercise power within their communities" (Naples 1998a, 18). As Barnett reports with respect to the civil rights movement, "the church conferred status on poor Black women who gave their time and personal commitment" (212). Religious affiliations and neighborhood churches are therefore often at the core of not only what creates a sense of community but also what provides a variety of structural supports to communal interdependence and mutual aid.

WHAT IS A COMMUNITY?

While motherwork and community work are vitally interdependent, "community" can mean many different things. The community workers Naples (1998a) interviewed in her study "defined 'good mothering' to comprise all actions, including social activisms, that addressed the needs of their children and community"(113).Their community was "variously defined as their racial-ethnic group, low-income people, or members of a particular neighborhood" (113). Naples, who addresses the differing conceptions of community (226), emphasizes that a community is constructed at the intersection of racial, ethnic, class, gender, and spatial relations. This means that it can be grounded in a sense of neighborhood surrounding one's household, and/or in one's racial-ethnic or class identification that may transcend one's particular neighborhood (239). Moreover, as Childers (1997) points out, especially with respect to poverty, "Communities of poor people do not spontaneously generate. They are created in a nexus of social, political, and economic forces that are sometimes regional, sometimes global, and almost always serve the interests of others besides poor women" (105). These forces shape one's experience and one's definition of community. "Community" therefore has a host of meanings and associations that are deeply embedded in collective consciousness. Not surprisingly, especially within social science discourse, community is a social construct that is full of ambivalent, ambiguous, and often contradictory meanings.[10]

Very much like "public family," the use of the summary term "community" can easily lend itself to denying power differentials and potential or actual conflicts within a community. For instance, by emphasizing the ideals of solidarity, mutual care, and a strong sense of belonging, especially within a community that is visibly marked or racialized, "community" can hide or obscure the "hierarchy within," that is, the power differential between women and men (Collins 1998, 222). The notion can also be used rather strategically by people who claim to be community representatives but who are actually only representing their personal interest in individual power positions.[11]

Community can also refer to a shared language, as in the case of the Latina/o community. This example of community, however, illustrates major problems. One is the conflict involved in the process of who defines whom by what terms, or whether "community" is a self-defined or externally imposed term. The original U.S. government term Hispanic lumped together everyone who came from any Latin American country, irrespective of vast national and cultural differences. Although the more recent term Latino is used by politically more progressive people (who nevertheless use the masculine noun as representing all people, female and male), it is a consciously chosen response to common oppression by the white Anglo system. Thus, similar to the term Hispanic it signifies a primarily political definition rather than a shared cultural identity.

Community can also refer to physical proximity where people share the same space or geographical area. A geographic, localized context can make a community a social living space and work site where "women can link family concerns to a wider network of resources" (Pardo 1998, 275). However, as the widespread phenomenon of residential segregation illustrates, in a racist, ethnocentric, and class-biased society, communities are also the result of a relationship between a specific, local context and the broader political-economic context in which it is inserted. All constructions of community are therefore "political constructions no matter who defines the boundaries" (Naples 1998b, 336). In

racially hypersegregated urban spaces, the notion of "community" is closely
related to "place," to where groups of people were forced to move because of
their racial or ethnic identity. It is also there where they develop a strong sense
of community and cultural identity (Haymes 1995). Cunningham and Curry
(1997), for instance, interviewed African Americans who live in one of Chicago's racially (and economically) segregated areas. They observed that "among
those interviewed we found no 'lone rangers.' The emphasis was on community
and African American culture" (77).

By looking at the way actual women regard community, and how they
struggle to "make community their own" (Garber 1995, 26), it is clear that political struggles combine a sense of home or place-bound community with a
community of purpose. Residential housing conditions give a particularly strong
example of how "community, locality, and domesticity" intersect. Organizing
co-ops or tenants groups, for instance, exemplifies "women's interests in linking
place and politics" where the forming of a community of purpose is part of the
women's political, that is, purposive activism (37). Whether geographical proximity makes for shared values fully depends on the particular history of a geographical region. As urban renewal and gentrification schemes demonstrate, city
planners and real estate markets also define geographical communities (cities
and neighborhoods), but in entirely market-driven terms. More organically developed communities whose market value is nil may therefore be torn apart.
Haymes (1995) describes urban renewal schemes as a battleground for Black
urban struggle because gentrification disenfranchises African Americans and
takes away their ownership of parts of the city.

Just as the meaning of community can vary, so can an individual's sense of
collective identity, belonging, or solidarity. Members of the Latina/o community, for instance, have multiple identities that shift depending on the specific
context in which that person finds herself. Naples gives the example of a Puerto
Rican community worker who variously defined her community as Latino or
Puerto Rican (1998a, 29). She was active in the Puerto Rican Civil Rights
Movement of the seventies, and due to the sexism she encountered in this
movement, she became a member of the National Conference of Puerto Rican
Women, and later, together with other women, organized a separate Latina
feminist organization, primarily in response to the exclusionary framework of
the white feminist movement (29–30).

Community workers may therefore have "emotionally engaged, albeit shifting definitions of community " (Naples 1998a, 192). Community work can be
"a constant struggle" in which people "address oppression in their own lives,
suffering in the lives of others, and their sense of solidarity or group kinships"
(Gilkes 1994, 213). This also means that community work can cover a wide
range of diverse tasks associated with combating racism, and with empowering
a community to survive, grow, and advance in a hostile society (230). In that
sense community forms "the grounds for . . . political commitments" and will
sustain "activism over periods of disillusionment and economic decline," as it

did for the many different community workers Naples interviewed (1998a, 192).

A political commitment can sustain community work through hard times, regardless of shifting definitions, shifting emphases on different aspects of community life, and the endless variety of tasks associated with this work. There are other, more troubling issues related to collective group identities, however. For instance, when a political commitment is missing, a group identity does not guide people to transcend their own narrow, exclusionary sense of community. How a community perceives or treats people who are moving into their community therefore depends on whether they are simply "newcomers" who nevertheless represent social-political or cultural commonalities, or whether they are "outsiders" marked by divisive difference. As Garber points out, "On a crude level, because interlopers may breach the consensual nature of the public decision making that is predicated on the sameness of citizenry, they can justifiably be shunned or silenced. Strangers might so threaten the community's perceived identity and economic self-interest . . . that certain people are denied entrance or driven out, often legally" (1995, 28). In Chicago, for instance, some of the public housing residents who were relocated into different neighborhoods were greeted with hostility or physical threats (Fischer 1999, 3). Clearly, racist and/or class-biased stereotypes play into the anxieties and fears resulting from the widespread and ongoing process of neighborhood deterioration. Rabrenovic (1995) gives another example of the way racial divisions affect the interpretation and therefore also political strategies of women activists. In Schenectady, New York, the fear accompanying deteriorating living conditions translated into "local collective actions to improve neighborhood conditions, despite major obstacles in their communities" (78). It was, however, mostly white women who formed an organization called Clean Sweep United, a name related to their main goal of pushing for "more sweeping law enforcement" (85). The women were concerned with the growing drug problem in their neighborhood. They fought for more police protection and an increase in arrests made instead of letting drug offenders off the hook through plea-bargaining (84). Because the women activists mostly blamed nonwhite people for bringing crime to their neighborhood, their political activism received, of course, no support from women with whom they did not share their whiteness, thus illustrating deep fissures in the web of communal responsibilities or sense of community.

FORMING CROSS-ALLIANCES

Clean Sweep United is only one example of the difficulties of transcending one's race and class identification, and of forming cross-alliances that try to bridge a host of structural and ideological divisions. These divisions certainly affect people's sense of identity, as illustrated by the difficulties people face when they are relocated into a neighborhood comprised of people with different racial-ethnic or class backgrounds. Group identity can be a source of strength and solidarity, especially to the extent to which it is shaped in a hostile environment, and it can be a source of hostility, consequently barricading one's group (neighborhood, community) against any outsiders seen as "others." Othering can take on the most directly hostile and violent form, as in the case of the Klan, whose hatred of religious and racial others relies on images of white Protestant women's and children's vulnerability (Blee 1991, 176).[12] By interviewing women who were former Klanmembers, and by noticing the perfunctory way they talked about their participation, it was brought home to Blee that "the racist, nativist venom of Klan politics percolated easily, unremarkably, throughout this world." In other words, it settled in the bone marrow of white Protestant communities (178).

However, it is not only the bone marrow of Protestant but also that of Catholic communities that seems to be affected by the poison of racism. In Boston white working-class women were furious at the thought of having their children bused to nonsegregated schools, and they screamed at Black schoolchildren— not in the South, and not in the 1920s, when the Klan came into existence, but in the 1970s. When busing children to schools outside their immediate neighborhood became public antisegregation policy, it met strong opposition from the parents and from many of Boston's teachers. Most were Catholic, upwardly mobile Irish Americans who, "imbued with conservative values . . . made the public schools into a paler, secular copy of the parochial schools they had experienced" (Wrigley 1998, 256). Although the Klan represents an extreme version of racist hatred, there is a discernible line of continuity to the racism of Boston's antibusing movement. This movement was carried mostly by white working-class mothers who were also the majority on the executive board of ROAR (Restore Our Alienated Rights), the main anti-antibusing organization (252). The women did not, however, simply organize because they wanted to defend racial purity on all levels of social and political existence, as the Klan members did. Instead, they were only interested in leaving things as they were. They wanted to stay within the culturally and racially insulated confines of their segregated neighborhoods. In other words, they engaged in a specific kind of political activism, "a right-wing political protest directed against changes in the racial status quo" (253).

The story of women activists in West Harlem, another racially segregated neighborhood, sets an impressive counterexample. Not only did the women challenge environmental racism and "the flagrant disregard for their quality of life," they also created "a critical fusion of traditional gendered roles with a new activism and a willingness to confront the male-dominated political machine" (Miller, Hallstein, and Quass 1996, 81). Moreover, the "local knowledge" of the older women who formed the backbone of this organization, the West Harlem Environmental Action (WHE ACT), was honored, and the organization broadened into a cohesive, organized group that introduced the concept of environmental racism in a citywide dialogue. The women later also organized "against multiple environmental assaults within the broader context of the environmental justice movement" (73).

I want to claim that it was their political goal, and not their attachment to a community segregated by class and race-ethnicity, that kept the organizers and participants of the Boston antibusing movement from reaching out, from trying to form alliances with people with whom they did not share class or ethnic identity—although they were widely supported by the majority of Bostonians. They were not interested in building a broad-based movement. As Wrigley writes, "The antibusing women undertook their activism in their normal surroundings. They did not expand their horizons by any geographic moves or by any new acquaintance with people very different from themselves" (283). The women also give a good example of the way maternal metaphors that are clearly rooted in emotionally charged concerns for the well-being of children can be chained to reactionary and destructive goals. In other words, although the concern for one's children's education (and thus their future) could build a bridge over class and race divisions, where it is engulfed by racialized fear and hatred, the spark of radical change turns into the fire of burning crosses.

While Clean Sweep United did not engage in the same kind of direct, open racism as ROAR, it nevertheless illustrates how racism insidiously asserts itself when political activism is not hooked up with an attempt to place issues plaguing a neighborhood into a larger social-political context. Thus, while women justifiably fought against a problem that was part of the devastation of their neighborhood and that posed a threat to themselves and to their children, they did so without taking into account and paying tribute to the larger political context. Without any sense of their own worldly limits, and of the way power relations on the macrolevel caused different kinds of problems for populations who differed in terms of class and/or race-ethnicity, "by concentrating solely on the consequences of poverty—drug and crime—and not on its causes—unemployment and racial discrimination—White women ignored issues that were important for minority women and their families" (Rabrenovic 1995, 83). The work of mother-activists was therefore aimed at ameliorating a threatening situation without, however, going beyond immediate practical considerations for this particular community—defined in the exclusionary terms of geographical location and racial-ethnic identity.

Evidently, white people, whether they are women or men, have quite different kinds of challenges to confront than non-white people when attempting to bridge a host of divisions produced by a white supremacist world. The commonality of discrimination, on the other hand, supports people who, despite vastly different cultural backgrounds, are lumped together or categorized/stigmatized as Other, as nonwhite, to build cross-class and cross-cultural alliances. Rabrenovic gives an example of how an ethnically defined community in Chelsea, Massachusetts, could form such alliances. Its members had different socioeconomic backgrounds, and they came from different countries: Puerto Rico, El Salvador, Honduras, Guatemala, Costa Rica, Colombia, the Dominican Republic, Vietnam, and Cambodia (90). Because they shared common concerns, people could come together in a common struggle against Boston University

(89). The university wanted to assume authority and responsibility for Chelsea's public schools. It placed a strong emphasis on early childhood education, and it therefore proposed a plan for instituting mandatory preschool and extended child-care programs for all children. One shared concern was that Boston University "was trying to supplant their families and their culture" (78). The Latina/o population in particular felt that schools did not address the needs of their children, thereby slighting mothers' ability to take care of their children. Above all, they had well-founded concerns that children would forget Spanish and would therefore become alienated from their communities because Boston University's proposal for mandatory pre-school and extended child-care programs emphasized early teaching of English. One of the proposal's desired "side effects" was to save money by reducing the need for bilingual education. Moreover, despite its formal commitment to a multicultural approach to education, the university did little to include representatives of ethnic communities in its negotiation with the City of Chelsea.

People were also concerned about the low status of Latinas/os, illustrated by the fact that they had no representation on the School Board.[13] It was the women who were the most active in organizing the struggle against Boston University. While it was hard for the women to mobilize needed resources and to connect with other immigrants who lived in more socially fragmented neighborhoods, the mothers became very active. They utilized their "social resources" in a narrower and broader sense:

Women did not have to learn that they needed to build an alliance but that they were part of the alliance from the beginning. They were successful in drawing on their social resources—ethnic ties and culture—to organize their ethnic community and to protect their family-based concerns. Over time, their goals widened: They no longer wanted simply to gain some control over services; they wanted to overcome the problems of political marginalization of the Latino population. Their strategy was to seek electoral representation and formal participation in the political process. (Rabrenovic, 93)

The Latina/o population of Chelsea crossed the boundaries of class and nationality based on a shared ethnic identity that was tightly linked to the commonality of social-cultural discrimination. An externally imposed discriminatory label formed the grounds for a politically defined collective identity that built a bridge across national, cultural, and class differences.

While Latinas in Chelsea formed alliances based on a shared political ethnic identity, Feldman, Stall, and Wright (1998) give an example of how poor African-American women took it upon themselves to build alliances with organizations and individual people who did not belong to their closely knit community. They write about the organizational work women activists have been engaged in at Wentworth Gardens, a Chicago public housing development, since the late 1950s. These women have been struggling against increasing state disinvestment and growing poverty in their community, and attempted to meet their own and their neighbor's everyday needs. Their efforts have ranged from informal social gatherings with neighbors and providing neighborly support (such as information sharing, errand running, and child care), to organizing more formal resident-initiated service programs (including grounds clean-ups, garden plantings, food and clothing distributions, youth and senior programs, crime-prevention and education programs, and organized sports activities), as well as sponsoring yearly celebrations and fund-raising efforts. (259–60)

The women activists at Wentworth Gardens built upon "women-centered organizing and protest strategies" (269), that is, an already existing fabric of social support. However, the women also became "increasingly aware that to improve public housing and disadvantaged communities in general, community-development processes must address not only the environmental and social viability of the community, but its economic viability as well" (258).

When they decided to establish a shopping center, it became necessary to go outside their own knowledge, expertise, and profound understanding of specific community needs, and to employ the technical knowledge or expertise from people who came from different educational, class, and racial-ethnic backgrounds. With minimal funding from the City of Chicago, the women were dependent on the donation of "all the technical assistance on the project, . . . including legal, architectural, economic development, community organizing, and funding application preparation and funds." The women employed the help of a community organizer with whom they had worked before. They also received the technical assistance of two members of local university centers because "of personal commitments gained through long-term involvements, and also because they had been impressed by the Wentworth Gardens activists' comradery, creativity, and tenacity in achieving their goals despite enormous economic and political obstacles" (270).

In the case of the activist women at Wentworth Gardens, the fragility of their various cross-alliances was certainly offset by their own sense of empowerment. This sense was nourished by their success in drawing on their own empirical knowledge and experience of the needs of their community, and by the technical knowledge, expertise, and insights they accumulated in the process of working with outside technical assistants. With respect to the insider/outsider relationship, the authors emphasize that

The increasing reliance on outside organizations and technical assistance, however, has not undermined grassroots democracy at Wentworth Gardens . . . While the shift from residents' past engagement in social reproduction and community organizing to this recent real-estate and economic development initiative poses substantial technical, economic, and political demands, it has not impeded residents in their ongoing women-centered organizing efforts to sustain the viability of their housing development. (271–72)

The women were clearly drawn into working with "outside 'experts' who became increasingly necessary as engagement in economic development grew" (259). However, they did not try to substitute larger economic development issues for the on-site service facilities they had developed and managed "to address their unmet community needs for child-care, laundry, and grocery services" (258). Thus, expanding the scope of their struggles called upon their reliance on outside technical and legal assistance, skills, and resources, but it enlarged rather than undermined their other community activities.

CREATING A NURTURING SPACE

Motherwork is place-bound, and so are related forms of collective struggle. Both are connected to a life-affirming subsistence orientation. Women-centered networking, nonhierarchical forms of organizing, and decentralized leadership styles are, in a way, the more visible and nameable layers of a subsistence orientation. This orientation grows out of the dailiness of mother/subsistence work that is bound to be attentive to a specific time and place. Motherwork is by nature place-bound, and it is therefore intimately connected to the provision of a homeplace. This provision is in need of a physical space that is conducive to the work associated with that provision. The separation of home and paid work, housing designs that represent the patriarchally defined needs of a heterosexual nuclear family, and racially segregated housing developments illustrate the strong link between larger social-economic institutions and the social and spatial structures in which motherwork takes place. Emotional social ties to a neighborhood are basic to women's place-bound collective engagements in local struggles, and working against many odds in a hostile environment also transposes the source of stability offered by a homeplace into the larger context of a social network.

Conflicts over space are directly connected to the question of who has the right and control over spatial resources. This is an ongoing struggle in the arena of public housing. Feldman, Stall, and Wright emphasize the importance of physical settings when assessing the political dimensions of maintaining households and communities (1998, 261). The public housing residents of Wentworth Gardens were therefore fighting for the rights "to develop, use, and manage the material and spatial resources of their housing development" (264).

This fight can take on the form of direct legal action. In May 1991 the Horner Mothers Guild, a group of more than twenty residents of the Henry Horner Annex, sued the Chicago Housing Authority (CHA). They charged that the agency had deliberately allowed their building to deteriorate to justify tearing it down. Basements were filled with tepid water, trash and junk littered the halls, which had no light bulbs, the incinerators were often backed up, and the buildings were infested with rats, mice, and roaches (Popkin et al. 2000, 94-97). As mentioned in chapter 2, four years later the parties to the suit signed an agreement to redevelop Horner in five phases including demolition, rehabilitation, and one-for-one replacement housing, a guarantee not given to the residents of any other public housing complex in Chicago (Oldweiler 1998, 12; see also Popkin et al. 2000). The women from Wentworth Gardens and from the Henry Horner Homes saw their power to effect change as being anchored in the empowering experiences of the everyday, and in the ongoing struggles to "create and sustain their homeplace and promote community viability" (Feldman, Stall, and Wright 1998, 265).

Women-centered environments build on the feminine tradition of creating a nurturing space (Reagon 1986, 87), or "feelings of home" (Naples 1998a, 106). Talking and writing about home "needs to hold in tension an awareness of the social processes linked to the production and organization of the cultural and metaphorical meanings accorded to the sphere of home" (Bowlby, Gregory, and McKie 1997, 347). Home is a complex, multifaceted and multilayered concept. Home is a social edifice that embodies meanings, values, and attributes that reflect the differing beliefs and experiences of its builders. Occupying a central but undervalued place within societies that endorse patriarchal values both formally and informally, the home provides a place within which identities and boundaries are learned, perpetuated, and challenged. It is both safe and dangerous, perpetual and evolving (347).

Home can be experienced as a space that nourishes a sense of belonging, a place of origin. Home can therefore be used "metaphorically in the demarcation and imagining of regional and racial identities and of nation states, just as the defense of a particular version of home and family is often a crucial element in ideologies of racial identities and nationalism" (347). Within the context of a racist society, a homeplace is therefore "a site of resistance" (hooks 1990b), and making a homeplace means constructing "a safe place where black people could affirm one another and by so doing heal many of the wounds inflicted by racist domination" (42).

Home is a highly gendered space, with a host of positive but also highly negative, often life-threatening implications. Bell hooks is fully justified in emphasizing that it has been women who have been doing, and have been expected to do, the life-affirming work of making a homeplace. As she writes, "Since sexism delegates to females the task of creating and sustaining a home environment, it has been primarily the responsibility of black women to construct domestic households as spaces of care and nurturance in the face of the brutal harsh reality of racist oppression, of sexist domination" (42). She denounces the patriarchal dismissal of the often colossal amount of effort that goes into the simple act of caring. In order to make her point as strongly as possible, she quotes Frederick Douglass's story of his enslaved mother's inability to tenderly care for him, watch over him, because she "was hired out a considerable distance from his place of residence." Although Douglass writes about how after work she traveled twelve miles to spend the night with her child, he does not even hint at acknowledging or understanding what it meant to travel this long distance after a grueling day of slave labor in order "to come to him in the night, just to hold him" (44).

This is certainly an extreme story. The sexual division of labor that puts patriarchal blinders on people's understanding of motherwork nevertheless continues to bolster the normalcy of an extreme. Underneath the structural violence of dismissing women/mothers' tremendous effort in doing the work of raising children lies the direct, open male violence against women in the home. Bluntly put, in its white Western version, home has been the traditional site of male violence against women, the silenced but always present dimension of sexism in its most pronounced form. It is normal to the extent to which it is widespread—and obviously increasing or intensifying.[14]

Hooks denounces the subordination of Black women by Black men not only because it damages "collective black solidarity" (48), but also because it destroys the tradition of the homeplace as a political site of resistance to a white supremacist system. It is a tradition that provides a safe place, a refuge to a family understood in the larger, communal sense of the word. She writes: "We are daily witnessing the disintegration of African-American family life that is grounded in a recognition of the political value of constructing homeplace as a site of resistance; black people daily perpetuate sexist norms that threaten our survival as a people" (48). In other words, the seed of radical change that is planted in the work of constructing a homeplace cannot sprout. It cannot spread into a protective communal life that carries the political work of challenging injustice in its many different manifestations.

Hooks emphasizes that it does not really matter that the role of creating a homeplace is assigned to women. It is more important to recognize that it was women who "took the conventional role and expanded it to include caring for one another, for children, for black men, in ways that elevated our spirits, that kept us from despair, that taught some of us to be revolutionaries able to struggle for freedom" (44). Clearly, hooks sees the "radical political dimension" of what I call a subsistence orientation, an orientation that is contained in women's conventional roles. Such an orientation is firmly wedded to subsistence work, to the construction of a homeplace "where all that truly mattered in life took place—the warmth and comfort of shelter, the feeding of our bodies, the nurturing of our souls. There we learned dignity, integrity of being; there we learned to have faith. The folks who made this life possible, who were our primary guides and teachers, were black women" (41–42).

Hooks's notion of homeplace influenced the authors of *A Tradition That Has No Name* (Belenky, Bond, and Weinstock). They also draw on a variety of writings that discuss or trace the history of "authentic public spaces" (Greene 1988), "free spaces" (Evans and Boyte 1986), "movement half-way houses" (Morris 1984), or "safe spaces" (Gamson 1996). Belenky, Bond, and Weinstock summarize core dimensions of these different concepts under the term "public homeplaces," places that lie between "private lives and large-scale institutions where ordinary citizens can act with dignity, independence, and vision" (1997,

164). These are places where values of cooperation and collaboration are nurtured, and where possibilities for creating a saner and safer world can be envisioned. Similarly, Kaplan writes that "by creating a third space that is neither public nor private, grassroots activists have opened up an arena in which human dignity, not national law or custom, prevails" (1997, 11).

POLITICS IN THE FLESH

Mother-activists and community othermothers are laboring in obscurity, in the invisible space of social life based on a value system that contradicts the dominant social norms of individual separateness, interests, and success. Instead, this value system emphasizes connectedness, interdependence, and common interests. It is a value system that is anchored in the materiality of subsistence work, intricately interlaced with a subsistence perspective. The political-economic and cultural dimensions of this kind of work are therefore inseparable as well.

A broad-based notion of "doing politics" is fully woven into a broad-based definition of work, which, in turn, becomes the basis for new politics. The political space of community othermothers thereby becomes a place that does—in a way—dismantle the public-private division, tearing the private sphere away from its neoliberal characterization as apolitical. The political space of community othermothers floods the traditional borders between public and private. It becomes a "third space" (Kaplan 1997) or a "third element" (Feldman, Stall, and Wright 1998). Political work taking place within this third dimension, this private/public in-between space, is revolutionary and threatening. That's why it is met with contempt, or with attempts (and often success) to suffocate it. And just like caring work, it is relegated to an invisible, apolitical private sphere.

Naming subsistence work reproductive rather than productive is in and of itself an outcome of a dichotomy that relies on the sexual division of labor. Just as motherwork is disregarded or devalued, so is political work emanating from it. From the perspective of what officially counts as political activism, it is therefore either kept in the shadows of invisibility, or it is ridiculed. Underneath this denigration lurks the abhorrence of the daily, bodily nature of motherwork in particular, and survival work in general. Just as a body that has the power to produce new life has to be controlled in indirect or direct forms of violence, so does work most strongly associated with it.

Political work that is intimately connected to body work is a "politics in the flesh." I am here using and expanding Cherríe Moraga's term "theory in the flesh," which "means one where the physical realities of our lives—our skin color, the land or concrete we grew up on, our sexual longings—all fuse to create a politic born of necessity" (Moraga and Anzaldúa 1981, 23). Moya points out that Moraga emphasizes the materiality of the body "by conceptualizing 'flesh' as the site on or within which the woman of color experiences the painful material effects of living in her particular social location" (1997, 145). Likewise, a politics in the flesh is rooted in the materiality of the body. Women/mothers have a visceral sense of what endangers the lives of children and their community, and their political actions against hunger or unhealthy, unsafe physical living spaces therefore involve the body as a source of knowledge. Because they recognize the importance of "local knowledge" and fuse it with "new energy and conviction," when women's agendas around quality of life issues are brought into the traditional male-dominated political arena what counts as the political is being transformed (Miller, Hallstein, and Quass 1997, 82).

A politics in the flesh is intricately linked to a subsistence orientation. It is transformative because it links the multifaceted, diverse tasks and responsibilities that comprise motherwork—seen from a holistic perspective—to a "creative cultural process of social change" (Gilkes 1994, 229). As Reagon writes, "Mothering here does not refer to biologically having babies out of your body," but rather finding "what is it that we nurture," "what are the unions we hold in our wombs? What do we have to transform?" (1986, 88). Reagon also states that "there is a need to create a new space, . . . larger than the space we now occupy," a space where Black people share "a commonness of humanity with other people and a unity with all that is living" (88–89).

To create such a larger space is a large task. It must, however, be anchored in the work that is place-bound, tied to the necessity of the body, and context-specific; work that is fully integrated in the everyday life of a culture; work where the spark of radical change contained in the care and nurture of life and of all that is living is allowed to ignite. Mother-activists or community other-mothers do put into practice what at times are only fragments of an alternative way of living, and what at other times are larger, more interwoven pieces. Placing motherwork, and thus subsistence rather than commodity production, at the center of such a vision of life, work, and culture requires taking a hard look at the devastating social and economic conditions that affect large segments of the population, and ultimately all of us living in this world. However, it also requires garnering feelings of hope by looking at traditions that have been counteracting the degrading or destructive imperatives of "our" system; seeing how these traditions are being kept alive under harsh circumstances, and how they are giving life to new ideas and initiatives; looking at daily survival struggles that involve insight, foresight, courage, strength, and knowledge entirely beyond the scope of our public discourse on poverty or welfare, or on politics or political action. Walker's essay "In Search of Our Mothers Gardens" (1983) shows vividly how her overburdened and overworked mother let her creative spark guide her in planting a garden on rocky soil where "whatever she planted grew as if by magic." It was a garden whose brilliant colors and original design clearly represented a piece of art that instilled in her daughter a legacy of respect for "all that illuminates and cherishes life" (204). She illustrates how the effort, the hard labor of making and letting grow, is imbued with the spiritual power of cherishing life in its many forms.

NOTES

1. In "The Unproductive Housewife" Folbre (1997) traces the history of the devaluation of work at home, especially as it shaped the notion of unproductive household labor, and, by the end of the nineteenth century, was therefore not counted in the U.S. census. This was a by-product of "a new definition of productive labor that valorized participation in the market and devalorized the nonmarket work central to many women's lives" (60).

2. Especially in *Grassroots Warriors* (1998a), but also in other writings, Naples reports on her longitudinal study of women community workers hired in Community Action Programs (CAP) during the War on Poverty, the corner stone of President Lyndon B. Johnson's Great Society Program.

3. See, for instance, Flammang's *Women's Political Voice* (1997) and the contributions to Cohen, Jones, and Tronto (1997) for substantive analyses and critiques of conventional understandings of women's political participation or political activism, especially as expressed in academic discourses.

4. Belenky, Bond, and Weinstock (1997) make similar observations. They write that organizations such as two Mothers Centers (one in Germany and one in the United States), the Center for Cultural and Community Development (a national network), and the National Congress of Neighborhood Women in Brooklyn, New York, "were largely ignored or misunderstood by traditional leaders, the media, funding agencies, and the general public" (159).

5. As the women involved in Boston's turbulent antibusing protests in the 1970s show, their strategic use of gender roles, such as helpless housewives or mothers, was also a form of protection against police attacks, especially when the women violated the rules about where to gather for marches (Wrigley 1998, 264).

6. Hernández (1997) and Taylor (1997) also report that the women persisted despite the fact that they had put themselves in grave danger, and that many disappeared or were kidnapped and battered.

7. See also Belenky, Bond, and Weinstock for their documentation of a "developmentally focused leadership" that calls for "creating a common language that is capable of articulating this alternative notion of leadership" (1997, 293–94).

8. See also Stack (1974, 60) for the origin of the term "fictive kin."

9. See also Cannon 1988, Collins 1998, and Higginbotham 1993.

10. Garber summarizes some of these complexities by describing how in academic writings "community is steeped in fraternal imagery and practices . . . that are most damaging because they conjure up something that has always been largely mythical" (1995, 28). Morris makes a similar point by criticizing university-based educators for romanticizing communities "in terms of a set of institutions (neighborhood, church, extended kin networks) that are defined by their marginality or subordination to the institutions of the economy and the state" (1996, 129). This is similar to what Spivak calls "essentializing the oppressed as nonideologically constructed subjects" (quoted in Alcoff 1991, 221).

11. However, as Fisher points out, conflict can also become a "dynamic training ground for democracy and political education" (1994, 213). In reference to McCourt's study of working-class women organizers (1977), he writes that "participation in such organizations helped members see the implications of their concerns and armed them with new information, greater self-confidence, and pride. In short, conflict empowers people for even a defeat against what most of the women saw as an 'all-powerful' power structure was often a psychic victory that led to continued efforts and greater involve-

ment" (213).

12. Blee's study of Klanswomen focuses on the first major Klan movement in the 1920s but also traces the emergence (and decline) of following movements: one between 1930 and the end of World War II, one in the 1950s, and the current one that dates back to the early 1980s and is linked up with extralegal terrorist and paramilitary groups (1991, 176). The women in the twenties movement had formed their own order, the Women of the Ku Klux Klan (WKKK). In the later movements women took on more supportive roles. Part of this shift in women's involvements and roles had to do with external political pressures on the Klan as it had fallen "into public disgrace and marginality" (175). Part of it also had to do more with the complex gender politics of the 1920s than those of modern right-wing movements that are currently linked to the Klan. According to Blee, "The WKKK's promotion of women's rights resembled the nativist strand of women's suffrage when it excluded nonwhite and non-Protestant women from the struggle for full citizenship for women" as many social reformers "strove to discipline unruly immigrants, and a segment of women's rights advocates subscribed to nativism and racism." At the same time, "the Klan used its agenda of women's rights to justify—even to require—vicious and brutal actions against blacks, Catholics, Jews, immigrants, and others," thereby reshaping and recontextualizing the earlier suffrage, temperance, or moral reform movements (177). Blee therefore sees a links between the progressive moments of the women's reactionary, hate-based Klan movement and the fluctuating political climate of the early twentieth century.

13. Today Latina/os are recognized as a force in the politics of the city.

14. See, for instance, Ann Russo's *Taking Back Our Lives* (2001), and the contributions to *Gender Violence* (O'Toole and Schiffman 1997) and *Transforming A Rape Culture* (Buchwald, Fletcher, and Roth 1993).

Conclusions

> We have the possibility to nurture a union between the knowledge we gather which is of the Black community and that of the larger society we live in. There is the need to create a new space, . . . larger than the space we now occupy, large enough for our people to continue as a people, sharing a commonness of humanity with other people and a unity with all that is living.
>
> We can choose to do this other job, mothering for our people. . . . It is in fact the blood and struggle of our people which created the space that we hold. We can choose to know that . . . we can choose to be mothers, nurturing and transforming a new space for a new people in a new time.
>
> —Bernice Johnson Reagon, *African Diaspora Women*

The broad claims about human needs and rights made by the new generation of women leaders Kaplan praises in her book *Crazy for Democracy* (1997) are anchored in the specific, local conditions of their families' and communities' lives. The women therefore continue the old tradition of women's place-bound social-political activism. Carrying out an invisible revolution is likewise not a new phenomenon. What is new, however, is that their struggles are confronting the "new world order" of a global economy, accompanied by fundamental changes in the social fabric of their particular society, culture, and nation state. Living in a world ruled by a predatory global economy creates next to insurmountable obstacles in the path of creating a nurturing space, but it also gives this work a sense of utmost urgency—when life is to be cherished rather than destroyed, created and sustained rather than exploited. In other words, the women and their allies are resisting the war against subsistence, that is, the local and global exploitation of subsistence work, and the ongoing destruction of its inner and outer survival base.

One of the most dramatic developments taking place within this new world order is the rapidly widening distance between the globalized economy and the social realm. International capitalism has not only fragmented social entities and communities, but the social has practically disappeared as a separate realm with its own right of existence. Public debates and various social or civic governing bodies and institutions that proclaim that right, and laws and regulations that politically sanction and therefore protect it, have withered away. Changes and developments in the social arena are more and more ruled by economic imperatives that are exclusively oriented towards winning and gaining a competitive advantage on the market. Such "turbo-capitalism" (Luttwak 1999) creates wealth because only one thing counts: profitable efficiency. The economic efficiency model is imposed upon the entire world, irrespective of the fact that this world is comprised of numerous social systems that are quite different from each other. Unfettered economic developments therefore almost automatically subsume everything: culture becomes marketable folklore, forests become timber mills, and so on. Society is sharply divided into winners (a few) and losers (many). Moreover, as Bales (1999) demonstrates in his survey of the spread of new forms of economic slavery, questions of public responsibility, and thus of morality, are strikingly absent.

Under the auspices of neoliberalism, the notion of a public social safety net that compensates for the negative workings of the free market has disappeared, making the market the sole arbiter of social life (de Goede 1996, Chomsky 1999). The economic underpinnings of the U.S. welfare reform, however, show another side of this apparent breaking away of social decision-making from a national political framework. By turning a poor mother's entitlement to public aid into a legal requirement to enter the labor market, the entitlement is transformed into an enforced supply of cheap labor. Although turbo-capitalism—also called "casino economy" (Barnet and Cavanagh 1994) or "manic capitalism" (Greider 1997)—does indeed represent an entirely unregulated, unfettered market, it does not simply usurp governmental decision-making power. According to Chomsky the "corporatization of America" (132) is the result of ongoing governmental support and interference that does away with protective barriers, supports the exploitation of labor and the environment, and allows poverty to increase unchecked. The corporatization of America therefore refers to a powerful government's collaboration with corporations. It subsidizes the welfare of the wealthy and does not even pretend to be primarily concerned with noncorporate interests. Underlying the myth of the "free" market and of freeing society from the evil of governmental interference is the reality of freeing up the private sector. In accordance with such a close collaboration of state and corporations, politics are more and more modeled after corporate strategies, and presumably democratic processes turn into spectacles on the political market where parties try to mass-produce votes.

In her analysis of welfare reform in the United States and New Zealand, Kingfisher observes that "the essence of privatization on the federal level [means] deregulation and delegitimization for social programs" (1996, 173). Not surprisingly, while the caseload of social workers declined dramatically by about 50 percent since the enactment of Personal Responsibility and Work Opportunity Reconciliation Act (PRWORA), this decline has not been matched by a drop in poverty. Among all other industrialized nations, the United States has the highest poverty rate for children (Chomsky, 28). [1]

The official disregard for the children of the poor is an integral part of the disregard for the poor in general, most of whom are women and the children for whom they are responsible. As our social-economic arrangements demonstrate, even in the richest country of the world, some children had better not be around. Once they are, all the fault and burden are placed on their mothers. As discussed throughout this book, many poor children are raised by solo mothers, that is, by a population officially defined as at-risk, deficient, broken, dysfunctional, morally suspect, or a menace to society. The concentration of poverty among children and women is therefore explained as an essentially *private* affair, as a result of failed individuals and failed families. The fact that it is "our" economy with its structural inequalities of access and opportunity that causes poverty on such a wide scale, that it is a *public* rather than private affair, never becomes an issue of public debate. Instead, it is our economy that is portrayed as the "suffering body," not "the individual poor body" (Kingfisher 1999, 5).

This is where neoliberal notions of the market and of possessive individualism where the winner takes all link up with old colonial imagery and practices. In other words, neoliberalism and neocolonialism go hand in hand. Not only does the welfare state continue to shrink, but poverty is "naturalized." Thus,

The non-poor represent society and civilization, maleness, "good"—that is, controllable—nature, order, autonomy and freedom, intentionality, morality and rationality; and the poor represent nature and savagery, femaleness, "bad"—or, uncontrollable—nature, disorder, need and necessity, want, desire, particularity, dependence, immorality, and irrationality. Gender is a key axis of this binary, with the various attributes on the "masculine" side having a positive valence in relation to those on the "feminine" side, which are hierarchically and definitively secondary. (Kingfisher 1999, 4)

This makes, of course, the savages by definition as unreformable as the welfare mothers who are constructed as lacking bodily discipline and suffering from the savage inability to defer sexual gratification (11). What comes in the guise of reforming the savages are actually strategies of controlling and disciplining them for the greater good of society, that is, the economic stakeholders. Where a sense of morality has been entirely usurped by market interests, the reformed welfare mother becomes the ex-welfarite or the "post-savage" who can now be more effectively exploited in the labor market. Welfare reform can be read as an employment strategy whose main goal is to expand the pool of cheap labor by adding reformed ex-welfarites (see Peck 2001). Not only is their unbridled sexuality now in the grip of a minimum wage ethic, but the workers are also tamed by the fear of losing any financial support once the welfare clock has been ticking beyond the allotted time.

In that respect welfare reform is part and parcel of a neocolonialism that reinvents the older colonial issue of transforming the poor into civilized, "proper (male) 'individuals' in order to become fully human/post-savage" (Kingfisher 1999, 11). While the old welfare regulations have been robbing women of this potential, welfare reform assists in their "moral uplift" through economic incorporation. Where welfare mothers cannot sufficiently subject themselves to this uplift, they join the legions of "America's Disappeared" (*The Nation*, 12 July 1999). To put it more bluntly, the colonial agenda of welfare reform feeds on a tension between uplift and annihilation:

Physical reformation/annihilation of poor "savages" can take place when welfare recipients lose all state support and end up homeless and hungry (and, in extreme cases, dead). Cultural reformation/annihilation can take place when dominant/colonial institutions condemn local practices or modes of social organization and forcibly impose different ones. Finally, spiritual or personal reformation/annihilation can take place in the process of convincing excluded people that they want to be in the center. (Kingfisher, 14)

The Kensington Welfare Rights Union has taken on the battle against this form of neolcolonialism. In October 1999 it kicked off The Poor People's Economic Human Rights Campaign and filed a petition before the Inter-American Commission on Human Rights, accusing the U.S. government of violating economic human rights by enacting and implementing PRWORA. It compiled the *Poor People's Human Rights Report* where it points to Article 23 of the *Universal Declaration of Human Rights* that was signed by countries of the United Nations in 1948, including the United States. This Article proclaims that "everyone has the right to work, to free choice of employment, to just and favorable conditions of work, and to protection against unemployment." It also states that "everyone who works has the right to just and favorable remuneration ensuring for himself and his family an existence worthy of human dignity, and supplemented, if necessary, by other means of social production" (*Poor People's Human Rights Report* 1999, 7).

The Poor People's Economic Human Rights Campaign asks individual people who have suffered violations under welfare cutbacks to become petitioners and to tell their stories to the organizers of this campaign in order to bring violations to light.[2] In other words, it is a social movement that draws on one of the poorest populations in the United States, a population that has little or no resources to participate in social movement activities. Poverty is heavily concentrated in certain urban residential areas where the collapse of much of the inner-city infrastructure exacerbates this scarcity of resources badly needed by community-based organizations or initiatives. Chicago's inner-city residential segregation along the lines of class and race, and its public housing policies, give a prime example of the fact that poor communities have to "address massive problems with scanty resources and the knowledge that most problems originate far beyond community borders. The mismatch is evident: organizations proliferate, but social conditions worsen" (Fisher 1994, 177–78).

The shedding of public responsibility manifests itself in several ways: the management of the Chicago Housing Authority (CHA) properties was privatized; in order to attract high-income renters, public housing stock is being reduced without, in turn, supplying a sufficient number of affordable low-income housing units; evictions are on the rise as a major replacement tool; Black poor women and their children are pushed into residential areas with an equally high concentration of poverty as well as racial-ethnic minorities; replacement housing is often rather shoddily built.[3] Most of the heads of households displaced from CHA public housing are Black women with children. In addition to being (and staying) poor, they are confronted by the legacy of a dual housing market.[4] By being pushed to the suburbs and relying on Section 8 vouchers, the women confront another unfair housing issue. Landlords can refuse to take Section 8 renters or they can refuse to renew the lease after a year. Not only do the women and their children leave their previous pockets of personal and communal support, but they are now asked to live like isolated nomads, making it next to impossible to rebuild any kind of community.

Load shedding of public responsibility also comes in the form of evicting social service programs housed in CHA buildings, such as youth and adult tutoring, drug prevention and intervention, food pantries, after-school teen programs, job training and placement, and others. In the fall of 2000 all these were eliminated in favor of "service connectors" to existing community-based programs, thus to an already overburdened pool of outside services. The responsibilities for connecting residents with various programs was handed over to the city Department of Human Serivce, but a year later a referral program is still not in place (*Chicago Tribune*, 27 July 2001).

In an article in the *Chicago Tribune* aptly titled "Home is Where the Problem is" (15 October 1998), McRoberts reports on several women residents' political struggles at the ABLA Homes, one of the public housing complexes currently undergoing a process of "revitalization." One of the women has been a tenant leader "who works closely with city agency officials to avoid drawn-out fights that have delayed redevelopment efforts at Cabrini-Green and other projects for several years." As the leader of the tenant council she also directs job-placement efforts, and many residents are thankful for this kind of visible, strong leadership. At the same time it is not only "savvy operators" but also informal community leaders whose "more traditional way of handling neighborhood affairs—'hollerin' at the children' who misbehave, as one elderly resident put it—will overcome the problems that remain despite long-term plans for a mixed-income neighborhood." In other words, tasks, responsibilities, and processes that are part and parcel of the invisible revolution of community othermothers do not become obsolete in public housing's redevelopment schemes. As a janitor at ABLA said by pointing at brick rowhouses right across the street from freshly rehabbed homes, "Only two things can happen: It will stay up like it is now, or it's going to end up like it is across the street." The brick houses across the street were hollowed-out wrecks.

No matter how redevelopment or revitalization schemes affect the lives of public housing residents, many women will continue to be friends, teachers, guides, or othermothers. And in the absence of money, access to information, and sociopolitical support, as political agents they will continue to rely on their own resourcefulness, their social-emotional ties, and their imagination and creativity. Their political work, however, will remain invisible unless it is acknowledged as such. Such an acknowledgment, of course, would require a host of social and cultural transformations. Above all, it would require placing subsistence at the center of individual and collective concerns. Only a subsistence orientation can discern and name the blatant but also insidious, destructive forces of the present global political-economic system where survival becomes a form of resistance. A subsistence orientation can shed light on the "economy of survival" that lies, hidden and denied, at the foundation of society (Melchiori 1997, 8). Melchiori points out that it is Third World women—whom she names "women in the South"[5]—who are redefining the "object" of political action:

Southern women's struggles have probably gone further ahead than any theories in inventing new forms of political action, and are able to impact both daily survival and the economic sphere on a global level, creating new policies. Their struggles, coming from the so-called subsistence economy which is traditionally outside the market, are clearly challenging globalization by proposing basic values for a different relationship between economic survival and social coexistence. (10)

Consequently, by defining social change in terms of developing a subsistence perspective, and by acting in accordance with its emphasis on life rather than on gaining the competitive edge, corresponding collective struggles can be seen as political struggles where "private" subsistence work is "going public."

Many feminists have documented how women all over the world create or lead political struggles where the traditional separation of public and private are meaningless (see, for instance, Miles 1996). The women, however, do not simply engage in alternative modes of political struggles but also acknowledge the importance of what is generally referred to as "the feminine." The feminine is here not simply understood as a social construct where crude nature is transformed into the sociality of a second nature. Rather, the feminine, or "woman," is seen as rooted in the physicality and materiality of bodies that are part of the first nature. Female bodiliness has unique potentials women do not have to free themselves from but can see and use in creative, self-affirming, non-patriarchal ways (von Werlhof 1996, 93). As von Werlhof points out, the term nature is related to the Latin verb *nascere*, which means "to be born" (93). Despite the attempts of male reproductive technologists to usurp the power of the female body, it is (still) women who give birth to new life. In Melchiori's words, "Something can be found which the human species has not yet figured out in a civil way: thinking through the meanings of birth, procreation, and sexuality and the link of such experiences with the original structure taken by the 'polis'" (8).

A rethinking of the feminine, and an acknowledgment of its natural or bodily foundation, is therefore not simply a private matter, but a matter of "creating the private sphere as a new space of political thinking and acting" (8). Women, the feminine—no matter how intertwined these terms and realities are with specific, culturally different positions—need space, a space to appear, a public space. As von Werlhof writes, "this is not a matter of publicity, public space in the conventional sense, but a matter of women creating their own public space" (154). Her example of a *Frauentreff*, a meeting of women in a rural area in Austria, illustrates a different meaning of "public." The term does not signify belonging to (and perishing) in conventional political arenas, but "standing outside the male concept of reality." A feminine public would therefore be "a matter of a women's public which is not necessarily hooked up with institutions. That's why we have a women's movement" (154). Melchiori summarizes the different groundings of such a public, and the possibilities for its emergence, with the following words:

We should not forget the spaces that political actions come from: the bodies and the private rooms; the dreams and the hysterical "words" that cannot be uttered in any language; the spaces of physical and moral violence against women which are alternatively places of protection or imprisonment; the spaces of families, nests, and cages; the spaces where care and love are difficult to separate from violence; and the spaces exiled from politics as well as those essential to its existence. (1997, 10)

As discussed by von Werlhof (and by others such as Mies and Shiva), creating a feminine public is possible only by developing a spiritually and emotionally different way of seeing oneself and the world, a different *Geisteshaltung*, a subsistence perspective. This means that the project of politics has to be rethought, and thus the host of meanings associated with the terms public and private. Where "public" refers to what is of concern to everyone, the history of African-American women is replete with examples of such a rethinking of the public/private dualism. It is also replete, however, with stories of discrimination and violence that make the political work of community othermothers, of everyday political activists, a work of survival and resistance. It also makes this work bear the radical seed of justice and freedom.

Black women who are perceived by their community as leaders of the struggle for group survival are described as educators. Their deep commitment to social justice is expressed in the interplay of political and educational activism, in their being "teacher/activists" (Collins 1990, 149). With its roots in the experience of slavery, education has traditionally been seen as a group effort. Communal values and ensuring the likelihood of cooperative interaction have been primary functions of Black mothers as educators of children (James 1993, 46). Since this work has a political dimension as it contributes to the formation of a democratic culture, the traditional boundaries between public and private are overflowing because what goes on in the private sphere of the household is of public concern to everyone. It is not the character deficiency of an individual mother, however, or the dysfunctional "culture of poverty" that is of public concern, but the shaping of democratic norms in the everyday life conditions and activities of mother-activists. As Hernández (1997) writes within the context of the Mothers' Movement in Argentina, "Issues such as power, action, change, citizenship, and community knit the web of meanings in political culture, providing a necessary articulation of everyday life experiences and setting the terms either for participation and continuous transformation or for disempowerment and stagnation" (28). What makes such continuous transformation and the creation of a counter-public possible, where politics collide with ethics, and where education collides with cultural work?

Although it is impossible to even try to answer a question of such magnitude, it is nevertheless possible to see the many different steps that can be taken in that direction, and the many different places where this can happen. Learning about new ways of subverting the public/private dualism, of creatively appropriating its flexible or fluid boundaries, is one of these steps. It involves many different processes, but all of them call for a fundamental rearranging of emotional, spiritual, and intellectual borders. Just as these borders are socially defined and delineated, processes whose goal is to rearrange or dismantle them are themselves in need of social support. Learning and unlearning have therefore always had an individual as well as collective dimension whose relative weight may shift back and forth, depending on the educational situation where this un/learning occurs.

For instance, formal education is an enclaved social public where all learners distinguish between their public and private selves. On the one hand this division can remain clear and absolute. On the other hand, it can be made more permeable—not in order to make the classroom a therapeutic, warm, and fuzzy place, but to utilize or create a *counterpublic* sphere. "Counter" here has a political-structural meaning. Learning processes that are centered around giving voice, validating or politicizing issues related to caring, raising children, and nourishing life cross public/private boundaries or make such crossing their explicit goal. In the literacy center the women's weekly meetings depended on a place whose safety was carefully constructed, and where the students' personal lives fully conflated with the themes and topics they offered each other as avenues for learning how to read and write. Their identities, tasks, responsibilities and learning desires were meshed with their roles as grand/mothers who wanted to be able to read to their children, and with their wish to obtain a GED, find employment, and escape the humiliation of the welfare system.

Trying to create a safe semipublic space in a college classroom, however, meets quite different challenges because the divisions between public and private spheres are fully institutionalized, manifested by the rather visible institutional power structure. These divisions also provide a certain degree of safety for the students who can set up their public selves as a shield against possible intrusions into their private lives. In my Motherwork course students are guided to investigate how poor motherworkers straddle the private and public world. The imperative to make the institutional framework more permeable is thematically and politically grounded in teaching and learning about raising children in poverty. By addressing the social as well as personal dimensions of the different ideological and material manifestations of motherwork, the privacy shield is difficult to uphold.

What Nelson describes as the "current fragility and fluidity of public-private boundaries" for family-daycare providers (1994, 202), and what Fraser sees as the "increased permeability of domestic and official-economic institutions" (1990b, 201) can be turned into positive possibilities. By acknowledging the interplay of these worlds, a hierarchical system of subordination and (super-) exploitation can be transformed and affirmed as a relationship of interdependence. However, only a different concept of work would allow for such an internal shifting of boundaries, a concept that does not feed off and reinforce the false dualism of public and private, and that acknowledges the social, economic, political, and cultural dimensions of all types of work, especially motherwork.

To journey through the emotional, intellectual, physical, and spiritual thickets of "learning our way out" would, of course, require a tremendous upheaval of the entire spectrum of social, economic, political, and cultural structures (Finger and Asún 2001). Above all, a global predatory economy would no longer feed the im/morality of the bottomline. Instead, discerning and focusing on the moral boundaries of care would become a concern for all.[6] Caring work would be taken out of the shadows of cultural invisibility or derogation, and its vital importance would be acknowledged. A focus on the process by which life is sustained would therefore include a public acknowledgment of the multitude of tasks, and the creative and productive processes involved in this kind of work.

By assuming a view from below, that is, the viewpoint of the survivors of the war against subsistence, subsistence can mean freedom, self-determination, preservation of our ecological foundations, and our cultural and biological diversity. Subsistence therefore expresses an appreciation of our continuity with nature. When work is seen as integrated in culture and where culture imbues everyday life, it also engages in a respectful, reciprocal, and cooperative relationship with the natural, biological foundations of life, or "nature." The fact that we are always tied to the "realm of necessity" (Arendt 1958), including the fact that we have bodies, that we are born and die, does therefore not simply indicate truly unfortunate limitations that call for scientific-technological transcendence or "liberation." Instead, where these limitations are acknowledged, and where the biological as well as cultural-spiritual abundance that accompanies such an acknowledgment is welcomed, a subsistence orientation can set the conditions for a sense of freedom that does not exploit and destroy but that nourishes and maintains within the very boundaries set by these limitations (Bennholdt-Thomsen and Mies 1999, 19–23).

Seen from that perspective, educational, social, and political action are all
part of a holistic practice that conjoins heart, mind, and soul. It is a practice
where our bodily connection with the natural world provides a major anchorage.
It is a practice where "paths are opening up for thinking, feeling, and acting according to our common experiences, different capabilities, and various potentials" (von Werlhof 1996, 178). It involves developing and utilizing subsistence
knowledge that not only manifests itself in the form of concrete skills, but also
entails an empathetic feel for the matter, for the other. Such knowledge is fed by
many sources. It is connected and dialogical rather than separate and monologi-
cal. Instead of universalizing or monopolizing, it allows diversity and multiplicity. It is fluid, provisional, changing knowledge, shunning the gesture of cer-
tainty or omnipotence. It is knowledge that is humble, accepting and respecting
limits, seeking to preserve and enhance rather than consume and destroy. It supports and releases into independence rather than fetters, imprisons, occupies,
and appropriates.

Seeing the interconnectedness of all life on earth, and therefore feeling responsible for its well-being, sounds like a utopian vision that confronts a heavily
divided and fragmented world. How such as vision can be upheld is, of course, a
question whose magnitude does not allow for equally grand answers. But it
allows looking for guidance to people who have taken small but significant
steps in a direction that points to such a future possibility, steps that can lead
away from the life-threatening or deadly individual and social fragmentation of
our world.

I am, for instance, reminded of Jenna, my research guide in the public housing projects. She told me about the emotional-spiritual challenge of being a
truth-teller because people don't want to hear the truth about what's really going
on in their own world and in the world at large; that she was "too Black," too
conscious, and too outspoken about racism. When Jenna visited me in my academic world, we compared notes on the difficulty of truth-telling in our respective work environments. By reaching the conclusion that we have to be capable
of facing and working through at times rather problematic conflicts, we discovered some common ground, despite our vastly different worlds. But this was
possible only because I had left my world many times and visited Jenna's, quietly listening, willing to be challenged or criticized, and fully respecting a world
I knew I could never fully understand no matter how hard I tried. This kind of
border-crossing, like any other, establishes ethical-cultural connections based on
an affirmation of and respect for life in its many different forms. Developing the
grounds for such fundamental respect, however, entails not only the hard work
of building bridges across social divides, but also of recognizing and respecting
divides that either cannot be bridged without a large-scale social-political upheaval, or that will always remain "incommensurable" differences. In Schutte's
words, placing "a high stake on the incommensurable as that which requires
recognition (rather than erasure or denigration in relation to a dominant culture)

is fundamental to acquiring an understanding, even if only a partial understanding, of the culturally differentiated 'other'" (1998, 63).

Melchiori (1997) discusses several levels and layers of difference often denied by women who attempt to build alliances. She suggests that instead of erasing these differences, they should acknowledge and analyze them. Some of these differences are lodged in "deepest desires," in "identities and belongings whose roots are often deeper than any gender belongings and whose dark sides we must face, even if with some bitterness" (8). There are also the "obscure roots of homeland, place, and culture," that is, "the fertile background of thoughts, values, and faiths which have contributed to our various and historically defined feminine identities" (9). Melchiori describes how women from Belgrade, Bosnia, and Gaza, as well as women immigrants in Canada, provide different interpretations of their bonds with a homeland by starting from their own daily lives. It is there where peace and war are made and destroyed, where the meaning of citizenship and belonging, and the meaning of being "rooted" are re-conceived, where the "normalcy" of these categories explodes (9). These women create political spaces in which traditional separations of public and private, productive and reproductive, economic and political, nature and nurture are confounded, "mixed up."

Bernice Johnson Reagon's thoughts bring to light the specificity *and* universality of a call for opening up and occupying a larger space, marking the internal and external divisions that have to be confronted in order to overcome them, and developing and nourishing a subsistence orientation. For me, the conclusions to her brief essay on "African Diaspora Women" (1986, 88–89), quoted at the beginning of this final chapter, are the conclusions of my book. They close the cycle of recognizing misery and destruction while simultaneously keeping faith in the possibility of remembering into the future, of unlearning the internal colonization of patriarchal bottom-line thinking, and discerning other possibilities.

NOTES

1. According to a study by The Urban Institute, one of every five children is poor (Acs and Gallagher 2000). The March supplement to the Current Population Survey (compiled by the U.S. Census Bureau) gives the following 1998 statistics: 13.5 million or 18.9 percent of people under eighteen years of age were poor, down from the 14.1 million and 19.9 percent reported for 1997. The supplement also reports that while the poverty rate decreased for whites and Hispanics, for Blacks it did not change between 1997 and 1998. At 26.1 percent in 1998, it remained at the lowest levels since 1959 (*Poverty in the United States 1998*). The overall poverty rate declined from 13.3 percent in 1997 to12.7 percent in 1998. A closer look at these numbers, however, reveals, that the decline of the overall poverty rate was mainly due to a sharp drop in the South, while it remained the same in other areas, including Illinois. In addition, a higher percentage of children lives below 50 percent of the poverty threshold.

2. See http://www.kwru.org for getting in touch with the Kensington Welfare Rights Union.

3. See chictrib@trib34.su-colo.bbnplanet.com for a series of articles regarding the "transformation" of public housing, and the relocation of many of its residents, in the *Chicago Tribune* (starting October 1998).

4. For a detailed analysis of the interplay of class and race with respect to fair housing in the Chicago Region, see Leachman et al. 1998.

5. What Melchiori calls Southern women is more broadly referred to as Third World women by Mohanty, that is, "both women from the geographical Third World and immigrant and indigenous women of color in the U.S." (1997, 7). While Mohanty acknowledges that "Third World" has become a problematic term, she claims that 'Third World' retains a certain heuristic value and explanatory specificity in relation to the inheritance of colonialism and contemporary neocolonial economic and geopolitical processes that the other formulations lack" (7). Other similar formulations like "North/South" and "advanced/underdeveloped nations" lose that dimension.

6. A number of feminist theorists have explored the characteristics of an ethic of care that expands the restrictive, sexist association with the feminized private sphere. See, for instance, Bowden 1997; Clement 1996; Tronto 1993; Walker 1998; and Wood 1994.

References

Abramovitz, Mimi. 1988. *Regulating the lives of women: Social welfare policy from colonial times to the present*. Boston: South End Press.
———. 1996. *Under attack, fighting back: Women and welfare in the United States*. New York: Monthly Review Press.
———. 1997. A not so hidden agenda. *The Women's Review of Books*. 14 (5):16–17.
Acs, Gregory and Megan Ghallager. 2000. Income inequality among America's children. Washington, D.C.: The Urban Institute.
Alarcón, Norma. 1990. The theoretical subject(s) of this bridge called my back and Anglo-American feminism. In *Making face, making soul:Haciendo cara.*, edited by G. Anzaldúa. San Francisco: Aunt Lute Foundation.
Albelda, Randy, and Nancy Folbre, and The Center for Popular Economics, eds. 1996. *The war on the poor*. New York: New Press.
Albelda, Randy, and Chris Tilly. 1994. It's not working: Why many single mothers can't work their way out of poverty. *Dollars and Sense*, November/December, 8–10.
Alcoff, Linda. 1991. The problem of speaking for others. *Cultural Critique* 20 (Winter): 5–32.
Amott, Teresa. 1993. *Women and the U.S. economy today*. New York: Monthly Review Press.
Amott, Teresa L., and Julie A Matthaei. 1996. A multi-cultural economic history of women in the United States. Boston: South End Press.
Anderson, Sarah, John Cavanagh, and Thea Lee. 1999. Ten myths about globalization. *The Nation* 269 (19):26–27.
Aptheker, Bettina. 1989. *Tapestries of life: Women's work, women's consciousness, and the meaning of daily experience*. Amherst: University of Massachusetts Press.
Arendt, Hannah. 1958. *The human condition*. Chicago: University of Chicago Press.
Aronowitz, Stanley, and Jonathan Cutler, eds. 1998. *Post-work*. New York and London: Routledge.

Ash, Daniel. 1994. Teen pregnancy is not a simple matter. *Chicago Tribune*, 28 September, p. 24.

Axinn, June M., and Amy E Hirsch. 1993. Welfare and the "reform" of women. *Families in Society* 74 (November):563–72.

Bales, Kevin. 1999. *Disposable people: New slavery in the global economy*. Berkeley: University of California Press.

Barnet, Richard J., and John Cavanagh. 1994. *Global dreams: Imperial corporations and the new world order*. New York: Simon and Schuster.

Barnett, Bernice McNair. 1995. Black women's collectivist movement organizations: Their struggles during the 'doldrums'. In *Feminist organizations: Harvest of the new women's movement*, edited by M. M. Ferree and P. Y. Martin. Chicago and London: University of Chicago Press.

Beasley, Chris. 1994. *Sexual economyths: Conceiving a feminist economics*. New York: St. Martin's Press.

Belenky, Mary Field, A. Lynne Bond, and Jacqueline S Weinstock. 1997. *A tradition that has no name: Nurturing the development of people, families, and communities*. New York: Basic Books.

Belenky, Mary Field, Blythe McVicker Clinchy, Nancy Rule Goldberger, and Jill Mattuck Tarule. 1986. *Women's ways of knowing: The development of self, voice, and mind*. New York: Basic Books Inc.

Bennholdt-Thomsen, Veronika. 1996. Women traders as promoters of a subsistence perspective: The case of Juchitán (Oaxaca), Mexico. In *Women, work, and gender relations in developing countries: A global perspective*, edited by P. Ghorayshi and C. Bélanger. Westport, CT: Greenwood Press.

Bennholdt-Thomsen, Veronika, and Maria Mies. 1999. *The subsistence perspective: Beyond the globalised economy*. London and New York: Zed Books.

Bettie, Julie. 2000. Women without class: *Chicas, cholas*, trash, and the presence/absence of class identity. *Signs* 26 (1):1–35.

Bhola, H. S. 1994. Women's literacy: A curriculum of assertion, resistance, and accomodation? *Convergence* 27 (2/3):41–50.

Blee, Kathleen M. 1991. *Women of the Klan: Racism and gender in the 1920s*. Berkeley: University of California Press.

———. 1997. Mothers in race-hate movements. In *The politics of motherhood: Activist voices from left to right*, edited by A. Jetter, A. Orleck, and D. Taylor. Hannover, NH: University Press of New England.

———. 1998. Reading racism: Women in the modern hate movement. In *No middle ground: Women and radical protest*, edited by K. Blee. New York and London: University of New York Press.

Blee, Kathleen M., ed. 1998. *No middle ground: Women and radical protest*. New York and London: University of New York Press.

Bleifuss, Joel. 1998. Corporate welfare reform. *In These Times*, 11 January, p. 9.

Boris, Eileen. 1993. The power of motherhood: Black and white activist women redefine the "political." In *Mothers of a new world: Maternalist politics and the origins of welfare states*, edited by S. Koven and S. Michel. New York: Routledge.

———. 1998. Scholarship and activism: The case of welfare justice. *Feminist Review* 24 (1):27–31.

———. 1999. When work is slavery. In *Women and welfare reform: Women's poverty, women's opportunities, and women's welfare*, edited by G. Mink. Washington, D.C.: Institute for Women's Policy Research.

Borland, Katherine. 1991. "That's not what I said": Interpretive conflict in oral narrative research. In *Women's words: The feminist practice of oral history*, edited by S. B. Gluck and D. Patai. New York and London: Routledge.

Bounds, Elizabeth M., Pamela K. Brubaker, and Mary E. Hobgood, eds. 1999. *Welfare policy: Feminist critiques*. Cleveland: Pilgrim Press.

Bourdieu, Pierre. 1984. *Distinction: A social critique of the judgment of taste*. Cambridge, Massachussetts: Harvard University Press.

Bowden, Peta. 1997. *Caring: Gender-sensitive ethics*. London: Routledge.

Bowlby, Sophie, Susan Gregory, and Linda McKie. 1997. "Doing home": Patriarchy, caring, and space. *Women's Studies International Forum* 20 (3):343–50.

Bowly, Devereux, Jr. 1978. *The poorhouse: Subsidized housing in Chicago, 1895–1976*. Carbondale and Edwardsville: Southern Illinois University.

Brah, Atvar, and Jane Hoy. 1989. Experiential learning: A new orthodoxy? In *Making sense of experiential learning: Diversity in theory and practice*, edited by S. W. Weil and I. McGill. Milton Keynes: The Society for Research into Higher Education & Open University Press.

Braidotti, Rosi. 1994. *Nomadic subjects: Embodiment and sexual difference in contemporary feminist theory*. New York: Columbia University Press.

Braidotti, Rosi, Ewa Charkiewicz, Sabine Häusler, and Saskia Wieringa. 1994. *Women, the environment and sustainable development: Towards a theoretical synthesis*. London: Zed Books.

Breitbart, Myrna Margulies, and Ellen-J Pader. 1995. Establishing ground: Representing gender and race in a mixed housing development. *Gender, Place, and Culture* 2 (1):5–20.

Brew, Angela. 1993. Unlearning through experience. In *Using experience for learning*, edited by D. Boud, R. Cohen and D. Walker. Buckingham: The Society for Research into Higher Education & Open University Press.

Brewer, Rose M. 1993. Theorizing race, class and gender: The new scholarship of black feminist intellectuals and black women's labor. In *Theorizing black feminisms: The visionary pragmatism of black women*, edited by S. M. James and A.P.A. Busia. New York and London: Routledge.

Brodkin, Karen. 1998. *How Jews became white folks and what that says about race in America*. New Brunswick, New Jersey, London: Rutgers University Press.

Brown, Elsa Barkley. 1989. African-American women's quilting: A framework for conceptualizing and teaching African-American women's history. *Signs* 14 (4):921–29.

———. 1993. Mothers of mind. In *Double stitch:Black women write about mothers & daughters*, edited by P. Bell-Scott, B. Guy-Sheftall, J. J. Royster, J. Sims-Wood, M. DeCosta-Willis, and L. P. Fultz. New York: Harper Perennial.

Brownworth, Victoria A. 1997. Life in the passing lane: Exposing the class closet. In *Queerly classed: Gay men & lesbians write about class*, edited by S. Raffo. Boston: South End Press.

Brunetiére, Dominique, Jeanette Metay, and Thierry Sylvestre. 1990. Is there an illiterate culture? In *ALPHA 90: Current research in literacy*, edited by J.-P. Hautecoeur. Québec: Ministère de l'Éducation.

Brunner, Otto. 1968. Das "ganze Haus" und die alteuropäische Ökonomik. In *Neue Wege der Sozial- und Verfassungsgeschichte*, edited by O. Brunner. Göttingen: Vandenhoeck U. Ruprecht.

Buchwald, Emilie, Pamela Fletcher, and Martha Roth, eds. 1993. *Transforming a rape culture*. Minneapolis: Milkweed Editions.

Busman, Deb. 1998. Representations of working-class "intelligence": Fiction by Jack London, Agnes Smedley, and Valerie Miner, and new scholarship by Carol Whitehill and Janet Zandy. *Women's Studies Quarterly* 26 (1 and 2):75–92.

Cancian, Maria, Robert Haveman, Thomas Kaplan, Daniel Meyer, and Barbara Wolfe. 1999. Work, earnings, and well-being after welfare: What do we know? Paper read at Conference on Welfare Reform and the Macroeconomy, sponsored by the Joint Center for Poverty Research, November 19–20, at Washington, D.C.

Canning, Kathleen. 1994. Feminist history after the linguistic turn: Historicizing discourse and experience. *Signs* 19 (2):368–404.

Cannon, Katie G. 1988. *Black womanist ethics*. Atlanta: Scholars Press.

Castern, Katie. 2000. What candidates are not saying about welfare reform. *PRAGmatics* 3 (2):14–16.

Changes in Illinois welfare law: The Illinois TANF program and other changes in public benefits. 1997. Chicago: The Poverty Law Project of the National Clearinghouse for Legal Services:.

Chicago Housing Authority. 1997. <http://www.thecha.org/>.

———. 2000. Plan for transformation: Improving housing in Chicago and the quality of life.

Childers, Mary M. 1997. A spontaneous welfare rights protest by politically inactive mothers: A daughter's reflection. In *The politics of motherhood: Activist voices from left to right*, edited by A. Jetter, A. Orleck, and D. Taylor. Hanover, NH: University Press of New England.

Chomsky, Noam. 1999. *Profit over people: Neoliberalism and global order*. New York: Seven Stories Press.

Chow, Esther Ngan-Ling, Doris Wilkinson, and Maxine Baca Zinn, eds. 1996. *Race, class, & gender: Common bonds, different voices*. Thousand Oaks: Sage Publications.

Christian, Barbara. 1990. The race for theory. In *Making face, making soul: Haciendo caras*, edited by G. Anzaldúa. San Francisco: Aunt Lute Foundation.

Clement, Grace. 1996. *Care, autonomy, and justice: Feminism and the ethic of care*. Boulder: Westview Press.

Code, Lorraine. 1998. How to think globally: Stretching the limits of imagination. *Hypatia* 13 (2):73–85.

Cohen, Cathy J., Kathleen B. Jones, and Joan C. Tronto, eds. 1997a. *Women transforming politics: An alternative reader*. New York and London: New York University Press.

———. 1997b. Politics: Sites of power/resistance. In *Women transforming politics: An alternative reader*, edited by C. J. Cohen, K. B. Jones, and J. C. Tronto. New York: Guilford Press.

Collins, Patricia Hill. 1990. *Black feminist thought: Knowledge, consciousness, and the politics of empowerment*. Boston: Unwin Hyman.

———. 1993. The meaning of motherhood and black mother-daughter relationships. In *Double stitch: Black women write about mothers & daughters*, edited by P. Bell-Scott, B. Guy-Sheftall, J. J. Royster, J. Sims-Wood, M. DeCosta-Willis, and L. P. Fultz.

————. 1994. Shifting the center: Race, class, and feminist theorizing about mother-hood. In *Mothering: Ideology, experience, and agency*, edited by E. N. Glenn, G. Chang, and L. R. Forcey. New York and London: New York University Press.

————. 1997. Comment on Hekman's "Truth and method: Feminist standpoint theory revisited": Where's the power? *Signs* 22 (2):375–81.

————. 1998. *Fighting words: Black women and the search for justice*. Minneapolis and London: University of Minnesota Press.

Collins, Sheila. 1996. *The politics of poverty and inequality*. New York: Monthly Review Press.

Cotterill, Pamela. 1992. Interviewing women: Issues of friendship, vulnerability, and power. *Women's Studies International Forum* 15 (5-6):593–606.

Crenshaw, Kimberlè Williams. 1997. Beyond racism and misogyny: Black feminism and 2 Live Crew. In *Women transforming politics: An alternative reader*, edited by C. J. Cohen, K. B. Jones, and J. C. Tronto. New York and London: New York University Press.

Cruikshank, Barbara. 1995. The will to empower: Technologies of citizenship and the war on poverty. *Socialist Review* 23 (4):29–55.

Cunningham, Phyllis, and Regina Curry. 1997. Learning within a social movement: The Chicago African-American experience. Paper read at the 38th Annual Adult Education Research Conference, May 16–18, at Stillwater, Oklahoma.

Dalla Costa, Mariarosa. 1995. Development and reproduction. *Common Sense* (17):11–33.

————. 1997. Some notes on neoliberalism, on land and on the food question. *Canadian Woman Studies/le cahiers de la femme* 17 (2):28–30.

Danziger, Sheldon. 2000. How they're faring: Work earnings under welfare reform. *Poverty Research News* 4 (5):5–7.

De Goede, Marieke. 1996. Ideology in the US welfare debate: Neo-liberal representations of poverty. *Discourse & Society* 7 (3):317–357.

DeParle, Jason. 1994. Better work than welfare. But what if there's neither? *New York Times Magazine*, 18 December, pp. 43, 49, 56, 58, 74.

————. 1998. Shrinking welfare rolls leave record high share of minorities. *New York Times*, 27 July, A1, A12.

————. 1999a. As welfare rolls shrink, load on relatives grows. *New York Times*, 21 February, A1, A24.

————. 1999b. Early sex abuse hinders many women on welfare. *New York Times*, 28 November, A1, A20, A21.

DeVault, Marjorie. 1997. Personal writing in social research: Issues of production and interpretation. In *Women's words: The feminist practice of oral history*, edited by S. B. Gluck and D. Patai. New York and London: Routledge.

————. 1999. *Liberating method: Feminism and social research*. Philadelphia: Temple University Press.

Dibernard, Barbara. 1996. Teaching what I'm not: An able-bodied woman teaches literature by women with disabilities. In *Teaching what you're not: Identity politics in higher education*, edited by K. J. Mayberry. New York and London: New York University Press.

DiFazio, William. 1998. Why there is no movement of the poor. In *Post-work*, edited by S. Aronowitz and J. Cutler. New York and London: Routledge.

Donovan, Aaron. 1999. At threshold of old age, still caring for children. *New York Times*, 5 December, A5, A12.

Dujon, Dian, and Ann Withorn. 1996. *For crying out loud: Women's poverty in the United States*. Boston: South End Press.

Duneier, Mitchell. 1992. *Race, respectability and masculinity*. Chicago: University of Chicago Press.

Ebert, Teresa L. 1996. *Ludic feminism and after: Postmodernism, desire, and labor in late capitalism*. Ann Arbor: University of Michigan Press.

Edelman, Marian Wright. 1994. *Wasting America's future: The Children's Defense Fund report on the cost of child poverty*. Boston: Beacon Press.

Edin, Kathryn, Laura Lein, Timothy Nelson, and Susan Clampet-Lundquist. 2000. Talking with low-income fathers. *Poverty Research News* 4 (2):10–12.

Ehrenreich, Barbara. 1997. Spinning the poor into gold: How corporations seek to profit from welfare reform. *Harper's Magazine* (August): 44–52.

Ellsworth, Elizabeth. 1997. *Teaching positions: Difference, pedagogy, and the power of address*. New York and London: Teachers College Press.

Enslin, Elizabeth. 1994. Beyond writing: Feminist practice and the limitations of ethnography. *Cultural Anthropology* 9 (4):537–68.

Esposito, Anthony. 1999. Class, race, and culture: Teaching intercultural communication. In *Teaching working class*, edited by S. L. Linkon. Amherst: University of Massachusetts Press.

Evans, Sarah M., and Harry C Boyte. 1998. *Free spaces: The sources of democratic change in America*. New York: Harper & Row.

Fanon, Franz. 1967. *Black skins, white masks*. New York: Grove Press.

Feldman, Roberta M., Susan Stall, and Patricia Wright. 1998. "The community needs to be built by us": Women organizing in Chicago public housing. In *Community activism and feminist politics: Organizing across race, class, and gender*, edited by N. A. Naples. New York and London: Routledge.

Ferree, Myra Marx, and Patricia Yancey Martin, eds. 1995. *Feminist organizations: Harvest of the new women's movement*. Philadelphia: Temple University Press.

Ferretti, Eileen. 1999. Between dirty dishes and polished discourse: How working-class moms construct identities. In *Teaching working class*, edited by S. L. Linkon. Amherst: University of Massachusetts Press.

Figueroa, Hector. 1999. Blood, sweat & shears: In the name of fashion. Exploitation in the garment industry. *NACLA report on the Americas* 29 (4):34–40.

Finger, Mathias, and José Manuel Asún. 2001. *Adult education at the crossroads: Learning our way out*. London and New York: Zed Books.

Fine, Michelle, and Lois Weis. 1998. *The unknown city: The lives of poor and working-class adults*. Boston: Beacon Press.

Fischer, Paul. 1999. Section 8 and the public housing revolution: Where will the families go? Chicago: Woods Fund.

Fisher, Robert. 1994. *Let the people decide: Neighborhood organizing in America*. New York: Twayne Publishers.

Flammang, Janet A. 1997. *Women's political voice: How women are transforming the practice and study of politics*. Philadelphia: Temple University Press.

Flynn, Gillian. 1999. Who's left in the labor pool? *Workforce* 78 (10):3–36.

Folbre, Nancy. 1993. Socialism, feminist and scientific. In *Beyond economic man: Feminist theory and economics*, edited by M. A. Ferber and J. A. Nelson. Chicago and London: University of Chicago Press.

———. 1994. *Who pays for the kids? Gender and the structures of constraint*. London and New York: Routledge.

————. 1997. The unproductive housewife: Her evolution in nineteenth-century economic thought. In *History and theory: Feminist research, debates, contestations*, edited by B. Laslett, R.-E. Joeres, M. J. Maynes, E. B. Higginbotham, and B.-N. Jeanne. Chicago and London: University of Chicago Press.

Frago, Charles. 1997. Altgeld's transportation lifeline cut. *Streetwise*, 14 October, p. 3.

Frankenberg, Ruth. 1993. *White women, race matters: The social construction of whiteness*. Minneapolis: University of Minnesota Press.

Fraser, Nancy. 1990a. Rethinking the public sphere: A contribution to the critique of actually existing democracy. *Social Text* 25 (6):56–79.

————. 1990b. Struggle over needs: Outline of a socialist-feminist critical theory of late-capitalist political culture. In *Women, the state, and welfare*, edited by L. Gordon. Madison: The University of Wisconsin Press.

————. 1995. What's critical about critical theory? In *Feminists read Habermas: Gendering the subject of discourse*, edited by J. Meehan. New York and London: Routledge.

From welfare to worse? Children, welfare reform, and local realities. 1998. Loyola University Center for Urban Research and Learning, Policy Research Action Group, Organization of the Northeast, Howard Area Community Center.

Funiciello, Theresa. 1990. The poverty industry: Do government and charities create the poor? *Ms. Magazine* 1 (3):33–40.

————. 1993a. The fifth estate: How and why the poverty industry distorts welfare issues and displaces the interests of people on welfare. In *Women and welfare reform: Women's poverty, women's opportunity, and women's welfare*, edited by G. Mink. Washington, D.C.: Institute for Women's Policy Research.

————. 1993b. *Dismantling the welfare system to end poverty in America*. New York: Atlantic Monthly Press.

Furman, Frida Kerner. 1997. *Facing the mirror: Older women and beauty shop culture*. New York and London: Routledge.

Fuss, Diana. 1989. *Essentially speaking: Feminism, nature and difference*. New York and London: Routledge.

Gamson, William A. 1996. Safe spaces and social movements. *Perspectives on Social Movements* 8:27–38.

Gans, Herbert J. 1991. *People, plans, and policies: Essays on poverty, racism, and the other national urban problems*. New York: Columbia University Press.

Garbarino, James, Kathleen Kostelney, and Nancy Dubrow, eds. 1991. *No place to be a child: Growing up in a war zone*. Lexington, MA: Lexington Books.

Garber, Judith A. 1995. Defining feminist community: Place, choice, and the urban politics of difference. In *Gender in urban research*, edited by J. Garber and R. S. Turner. Thousand Oaks: Sage Publications.

Garfinkel, Harold. 1956. Conditions of successful degradation ceremonies. *American Journal of Sociology* 61 (5):420–24.

Gelpi, Barbara C., Nancy C. M. Hartsock, Clare C. Novak, and Myra H. Strober. 1986. *Women and poverty*. Chicago: University of Chicago Press.

Gerschlager, Caroline, and Peter Heintel. 1993. Der kalte Blick der Ökonomie: 30 Gespräche. In *Der kalte Blick der Ökonomie: 30 Gespräche*, edited by A. Bammé, W. Berger, C. Gerschlager, and L. Gubitzer. München and Wien: Profil Verlag.

Gibbs, Lois, An Interview With. 1997. "What is your wife trying to do—shut down the chemical industry?": The housewives of Love Canal. In *The politics of mother-*

hood: Activist voices from left to right, edited by A. Jetter, A. Orleck, and D. Taylor. Hanover, NH: University Press of New England.

Gilkes, Cheryl Townsend. 1994. "If it wasn't for the women . . . ": African American women, community work, and social change. In *Women of color in U.S. society*, edited by M. B. Zinn and B. T. Dill. Philadelphia: Temple University Press.

Glazer, Nona Y. 1984. Servants to capital: Unpaid domestic labor and paid work. *Review of Radical Political Economics* 161 (1):61–87.

Glenn, Evelyn Nakano. 1994. Social constructions of mothering: A thematic overview. In *Mothering: Ideology, experience, and agency*, edited by E. N. Glenn, G. Chang, and L. R. Forcey. New York and London: Routledge.

———. 1997. From servitude to service work: Historical continuities in the racial division of paid reproductive labor. In *History and theory: Feminist research, debates, contestations*, edited by B. Laslett, R.-E. Joeres, M. J. Maynes, E. B. Higginbotham, and J. Barker-Nunn. Chicago and London: University of Chicago Press.

Golden, Renny. 1997. *Disposable children: America's welfare system*. Belmont, CA: Wadsworth Publishing Company.

Gordon, Danielle, and James Ylisela, Jr. 1998. Court ruling puts more teeth in public housing plan. *Chicago Reporter* 27 (3):1, 6, 17.

Gordon, Linda. 1988. What does welfare regulate? *Social Research* 55 (4):609–30.

———. 1994a. What future for social policy? Welfare reform: A history lesson. *Dissent* (Summer):323–28.

———. 1994b. *Pitied but not entitled: Single mothers and the history of welfare*. Cambridge, MA: Harvard University Press.

———, ed. 1990. *Women, the state, and welfare*. Madison: University of Wisconsin Press.

Gorelick, Sherry. 1991. Contradictions of feminist methodology. *Gender and Society* 5:459–77.

Greene, Maxine. 1988. *The dialectic of freedom*. New York: Teachers College Press.

Greenhouse, Steven. 1998. Many participants in workfare take the place of city workers. *New York Times*, 13 April, A1, A25.

Gregory, Steven. 1998. *Black corona: Race and the politics of place in an urban community*. Princeton, NJ: Princeton University Press.

Greider, William. 1997. *One world, ready or not: The manic logic of global capitalism*. New York: Simon & Schuster.

Griffin, Christine. 1996. Experiencing power: Dimensions of gender, "race," and class. In *Practicing feminism: Identity, difference, and power*, edited by N. Charles and F. Hughes-Freeland. New York and London: Routledge.

Grossman, Karl. 1993. Environmental racism. In *The "racial" economy of science: Toward a democratic future*, edited by S. Harding. Bloomington and Indianapolis: Indiana University Press.

Grumman, Cornelia. 1999. Welfare caseload slashed in 2 years. *Chicago Tribune*, 27 June, pp. 1, 11.

Habermas, Juergen. 1989. *The structural transformation of the public sphere: An inquiry into a category of bourgeois society*. Translated by T. Burger and F. Lawrence. Cambridge, MA: MIT Press.

Hacker, Andrew. 1992. *Two nations*. New York: Ballantine Books.

Hall, John R. 1997. *Reworking class*. Ithaca and London: Cornell University Press.

Hanney, Suzanne. 1999. Winter relocation has CHA residents wary. *Streetwise*, 28 September–11 October, pp.1, 3.

Haraway, Donna. 1988. Situated knowledges: The science question in feminism and the privilege of partial perspective. *Feminist Studies* 14 (3):575–99.

———. 1991. *Simians, cyborgs, and woman: The reinvention of nature.* New York and London: Routledge.

Harcourt, Wendy. 1994. *Feminist perspectives on sustainable development.* London and New Jersey: Zed Books.

Harding, Sandra. 1991. *Whose science? Whose knowledge? Thinking from women's lives.* Ithaca: New York University Press.

———. 1998. *Is science multicultural? Postcolonialism, feminism, and epistemologies.* Bloomington and Indianapolis: Indiana University Press.

Hardy-Fanta, Carol. 1997. Latina women and political consciousness: La chispa que prende. In *Women transforming politics: An alternative reader,* edited by C. J. Cohen, K. B. Jones, and J. C. Tronto. New York and London: New York University Press.

Harrington, Michael. 1963. *The other America: Poverty in the United States.* New York: Penguin Books.

Harris. 1993. Work and welfare among single mothers in poverty. *American Journal of Sociology* 99 (3):317–52.

Hart, Mechthild U. 1990. Liberation through consciousness raising. In *Fostering critical reflection in adulthood:A guide to transformative and emancipatory learning,* edited by J. Mezirow. San Francisco: Jossey-Bass.

———. 1992. *Working and educating for life: Feminist and international perspectives on adult education.* New York and London: Routledge.

———. 2001. Transforming boundaries of power in the classroom: Learning from *la mestiza.* In *Power in practice: Adult Education and the struggle for knowledge and power in society,* edited by R. Cervero and A. Wilson. San Francisco: Jossey-Bass.

Hartsock, Nancy C. 1983. The feminist standpoint: Developing the grounds for a specifically feminist historical materialism. In *Discovering reality: Feminist perspectives on epistemology, metaphysics, and philosophy,* edited by S. Harding and M. B. Hintikka. Boston: Reidel.

Hautecoeur, Jean-Paul, ed. 1996. *ALPHA 96: Basic education and work.* Hamburg: Unesco Institute for Education & Culture Concepts Inc.

———, ed. 1990. *ALPHA 90: Current research in literacy.* Québec: Ministère de Él'ducation.

Haymes, Stephen. 1995. *Race, culture, and the city: A pedagogy for black urban struggle.* Albany: SUNY Press.

Helmbold, Lois Rita. 1998. No passing zone. *The Women's Review of Books,* pp. 15,16.

Hernández, Adriana. 1997. *Pedagogy, democracy and feminism: Rethinking the public sphere.* New York: State University of New York Press.

Hertz, Rosanna, ed. 1997. *Reflexivity & voice.* Thousand Oaks: Sage Publications.

Hess, Alfred G. 1999. School reform struggles in an era of accountability. *PRAGmatics: The Journal of Community-Based Research* 2 (4):3–5.

Higginbotham, Evelyn Brooks. 1992. African-American women's history and the metalanguage of race. *Signs* 17 (2):253–54.

———. 1993. *Righteous discontent: The women's movement in the black baptist church, 1880–1920.* Cambridge, MA: Harvard University Press.

Hirsch, Arnold R. 1998. *Making the second ghetto: Race and housing in Chicago, 1940–1960*. Chicago: Chicago University Press.

Hirsch, Marianne. 1997. Feminism at the maternal divide: A diary. In *The politics of motherhood: Activist voices from left to right*, edited by A. Jetter, A. Orleck and D. Taylor. Hanover, NH: University Press of New England.

Holloway, Karla. 1995. *Codes of conduct: Race, ethics, and the color of our character*. New Brunswick, NJ: Rutgers University Press.

Holzer, Harry J. 1998. Employer demand for welfare recipients and the business cycle: Evidence from recent employer surveys. Paper read at Conference on Welfare Reform and the Macroeconomy, November 19–20, at Washington, D.C.

Hondagneu-Sotelo, Pierette. 1994. Regulating the unregulated?: Domestic workers' social networks. *Social Problems* 41 (1):50–64.

———. 1998. Latina immigrant women and paid domestic work. In *Community activism and feminist politics: Organizing across race, class, and gender*, edited by N. A. Naples. New York and London: Routledge.

hooks, bell. 1989. *Thinking feminist, thinking black*. Boston: South End Press.

———. 1990a. Talking back. In *Making face, making soul: Haciendo caras*, edited by G. Anzaldúa. San Francisco: Aunt Lute Foundation.

———. 1990b. *Yearning: Race, gender, and cultural politics*. Boston: South End Press.

———. 1994. *Teaching to transgress: Education as the practice of freedom*. New York and London: Routledge.

Horowitz, Ruth. 1995. *Teen mothers: Citizens or dependents?* Chicago: University of Chicago Press.

Houppert, Karen. 1999. You're not entitled! Welfare "reform" is leading to government lawlessness. *The Nation* 269 (13):11–25.

Hurtado, Aïda. 1996. Strategic suspensions: Feminists of color theorize the production of knowledge. In *Knowledge, difference, and power: Essays inspired by women's ways of knowing*, edited by N. R. Goldberger, J. M. Tarule, B. M. Clinchy, and M. F. Belenky. New York: Basic Books.

Jackson, Sandra, and José Solís Jordán, eds. 1999. *I've got a story to tell: Identity and place in the academy*. New York: Peter Lang.

James, Stanlie M. 1993. Mothering: A possible black feminist link to social transformation. In *Theorizing black feminisms: The visionary pragmatism of black women*, edited by S. M. James and A. P.A. Busia. New York and London: Routledge.

Jameson, Elizabeth, and Susan Armitage, eds. 1997. *Writing the range: Race, class, and culture in the women's west*. Norman and London: University of Oklahoma Press.

Jarrett, Robin L. 1994. Living poor: Family life among single parent, African-American women. *Social Problems* 41 (1):30–49.

Jensen, Barbara. 1998. The silent psychology. *Women's Studies Quarterly* 26 (1/2):202–15.

Jetter, Alexis, Anneliese Orleck, and Diana Taylor, eds. 1997. *The politics of motherhood: Activist voices from left to right*. Hanover, NH: University Press of New England.

Jezierski, Louise. 1995. Women organizing their place in restructuring economies. In *Gender in urban research*, edited by J. Garber and R. S. Turner. Thousand Oaks: Sage Publications.

Jones, Ann. 1994. *Next time, she'll be dead*. Boston: Beacon Press.

Jones, Leland, Lloyd Newman, and David Isay. 1997. *Our America: Life and death on the south side of Chicago*. New York: Scribner.

Joseph, Lawrence B, ed. 1999. *Families, poverty, and welfare reform: Confronting a new policy era.* Chicago: Center for Urban Research and Policy Studies, Irving B. Harris Graduate School of Public Policy Studies, University of Chicago: University of Illinois Press.

Kadi, Joanna. 1996. *Thinking class: Sketches from a cultural worker.* Boston: South End Press.

Kamin, Blair. 1995a. An elusive blend. *Chicago Tribune*, 20 June, pp. 1, 12.

———. 1995b. Housing that works. *Chicago Tribune*, 18 June, pp. 1, 9.

Kaplan, Temma. 1995. Female consciousness and collective action: The case of Barcelona, 1910–1918. In *Rethinking the political: Gender, resistance, and the state*, edited by B. Laslett, J. Brenner, and Y. Arat. Chicago: Chicago University Press.

———. 1997. *Crazy for democracy: Women in grassroots movements.* New York and London: Routledge.

Karamcheti, Indira. 1996. Caliban in the classroom. In *Teaching what you're not: Identity politics in higher education*, edited by K. J. Mayberry. New York and London: New York University Press.

Karp, Sarah. 2000. Minorities off welfare get few jobs. *Chicago Reporter* 29 (1):1, 7–10.

Katz, Michael B. 1989. *The undeserving poor: From the war on poverty to the war on welfare.* New York: Pantheon Books.

Kenway, Jane, and Helen Modra. 1992. Feminist pedagogy and emancipatory possibilities. In *Feminism and critical pedagogy*, edited by C. Luke and J. Gore. New York and London: Routledge.

Kim, Marlene. 1996. The working poor and welfare recipiency. *Poverty & Race* 5 (1):7–8.

Kingfisher, Catherine P. 1996. *Women in the American welfare trap.* Philadelphia: University of Pennsylvania Press.

———. 1999. Rhetoric of (female) savagery: Welfare reform in the United States and Aotearoa/New Zealand. *NWSA Journal* 11 (1):1–20.

Kirsch, Gesa E. 1999. *Ethical dilemmas in feminist research: The politics of location, interpretation, and publication.* New York: State University of New York Press.

Kittay, Eva Feder. 1998. Dependence, equality, and welfare. *Feminist Review* 24 (1):32–43.

———. 1999. Welfare, dependency, and a public ethic of care. In *Whose welfare?*, edited by G. Mink. Ithaca and London: Cornell University Press.

Koonz, Claudia. 1997. Motherhood and politics on the far right. In *The politics of motherhood: Activist voices from right to left*, edited by A. Jetter, A. Orleck, and D. Taylor. Hanover, NH: University Press of New England.

Kotlowitz, Alex. 1991. *There are no Children Here: The story of two boys growing up in the other America.* New York: Doubleday.

Krauss, Celene. 1998. Challenging power: Toxic waste politics and the politicization of white, working-class women. In *Community activism and feminist politics: Organizing across race, class, and gender*, edited by N. A. Naples. New York and London: Routledge.

Krojec, Valerie Dawkins, Paula Jordon Bloom, Tery Talan, and Douglas Clark. 2001. *Who's caring for the kids? The status of the early childhood workforce in Illinois.* Chicago: Joint Poject by the Center for Early Childhood Leadership, National Louis University, and Illinois Network of Child Care Resources and Referral Agencies.

LaDuke, Winona, An Interview With. 1997. Reclaiming culture and the land: Motherhood and the politics of sustaining community. In *The politics of motherhood: Voices from left to right*, edited by A. Jetter, A. Orleck, and D. Taylor. Hanover, NH: University Press of New England.

Lamont, Michele, and Annette Lareau. 1988. Cultural capital: Allusions, gaps and glissandos in recent theoretical developments. *Sociological Theory* 6 (Fall):153–68.

Lavelle, Robert. 1995. *America's new war on poverty*. San Francisco: KQED Books.

Leachman, Mike, Phil Nyden, Bill Peterman, and Darnell Coleman. 1998. Black, white, and shades of brown: Fair housing and economic opportunity in the Chicago region. Chicago: Leadership Council For Metropolitan Open Communities.

Lemann, Nicholas. 1991. *The promised land: The great black migration and how it changed America*. New York: Vintage Books.

Lemke-Santangelo, Gretchen. 1996. *Abiding courage: African American migrant women and the east bay community*. Chapel Hill: University of North Carolina Press.

Lewin, Tamat. 1998. From welfare roll to child care worker. *New York Times*, 12 April, A1, A14.

Linkon, Sherry Lee, ed. 1999. *Teaching working class*. Amherst: University of Massachusetts Press.

Lloyd, Susan, and Nina Taluc. 1999. The effects of male violence on female employment. *Violence Against Women* 5 (4):370–92.

Lopoo, Len. 2000. Welfare reform and the macro-economy. *Poverty Research News* 4 (1):15–17.

Lorde, Audre. 1984. *Sister outsider: Essays and speeches*. Trumansburg, NY: Crossing Press.

———. 1988. *A burst of light*. Ithaca, NY: Firebrand Books.

Louie, Miriam Ching Yoon. 2001. *Sweatshop warriors: Immigrant women workers take on the global factory*. Cambridge: South End Press.

Loury, Alden K. 2000a. Fatherhood, ready or not. *Chicago Reporter* 29 (4): 8–9.

———. 2000b. Fighting the odds. *Chicago Reporter* 29 (4):3–7.

Lugones, Maria. 1990. Playfulness, "world"-traveling, and loving perception. In *Making face, making soul: Haciendo caras*, edited by G. Anzaldúa. San Francisco: Aunt Lute Foundation.

Luttrell, Wendy. 1997. *Schoolsmart and motherwise: Working-class women's identity and schooling*. New York and London: Routledge.

Luttwak, Edward. 1999. *Turbo-capitalism: Winners and losers in the global economy*. New York: HarperCollins Publishers.

Lyderson, Karl. 1998. Slowly poisoned. Altgeld residents sick over EPA decision. *Streetwise*, 4 August–11 August, pp. 1, 2.

Maher, Frances A., and Mary Kay Thompson Tetreault. 1994. *The feminist classroom: An inside look at how professors and students are transforming higher education for a diverse society*. New York: Basic Books.

———. 1996. Women's ways of knowing in women's studies, feminist pedagogies, and feminist theory. In *Knowledge, difference, and power: Essays inspired by women's ways of knowing*, edited by N. R. Goldberger, J. M. Tarule, B. M. Clinchy, and M. F. Belenky. New York: Basic Books.

Mantsios, Gregory. 1996. Rewards and opportunities: The politics and economics of class in the U.S. In *The meaning of difference: American constructions of race, sex and gender, social class, and sexual orientation*, edited by K. E. Rosenblum and T.-M. Travis. New York: McGraw Hill.

Marsh, Jordan. 1997. The gang way. *Reader* 26 (44):18–20, 24.

Marshall, Barbara L. 1994. *Feminism, social theory and social change.* Boston: Northeastern University Press.

Massey, Douglas S., and Mary J Fischer. 1998. Where we live, in black and white. *The Nation* 267 (20):25.

Mayberry, Katherine J., ed. 1996. *Teaching what you're not: Identity politics in higher education.* New York and London: New York University Press.

McCourt, Kathleen. 1977. *Working-class women and grass-roots politics.* Bloomington and Indianapolis: Indiana University Press.

McIntosh, Peggy. 1995. White and male privilege: A personal account of coming to see correspondences through work in women's studies. In *Race, class, and gender,* edited by M. L. Andersen and P. H. Collins. Belmont, CA: Wadsworth Publishing Company.

McRoberts, Flynn. 1998a. Home is where the problem is. *Chicago Tribune,* 25 October, pp. 1, 18–19.

———. 1998b. Move from CHA high-rise can involve a leap of faith. *Chicago Tribune,* 2 September, pp. 1, 12.

McRoberts, Flynn, and Terry Wilson. 1998. CHA has 9 of 10 poorest areas in U.S., study says. *Chicago Tribune,* 21 January, pp. 1, 6.

Melchiori, Paola. 1996. Women, civil society and feminist political practices: Which critique of the democratic conceptual frame? Paper read at 6th International Interdisciplinary Congress on Women, April 22–26, at Adelaide, Australia.

———. 1997. Messages from Huairou: Notes for a redefinition of spaces of politics. *Canadian Women's Studies/les cahiers de la femme* 17 (2):6–11.

Michel, Sonya. 1998. Childcare and welfare (in)justice. *Feminist Studies* 24 (1):44–54.

Michelson, Elana.1996a. "Auctoritee" and "experience": Feminist epistemology and the assessment of experiential learning. *Feminist Studies* 22 (3):627–55.

———. 1996b. Ususal suspects: Experience, reflection and the (en)gendering of knowledge. *International Journal of Lifelong Education* 15 (6):438–54.

———. 1998. Re-membering: The return of the body to experiential learning. *Studies in Continuing Education* 20 (2):217–33.

Mies, Maria. 1982. *The lace makers of Narsapur: Indian housewives produce for the world market.* London: Zed Press.

———. 1986. *Patriarchy and accumulation on a world scale.* London: Zed Press.

———. 1991. Women's research or feminist research? The debate surrounding feminist science and methodology. In *Beyond methodology: Feminist scholarship as lived research,* edited by J. A. Cook and M. M. Fonow. Bloomington and Indianapolis: Indiana University Press.

———. 1996. Globalisation of the economy and women's work in a sustainable society. Paper read at 6th International Interdisciplinary Congress on Women, April 22–26, at Adelaide, Australia.

———. 1997. Do we need a new "moral economy"? *Canadian Woman Studies/les cahiers de la femme* 17 (2):12–20.

Mies, Maria, and Vandana Shiva. 1993. Ecofeminism. London and New Jersey: Zed Books.

Miles, Angela. 1996. *Integrative feminisms: Building global visions, 1960s–1990s.* New York and London: Routledge.

Miller, Vernice, Moya Hallstein, and Susan Quass. 1996. Feminist politics and environmental justice: Women's community activism in West Harlem, New York. In

Feminist political ecology: Global issues and local experiences, edited by D. Rocheleau, B. Thomas-Slayter and E. Wangari. New York and London: Routledge.

Mink, Gwendolyn. 1993. Women and welfare reform: Women's poverty, women's opportunities, and women's welfare. Paper read at A Policy Conference to Break Myths and Create Solutions, October 23, at Washington, D.C.

———. 1998a. The lady and the tramp (II): Feminist welfare politics, poor single mothers, and the challenge of welfare justice. *Feminist Studies* 24 (1):55–64.

———. 1998b. *Welfare's end.* Ithaca and London: Cornell University Press.

———. 1999. *Whose welfare?* Ithaca and London: Cornell University Press.

Mistry, Rashmita, Danielle Crosby, Aletha Huston, David Casey, and Marika Ripke. 2000. Lessons from new hope: The impact on children's well-being. *Poverty Research News* 4 (4):4, 6–7.

Moberg, David. 1999. Bringing down niketown. *The Nation* 268 (21):15–19.

Moffitt, Robert, and Jennifer Roff. 2000. The diversity of welfare leavers. Baltimore, MD: John Hopkins University, Welfare, Children & Families Study (Policy Brief 00–2).

Mohanty, Chandra Talpade. 1991. Cartagrophies of struggle: Third world women and the politics of feminism. In *Third world women and the politics of feminism,* edited by C. T. Mohanty, A. Russo and L. Torres. Bloomington and Indianapolis: Indiana University Press.

———. 1997. Women workers and capitalist scripts: Ideologies of domination, common interests, and the politics of solidarity. In *Feminist genealogies, colonial legacies, democratic futures,* edited by J. M. Alexander and C. T. Mohanty. New York and London: Routledge.

Moraga, Cherríe, and Gloria Anzaldúa, eds. 1981. *This bridge called my back: Writings by radical women of color.* Watertown, MA: Persephone Press.

Morris, Aldon D. 1984. *The origins of the civil rights movement: Black communities organizing for social change.* New York: Free Press.

Morris, Elizabeth. 1996. Community in theory and practice: A framework of intellectual renewal. *Journal of Planning Literature* 11 (1):127–51.

Moya, Paula M. 1997. Postmodernism, "realism," and the politics of identity: Cherríe Moraga and Chicana feminism. In *Feminist genealogies, colonial legacies, democratic futures,* edited by J. M. Alexander and C. T. Mohanty. New York and London: Routledge.

Mullings, Leith. 1994. Images, ideology, and women of color. In *Women of color in U.S. society,* edited by M. B. Zinn and B. T. Dill. Philadelphia: Temple University Press.

Naples, Nancy A. 1992. Activist mothering: Cross-generational continuity in the community work of women from low-income neighborhoods. *Gender & Society* 5 (3):441–63.

———. 1996. A feminist revisiting of the insider/outsider debate: The outsider phenomenon in rural Iowa. *Qualitative Sociology* 19 (1):83–106.

———. 1998a. *Grassroots warriors: Activist mothering, community work, and the war on poverty.* New York and London: Routledge.

———. 1999. Towards comparative analyses of women's political praxis: Explicating multiple dimensions of standpoint epistemology for feminist ethnography. *Women and Politics* 20 (1):29–57.

———, ed. 1998b. *Community activism and feminist politics: Organizing across race, class, and gender.* New York and London: Routledge.

Narayan, Uma. 1997. *Dislocating cultures: Identities, traditions, and third world feminism.* New York and London: Routledge.

Navarro, Mireya. 1996. Teen-age mothers viewed as abused prey of older men. *New York Times,* 19 May, A1, A19.

Nelson, Barbara. 1990. The origins of the two-channel welfare state: Workmen's compensation and mother's aid. In *Women, the state, and welfare,* edited by L. Gordon. Madison: The University of Wisconsin Press.

Nelson, Cary, and Lawrence Grossberg, eds. 1988. *Marxism and interpretation of culture.* Urbana: University of Illinois Press.

Nelson, Lynn Hankinson. 1993. Epistemological communities. In *Feminist epistemologies,* edited by L. Alcoff and E. Potter. New York and London: Routledge.

Nelson, Margaret K. 1994. Family day care providers: Dilemmas of daily practice. In *Mothering: Ideology, experience, and agency,* edited by E. N. Glenn, G. Chang, and L. R. Forcey. New York and London: Routledge.

Noddings, Nel. 1991. Stories in dialogue: Caring and interpersonal reasoning. In *Stories lives tell: Narrative and dialogue in education,* edited by C. Witherell and N. Noddings. New York: Teachers College Press.

Oldweiler, Cory. 1998. Going to bat for public housing residents. *Chicago Reporter* 27 (8):11–13.

Omi, Michael, and Howard Winant. 1986. *Racial formation in the United States from the 1960s to the 1980s.* New York: Routledge.

O'Neill, Robert. 1997a. ABLA remake hits snag. *Chicago Reporter* 26 (8):3.

———. 1997b. Condemned. *Chicago Reporter* 26 (6):6–9.

———. 1997c. Oh yes, they can take that away from me. *Chicago Reporter* 26 (1):1, 7.

Orleck, Anneliese. 1997a. "If it wasn't for you, I'd have shoes for my children": The political education of Las Vegas welfare mothers. In *The politics of motherhood: Activist voices from left to right,* edited by A. Jetter, A. Orleck, and D. Taylor. Hanover, NH: University Press of New England.

———. 1997b. Overview: Mothers and the politics of feeding hungry children. In *The politics of motherhood: Activist voices from left to right,* edited by A. Jetter, A. Orleck, and D. Taylor. Hanover, NH: University Press of New England.

———. 1997c. Tradition unbound: Radical mothers in international perspective. In *The politics of motherhood: Activist voices from left to right,* edited by A. Jetter, A. Orleck, and D. Taylor. Hanover, NH: University Press of New England.

O'Toole, Laura L, and Jessica R Schiffman, eds. 1997. *Gender violence: Interdisciplinary perspectives.* New York and London: New York University Press.

Pardo, Mary. 1995. Doing it for the kids: Mexican American community activists, border feminists? In *Feminist organizations: Harvest of the new women's movement,* edited by M. M. Ferree and P. Y. Martin. Philadelphia: Temple University Press.

———. 1998. Creating community: Mexican women in Eastside Los Angeles. In *Community activism and feminist politics: Organizing across race, class, and gender,* edited by N. A. Naples. New York and London: Routledge.

Pari, Caroline. 1999. "Just American"? Reversing ethnic and class assimilation in the academy. In *Teaching working class,* edited by S. L. Linkon. Amherst: University of Massachusetts Press.

Parker, Jaclyn H. 1993. Men in families: New roles, new challenges. *SSA MAGAZINE* 5 (1):2–5.

Patai, Daphne. 1991. U.S. academics and third world women: Is ethical research possible? In *Women's words: The feminist practice of oral history*, edited by S. B. Gluck and D. Patai. New York and London: Routledge.

Pateman, Carole. 1989. *The disorder of women*. Stanford: Stanford University Press.

Pavetti, LaDonna A. 1998. What will the states do when jobs are not plentiful? Policy and implementation changes. Paper read at Conference on Welfare Reform and the Macroeconomy, November 19–20, at Washington, D.C.

Peake, Linda J. 1997. Toward a social geography of the city: Race and dimensions of urban poverty in women's lives. *Journal of Urban Affairs* 19 (3):335–61.

Pearce, Diana. 1990. Welfare is not for women: Why the war on poverty cannot conquer the feminization of poverty. In *Women, the state, and welfare*, edited by L. Gordon. Madison: University of Wisconsin Press.

Peck, Jamie. 2001. *Workfare States*. New York and London: The Guilford Press.

Peltz, Jennifer. 1999. Living at CHA site called health hazard. *Chicago Tribune*, 24 October, p. 1.

Peters, Suzanne. 1985. Reflections on studying mothering, motherwork, and mothers' work. Paper read at Motherwork Workshop, October, at Institut Simone de Beauvoir, Concordia University, Montreal.

Peterson, Nancy J. 1996. Redefining America: Literature, multiculturalism, pedagogy. In *Teaching what you're not: Identity politics in higher education*, edited by K. J. Mayberry. New York and Lodnon: New York University Press.

Pettiway, Leon E. 1997. *Workin' it: Women living through drugs and crime*. Philadelphia: Temple University Press.

Phillips, Lynn. 1996. Toward postcolonial methodologies. In *Women, work, and gender relations in developing countries: A global perspective*, edited by P. Ghorayshi and C. Bélanger. Westport, CT: Greenwood Press.

Pitts, Leonard, Jr. 1999. *Becoming dad: Black men and the journey to fatherhood*. Atlanta: Lonstreet.

Piven, Frances Fox. 1999. Welfare and work. In *Whose welfare?*, edited by G. Mink. Ithaca and London: Cornell University Press.

Polakow, Valerie. 1993. *Lives on the edge: Single mothers and their children in the other America*. Chicago: University of Chicago Press.

Pollitt, Katha. 1999. Let them sell lemonade. *The Nation* 268 (6):11.

Poor people's human rights report on the United States. 1999. Philadelphia: Kensington Welfare Rights Union.

Popkin, Susan, Victoria E. Gwiasda, Lynn M. Olson, Dennis P. Rosenbaum, and Larry Buron. 2000. *The hidden war: Crime and the tragedy of public housing in Chicago*. New Brunswick, NJ and London: Rutgers University Press.

Popkin, Susan, and Lynn Olson. 1995. Sweeping out drugs and crime: Residents' views of the Chicago Housing Authority's public housing drug elimination program. *Crime & Delinquency* 41 (1):73–99.

Poverty in the United States. 1998. U.S. Bureau of the Census.

Pryse, Marjorie. 1998. Critical interdisciplinarity, women's studies, and cross-cultural insight. *NWSA Journal* 10 (1):1–22.

Puntenney, Deborah L. 1997. The impact of gang violence on the decisions of everyday life: Disjunctions between policy assumptions and community conditions. *Journal of Urban Affairs* 19 (2):142–61.

Quadagno, Jill. 1994. *The color of welfare: How racism undermined the war on poverty*. New York: Oxford University Press.

Rabrenovic, Gordana. 1995. Women and collective action in urban neighborhoods. In *Gender in urban research*, edited by J. Garber and R. S. Turner. Thousand Oaks: Sage Publications.

Raffo, Susan. 1997. *Queerly classed: Gay men & lesbians write about class*. Boston: South End Press.

Raphael, Jody. 1995. Domestic violence and welfare reform. *Poverty & Race* 4 (4):19–20.

Raphael, Jody, and Richard M. Tolman. 1997. Trapped by poverty, trapped by abuse. New evidence documenting the relationship between domestic violence and welfare. Chicago and Ann Arbor, Michigan: A collaborative project of the Taylor Institute and the University of Michigan Research Development Center on Poverty Risk and Mental Health.

Reagon, Bernice Johnson. 1986. African Diaspora women: The making of cultural workers. *Feminist Studies* 12 (1):77–89.

Reay, Diane. 1997. Feminist theory, habitus, and social class: Disrupting notions of classlessness. *Women's Studies International Forum* 20 (2):225–33.

Rector, Robert. 1994. Combating family disintegration, crime and dependence: Welfare reform and beyond: The *Heritage Foundation Backgrounder*, 8 April.

Rental housing assistance-the worsening crisis: A report to Congress on worst case housing needs. 2000. U.S. Department of Housing and Urban Development.

Ribbens, Jane. 1989. Interviewing—an "unnatural situation"? *Women's Studies International Forum* 12 (6):579–92.

Rich, Adrienne. 1979. *On lies, secrets, and silence*. New York: W. W. Norton.

———. 1986. *Blood, Bread, and Poetry: Selected Prose*. New York: W. W. Norton.

Roberts, Dorothy. 1997. *Killing the black body: Race, reproduction, and the meaning of liberty*. New York: Pantheon Books.

———. 1999. Welfare's ban on poor motherhood. In *Whose welfare?*, edited by G. Mink. Ithaca and London: Cornell University Press.

Rodrigues, Luis. 1994. Turning youth gangs around. *The Nation* 259 (17):605–609.

Rogal, Brian J. 1998. CHA tenant evictions jump as buildings fall. *Chicago Reporter* 27 (11):1, 6–9.

Rollins, Judith. 1985. *Between women: Domestics and their employers*. Philadelphia: Temple University Press.

Roy, Kevin. 2000. Fathers on the margins of work and family: The paternal involvement project. *Poverty Research News* 4 (2):15–18.

Rubinowitz, Leonard S., and James E. Rosenbaum. 2000. *Crossing the class and color line: From public housing to white suburbia*. Chicago and London: University of Chicago Press.

Ruddick, Sarah. 1989. *Maternal thinking: Toward a politics of peace*. New York: Ballantine Books.

———. 1997. Rethinking "maternal' politics. In *The politics of motherhood: Activist voices from left to right*, edited by A. Jetter, A. Orleck, and D. Taylor. Hanover, NH: University Press of New England.

Russo, Ann. 2001. *Taking back our lives: A call to action for the feminist movement*. New York and London: Routledge.

Saeger, Joni. 1996. "Hysterical housewives" and other mad women: Grassroots environmental organizing in the United States. In *Feminist political economy: Global issues and local experiences*, edited by D. Rocheleau, B. Thomas-Slayter, and E. Wangari. New York and London: Routledge.

Schein, Virginia. 1995. *Working from the margins: Voices of mothers in poverty.* Ithaca and London: Cornell University Press.

Schutte, Ofelia. 1998. Cultural alterity: Cross-cultural communication and feminist theory in north–south contexts. *Hypatia* 13 (2):53–72.

Schwarz, John E., and Tomas J. Volgy. 1992. *The forgotten Americans.* New York and London: W. W. Norton.

Schweickart, Patrocinio P. 1996. Speech is silver, silence is gold: The asymmetrical intersubjectivity of communicative action. In *Knowledge, difference, and power: Essays inspired by women's ways of knowing,* edited by N. R. Goldberger, J. M. Tarule, B. M. Clinchy, and M. F. Belenky. New York: Basic Books.

Scott, Ellen K., Kathryn Edin, Andrew S. London, and Joan Maya Mazelis. 2000. Welfare reform and the work–family tradeoff. *Poverty Research News* 4 (4):9–11.

Scott, Joan Wallach. 1991. The evidence of experience. *Critical Inquiry* 17:773–97.

Scott, Kesho Yvonne. 1991. *The habit of surviving.* New York: Ballantine Books.

Shiva, Vandana. 1989. *Staying alive: Women, ecology and development.* London: Zed Books.

———. 2000. *Stolen harvest: The hijacking of the global food supply.* Cambridge, MA: South End Press.

Sidel, Ruth. 1996. *Keeping women and children last: America's war on the poor.* New York: Penguin Books.

Simpson, Burney. 1996. City plots new West Side story. *Chicago Reporter* 25 (8):1, 8–10.

Smith, Dorothy E. 1987. The everyday world as problematic: A feminist sociology. Boston: Northeastern University Press.

———. 1997. Comment on Hekman's "Truth and method: Feminist standpoint theory revisited." *Signs* 22 (2):392–98.

Smith, Ruth. 1999. Decentering poverty. In *Welfare policy: Feminist critiques,* edited by E. M. Bounds, P. K. Brubaker and M. E. Hobgood. Cleveland: Pilgrim Press.

Smith, Zira. 1994. Self-employment skills training. Educational survival strategy for adults with low skills: A model for oral instruction. Unpublished dissertation, Northern Illinois University, Dekalb, Illinois.

Soros, George. 1998. *The crisis of global capitalism: Open society endangered.* New York: Public Affairs.

Spalter-Roth, Roberta M., and Heidi I. Hartmann. 1995. Dependence on men, the market, or the state: The rhetoric and reality of welfare reform. *Journal of Applied Social Sciences* 18 (1):55–70.

Sparks, Elizabeth. 1998. Against all odds: Resistance and resilience in African American welfare mothers. In *Mothering against the odds: Diverse voices of contemporary mothers,* edited by C. G. Coll, J. L. Surrey, and K. Weingarten. New York: Guilford Press.

Stacey, Judith. 1991. Can there be a feminist ethnography? In *Women's words: The feminist practice of oral history,* edited by S. B. Gluck and D. Patai. New York and London: Routledge.

Stack, Carol B. 1974. *All our kin: Strategies for survival in a black community.* New York: Harper & Row.

Stack, Carol B., and Linda M. Burton. 1994. Kinscripts: Reflections on family, generation, and culture. In *Mothering: Ideology, experience, and agency,* edited by E. N. Glenn, G. Chang, and L. R. Forcey. New York and London: Routledge.

Stern, Susan Parkinson. 1998. Conversation, research, and struggles over schooling in an African American community. In *Community activism and feminist politics: Organizing across race, class, and gender*, edited by N. A. Naples. New York and London: Routledge.

Stone-Mediatore, Shari. 1998. Chandra Mohanty and the revaluing of "experience." *Hypatia* 13 (2):116–33.

Street, Paul. 1998. The poverty of workfare: Dubious claims, dark clouds, and a silver lining. *Dissent* 45 (4):53–59.

Summers, Barbara, ed. 1989. *I dream a world: Portraits of black women who changed America*. New York: Stewart Tabory & Chang.

Swiss, Deborah J., and Judith P. Walker. 1993. *Women and the work/family dilemma: How today's professional women are finding solutions*. New York: J. Wiley.

Sylvester, Christine. 1995. African and western feminisms: World-traveling the tendencies and possibilities. *Signs* 20 (4):941–69.

Tarule, Jill Mattuck. 1996. Voices in dialogue: Collaborative ways of knowing. In *Knowledge, difference, and power: Essays inspired by women's ways of knowing*, edited by N. R. Goldberger, J. M. Tarule, B. M. Clinchy, and M. F. Belenky. New York: Basic Books.

Taylor, Diane. 1997. Making a spectacle: The mothers of the Plaza de Mayo. In *The politics of motherhood: Activist voices from left to right*, edited by A. Jetter, A. Orleck and D. Taylor. Hanover, NH: University Press of New England.

Teenage pregnancy and the welfare reform debate. 2000. Alan Guttmacher Institute Policy Papers. <www.agi-usa.org>.

Thorne, Barrie, and Marilyn Yalom, eds. 1992. *Rethinking the family: Some feminist questions*. Boston: Northeastern University Press.

Tilly, Louise, and Patricia Gurin. 1990. Women, politics, and change. In *Women, politics, and change*, edited by L. Tilly and P. Gurin. New York: Russell Sage.

Townsend, Janet Gabriel, with other authors. 1999. Empowerment matters: Understanding power. In *Women and power: Fighting patriarchy and poverty*, edited by J. G. Townsend, E. Zapata, J. Rowlands, P. Alberti, and M. Mercado. London and New York: Zed Press.

Toy, Vivien S. 1998. Tough workfare rules used as way to cut welfare rolls. *New York Times*, 15 April, A1, A24.

Tronto, Joan C. 1993. *Moral boundaries: A political argument for an ethic of care*. New York and London: Routledge.

Tucker, Robert C, ed. 1978. *The Marx-Engels reader*. 2nd ed. New York: W. W. Norton.

Tucker, Susan. 1988. *Telling memories among southern women*. Baton Rouge and London: Louisiana State University Press.

Two sides of the coin. 1994. Chicago: Women Employed Institute and Office for Social Policy Research, Northern Illinois University.

2001 report on Illinois poverty. Chicago: Illinois Poverty Summit, facilitated by Heartland Alliance for Human Needs & Human Rights.

Vanderbosch, Jane. 1997. Notes from the working class. In *Queerly classed: Gay men & lesbians write about class*, edited by S. Raffo. Boston: South End Press.

Venkatesh, Sudhir Alladi. 1997. Invisible community: Inside Chicago's public housing. *The American Prospect* (34):35–40.

———. 2000. *American project: The rise and fall of a modern ghetto*. Cambridge, MA: Harvard University Press.

Von Werlhof, Claudia. 1991. *Was haben die Hühner mit dem Dollar zu tun?* München: Verlag Frauenoffensive.

——. 1993a. Im Grunde gibt es vor lauter Ökonomie keine Kultur mehr. In *Der kalte Blick der Ökonomie,* edited by A. Bammé, W. Berger, C. Gerschlager, and L. Gubitzer. München and Wien: Profil Verlag.

——. 1993b. Subsistenz: Abschied vom ökonomischen Kalkül. Paper read at Humboldt Universität, January 25, at Berlin.

——. 1994a. Die Zukunft der Entwicklung und die Zukunft der Subsistenz oder Subsistenz statt Entwicklung. *Innsbrucker Geographische Studien* 21 (Lateinamerika—Krise ohne Ende?):161–70.

——. 1994b. Logik und Denkschranken neuzeitlicher Naturbeherrschung. Gibt es Perspektiven ihrer Überwindung? In *Wie ist qualitatives Wachstum möglich? Protokoll des 3. Kempfhausener Gesprächs.* Kempfhausen: Das Kommunikations-Forum der Hypo-BANK.

——. 1996. *Mutter-Los: Frauen im Patriarchat zwischen Angleichung und Dissidenz.* München: Frauenoffensive.

Waldman, Linda, ed. 1993. *My neighborhood: The words and pictures of inner-city children.* Chicago: Hyde Park Bank Association.

Walker, Alice. 1983. *In search of our mothers' gardens.* San Diego: Harcourt, Brace, Jovanovich.

Walker, Margaret Urban. 1998. *Moral understandings: A feminist study in ethics.* New York and London: Routledge.

Wallerstein, Immanuel. 1979. *The capitalist world economy.* Cambridge: Cambridge University Press.

Welfare reform at age one: Early indicators of impact on clients and agencies. 1998 (June). Chicago: Work, Welfare, and Families, the Chicago Urban League, and The Center for Urban Economic Development, University of Illinois.

West, Guida, and Rhoda Lois Blumberg. 1990a. Reconstructing social protest from a feminist perspective. In *Women and social protest,* edited by G. West and R. L. Blumberg. New York: Oxford University Press.

——. 1990b. *Women and social protest.* New York: Oxford University Press.

Williams, Patricia. 1995. *The rooster's egg: On the persistence of prejudice.* Cambridge, MA: Harvard University Press.

Willis, Ellen. 1999. *Don't think, smile! Notes on a decade of denial.* Boston: Beacon Press.

Willow, Morgan Grayce. 1997. Class struggles. In *Queerly classed: Gay men & lesbians write about class,* edited by S. Raffo. Boston: South End Press.

Wilson, William Julius. 1996. *When work disappears: The world of the new urban poor.* New York: Alfred A Knopf.

Winant, Howard. 1994. *Racial conditions.* Minneapolis: University of Minnesota Press.

Winkler, Barbara Scott. 1996. Straight teacher/queer classroom: Teaching as an ally. In *Teaching what you're not: Identity politics in higher education,* edited by K. J. Mayberry. New York and London: New York University Press.

Wolf, Diane L. 1996. *Feminist dilemmas in fieldwork.* Boulder: Westview Press.

Wood, Julia T. 1994. *Who cares? Women, care, and culture.* Carbondale and Edwardsville: Southern Illinois University Press.

Working-Class Studies. 1995. Special issue of *Women's Studies Quarterly* 23 (1 and 2).

Wright, Erik Olin. 1997. Rethinking, once again, the concept of class structure. In *Reworking class,* edited by J. R. Hall. Ithaca and New York: Cornell University Press.

Wrigley, Julia. 1998. From housewives to activists: Women and the division of political labor in the Boston antibusing movement. In *No middle ground: Women and radical protest*, edited by K. Blee. New York and London: University of New York Press.

Young, Gay, and Bette J. Dickerson, eds. 1994. *Color, class & gender: Experiences of gender*. London: Zed Books.

Zandy, Janet. 1998. Traveling working class. *Women's Studies Quarterly* 26 (1 and 2):228–42.

Zinn, Maxine Baca. 1992. Family, race, and poverty in the eighties. In *Rethinking the family: Some feminist questions*, edited by B. Thorne and M. Yalom. Boston: Northeastern University Press.

Zinn, Maxine Baca, and Bonnie Thornton Dill, eds. 1994. *Women of color in U.S. society*. Philadelphia: Temple University Press.

Index

About the Author

MECHTHILD U. HART is Associate Professor at the School for New Learning, DePaul University. Her teaching and writing has focused on motherwork within the larger political and economic context of sexual, racial-ethnic, and international divisions of labor. She also works in the area of educational theory, where she concentrates on the political and pedagogical implications of educational practices that are anchored in an acknowledgment of life-affirming work.